DEMOCRACY, BUREAUCRACY AND PUBLIC CHOICE

Economic Explanations in Political Science

PATRICK DUNLEAVY

Department of Government, London School of Economics and Political Science

HARVESTER WHEATSHEAF

New York   London   Toronto   Sydney   Tokyo   Singapore

First published 1991 by
Harvester Wheatsheaf
66 Wood Lane End, Hemel Hempstead
Hertfordshire HP2 4RG
A division of
Simon & Schuster International Group

© Patrick Dunleavy, 1991

Typeset in 10/12 Plantin
by Keyset Composition, Colchester

Printed and bound in Great Britain by
BPCC Wheatons Ltd, Exeter

British Library Cataloguing in Publication Data

Dunleavy, Patrick. 1952–
    Democracy, bureaucracy and public choice:
    economic explanations in political science.
    1. Politics. Collective choice
    I. Title
    320.019
    ISBN 0-7450-0167-X
    ISBN 0-7450-0233-1 pbk

---

1 2 3 4 5 95 94 93 92 91

CONTENTS

v

Contents

vi

FIGURES

vii

Figures

TABLES

PREFACE

When I first began working on some of the ideas in this book, my attitudes towards public choice theory were wholly critical. My idea was to develop an *ad hominem* critique of some key rational choice models, to show that they were internally inconsistent and ideologically slanted, and to do what I could to demonstrate that this was only a speciously attractive research programme. My own work in public choice was to be merely a ladder used to reach this limited goal, later to be kicked down when it was no longer needed. Instead, ten years later, much of my research has been restructured around a particular kind of institutional public choice method. I now recognize the value of instrumental models as a mode of thinking clearly about the manifold complexities of political life, and could not pursue research without using them. Yet my scepticism about the scientific status of much liberal political economy remains, especially about its close links with the new right in practical politics.

The way in which public choice has developed as an alternative political science carries twin dangers. On the one hand, practitioners in the field often display a thrust towards premature formalization. Major theoretical works emerge, and spawn an increasing technical literature in which some of the key works' starting assumptions are progressively lost to view. Questions about inherently messy empirical applications are pushed aside by the pace of the development of formal models, and existing empirical knowledge is often pointlessly impugned or ignored in the process. On the other hand, political scientists using alternative approaches in fields colonized by public choice often react defensively, sidelining public choice contributions, and making only very generalized or basic criticisms of the methods employed or the results obtained. The resulting 'dialogue of the deaf' is unsatisfactory because it means that rigorous scrutiny of public choice is thin on the ground, while the empirical applicability of recon-structed public choice models is rarely appreciated. The purpose of this

xi

Preface

book is to contribute towards the development of a more fruitful and critical interaction.

The first part of the book to be written was a joint paper with Hugh Ward published in 1981: its basic ideas are now incorporated into Chapters 4 and 5. I owe a great debt to Hugh which I am proud to acknowledge here: without his input I would never have had the confidence to launch upon this venture or to sustain it through several bad patches. Closely rivalling Hugh's influence in these pages is that of Bob Goodin, who both as a friend and an editor constantly identified arguments needing attention and suggested avenues for further thought.

My colleagues at the London School of Economics and Political Science, Brendan O'Leary, Brian Barry and Desmond King, very generously undertook to read and comment on the whole draft of the text, and Christopher Hood read all of Part II. Their detailed and helpful reactions triggered a major rewrite which delayed the book a further six months, indicating only too well the extent to which I am in their debt.

My third acknowledgement is to the M.Sc. and doctoral students who attended my public policy seminars at the London School of Economics throughout the 1980s. They put up with numerous early variants of my ideas and patiently explained to me why they would not do. Their reactions, interests and seminar demands stimulated virtually all of the better ideas contained here, and at the same time broadened my education in comparative politics.

I am grateful also to all the many professional colleagues who criticized earlier versions of these ideas at PSA (Political Studies Association) Conferences and as journal editors and referees, especially Christopher Pollit, Rod Rhodes, George Jones, Anthony King, Ivor Crewe and Wyn Grant. Edward Elgar helped me to define the initial idea for the book, while Clare Grist of Harvester Wheatsheaf provided the external drive needed to get it finished long after it was initially promised. Gordon Tullock and two other anonymous American reviewers stimulated many changes late on in the preparation of the text for which I am very grateful.

Finally, I thank Sheila Dunleavy for help and encouragement too vast to be quantified. In a period when it is fashionable to make fun of the structuralist maxim that authors do not *write* books, I, at least, am acutely aware that anything worthwhile in these pages is a collective achievement.

Patrick Dunleavy
London School of Economics
and Political Science

ACKNOWLEDGEMENTS

I thank the editors and publishers of two journals for permission to reuse passages from my papers which they originally published.
1. *The British Journal of Political Science* published by Cambridge University Press for:
(a) 'Bureaucrats, budgets and the growth of the state: reconstructing an instrumental model', *British Journal of Political Science* (1985), vol. 15, no. 3, pp. 299–328.
(b) 'Group identities and individual influence: reconstructing the theory of interest groups', *British Journal of Political Science* (1988), vol. 18, no. 1, pp. 21–49.
2. *Public Administration* published by Basil Blackwell for:
(a) 'Explaining the privatization boom: public choice versus radical approaches', *Public Administration* (1986), vol. 64, no. 2, pp. 13–34.
(b) 'The architecture of the British central state: Part I, Framework for analysis', *Public Administration* (1989), vol. 67, no. 3, pp. 249–75.
(c) 'The architecture of the British central state: Part II, Empirical findings', *Public Administration* (1989), vol. 67, no. 4, pp. 391–417.
I thank Hugh Ward for generously allowing me to reuse material from the following co-authored paper in Chapters 4 and 5, and the *British Journal of Political Science* and Cambridge University Press for their permission to reproduce passages from it: P. Dunleavy and H. Ward, 'Exogenous voter preferences and parties with state power: some internal problems of economic models of party competition', *British Journal of Political Science* (1981), vol. 11, no. 3, pp. 351–80.
In addition, the author and publishers thank John Wiley & Sons for permission to reproduce Figure 19 from p. 98 of David Robertson's *A Theory of Party Competition* (London: Wiley & Sons, 1976).

Chapter 1

INTRODUCTION: INSTITUTIONAL PUBLIC CHOICE THEORY AND POLITICAL ANALYSIS

In the last twenty years more and more social scientists have begun using concepts and methods derived from economics to explain political phenomena. A new field of research has grown up which attempts to model collective decision-making in liberal democracies much as conventional economists analyze consumers' and firms' behaviour in private markets. This approach is variously known as 'political economy' (because it straddles the disciplines of economics and political science); 'public choice theory' (because it focuses on public or collective choices as opposed to the private choices of individuals analyzed by conventional micro-economics); or 'rational choice theory' (because it develops from the assumption that people are rational actors). There is a basic cleavage within public choice between the more abstract modelling work which I term the 'first principles' literature, and the more applied work which I term 'institutional public choice'.

First principles analysis uses techniques such as game theory and algebraic economics to analyze multiple puzzles about individual behaviour, or to make sweeping assumptions about how large groups of people behave in order to explore a whole society's development. A great deal of this literature does not connect well with the traditional preoccupations of political science. The abstract conjunctures which are modelled are often so stripped down, so uncomplicated and so unambiguously specified, that in many cases it is hard to think of analogous political situations. Even when reasonably close-fitting empirical examples can sometimes be found, translating 'real life' into 'first principles' analysis is so difficult that we end up able to explain only small slices of the political process disconnected from each other. This literature has added to the political science repertoire some interesting 'apt illustrations' and some important insights into isolated pieces of decision-making (for example, Tzserbelis, 1990). But it has not otherwise changed the ways in which political scientists picture the

1

continuous operations of political institutions, nor defined any distinctive picture of the whole political system.

Institutional public choice has had a much broader impact, both on political science and on practical policy-making. A substantial body of work now offers a coherent picture of almost all aspects of the political process and government institutions. Writers such as Mancur Olson, Anthony Downs and William Niskanen do not use very complicated first principles reasoning, nor describe only the behaviour of abstract algebraic entities. Instead, they offer a compelling, applied and relatively detailed account of how the core processes of liberal democratic politics operate. These writers and their imitators and critics have analyzed why people join interest groups, how voters choose between parties at election time, how coalitions form in committees and legislatures, how bureaucracies make policy and how sub-national governments deliver policy outputs to citizens.

THE STRENGTHS AND LIMITS OF PUBLIC CHOICE

This book has three somewhat paradoxical aims: firstly, to broaden awareness of the scope and power of institutional public choice accounts; secondly, to criticize these models by exposing their unspoken and contestable assumptions and right-wing leanings; and thirdly, to reconstruct key public choice models so as to demonstrate that a properly grounded instrumental account need not produce these sorts of conclusions.

The strengths of institutional public choice theory

These insights have seldom been set out in an accessible, compelling and clear-cut way. Most introductions to the field have been written by enthusiastic propagandists of the genre, usually economists, who have concentrated far more on 'first principles' elements than on the areas most useful to political scientists (Mueller, 1979, 1989). When applications to empirical political contexts have been made they are generally crudely specified, and show little awareness of or openness to political science research carried out from alternative perspectives (Tullock, 1976). At the same time, the specialized expertise needed to enter the public choice field has created a considerable barrier to analysis by outsiders. Some outside authors have attacked public choice theory's values and philosophical orientation, rather than engaging in any detailed debate with the views being challenged (Self, 1985, pp. 47–8; Etzioni, 1988; Hindess, 1988, 1989). Only a few introductory surveys by political scientists avoid these twin dangers – and they are chiefly concerned to expound public choice work rather than to probe its limitations critically (McLean, 1982, 1987; Laver, 1981; Abrams, 1980).

As a result it is still very common outside the United States for political scientists who do not themselves use public choice methodology to dismiss it as of marginal interest for the discipline as a whole. Even in the US the prominence of public choice in leading political science journals is based on a fairly small group of authors and studies. Public choice theory is widely seen by political scientists as simply another abstruse specialism produced by overdeveloping particular techniques without putting equal effort into showing how they can add to our substantive knowledge about central topics in political life. Public choice may be a legitimate field to work in 'if you like that kind of thing', but it is still not regarded as a basic intellectual position which has to be regularly or seriously considered in describing the behaviour of political systems and structures. This stance sits very oddly with the diffusion of soft public choice concepts across most areas of contemporary political science, and the extensive acceptance of public choice reasoning and conclusions by other policy-relevant professions and some types of politicians. By setting out institutional public choice theory in a convincing way I hope to show why its assumptions and conceptions have increasingly come to dominate both a large area of 'forefront' research in political science and many policy debates in practical politics.

Public choice premisses

In the existing literature these assumptions are presented as few, parsimonious and uncontentious. The 'rational actor' model at the heart of all public choice accounts assumes that:

- people have sets of well-formed preferences which they can perceive, rank and compare easily;
- their preference orderings are transitive or logically consistent, so that if someone prefers socialism to liberalism, and liberalism to fascism, then they will also prefer socialism to fascism;
- people are 'maximizers' who always seek the biggest possible benefits and the least costs in their decisions. They act rationally when they pursue their preferences in an efficient manner and maximize benefits net of costs. On this formal definition, someone behaves 'rationally' if they optimize their preferences in a consistent fashion, however substantively ill-advised we may judge their preferences to be; and
- people are basically egoistic, self-regarding and instrumental in their behaviour, choosing how to act on the basis of the consequences for their personal welfare (or that of their immediate family).

Public choice exponents commonly defend these premisses as uncontroversial and not implying any substantive value judgements – even when the argument that people are basically self-interested in their behaviour is held to apply irrespective of the social role that people may be occupying

3

(for example, as voters, interest group members, politicians or bureaucrats).

However, there is an increasing recognition even among economists that their notion of 'rational economic man' (or woman) is too often 'introduced furtively' and left under-specified. The rational actor is usually 'an abstract and shadowy figure' who 'lurks in the assumptions' rather than being explicitly described (Hollis and Nell, 1975, pp. 53–5). In addition to the assumptions above which are formally described there are typically a whole series of additional subtle and diffuse premisses which are not often explicitly acknowledged. In consequence non-expert readers may have little idea what these hidden assumptions are, or how much they skew or limit public choice analyses. For example, I show in later chapters that virtually all public choice theories involve very restrictive premisses.

On the demand-side:
- they assume that people possess a great deal of prior knowledge in making political decisions, equivalent to assuming that they are perfectly informed; and
- they require people's preferences to be fixed exogenously and to be unaffected by their participation in the political choice processes being analyzed.

On the supply-side:
- they make 'heroic' assumptions about the extent to which collective entities (such as firms, parties, or bureaucracies) can be treated as unitary actors for the purpose of analysis; and
- they model political decision-makers as actors with only a single maximizing course of action open to them.

The mechanisms for coping with these and other problems remain hotly contested in debates about the methodology of conventional economics (Blaug, 1980; Caldwell, 1984). However, translating these assumptions into political contexts – applying them to choices about issues remote from people's everyday experiences and made in collective processes radically different from economic markets – clearly raises difficulties of a new order of magnitude.

The conservative value-bias of public choice theory

Implicit or unacknowledged premisses largely account for this characteristic political linkage. Over the last two decades institutional public choice has played a significant role in the development of political debates in the United States, Britain, Australia, New Zealand and Western Europe. It has been taken up enthusiastically by the key intellectuals and pressure groups who have drafted arguments, policy proposals and speeches for strongly conservative politicians such as Ronald Reagan and Margaret Thatcher.

Introduction

Throughout this book I use the description 'new right' as a useful summary label for their combination of economic neo-liberalism and social conservatism which seemed so politically successful in the 1980s (King, 1987, Chapters 2 and 7; Green, 1987; Barry, 1987a; Hoover and Plant, 1988). Particularly important in securing a rapid breakthrough for new right approaches has been public choice theory's fusion of positive theory and empirical work on the one hand, and of prescriptive theory and policy analysis on the other. Long-running right-wing suspicions of liberal democracy have been rephrased in intellectually attractive terms, considerably extending their social appeal and mass media plausibility.

Academically also, institutional public choice work has formed the core of a coherent and influential new right theory of the state (Dunleavy and O'Leary, 1987, pp. 72–135). Perhaps as important, however, the elements of institutional public choice which have most extensively crossed over to influence the development of mainstream political science have been preponderantly right-wing in their political coloration. A subtly skewed development of knowledge about liberal democratic processes has been fostered by the overwhelming predominance of new right and neo-conservative thinking amongst exponents of public choice theory. Illuminating those public choice concepts and implicit assumptions is a key objective of this book.

Public choice methodology, however, is not intrinsically tied to right-wing political values. There have been some smaller counter-currents in the public choice literature, developed by authors who do not share the views. Some key writers on institutional public choice have been pluralists (such as Downs and to a lesser degree Tiebout) or élite theorists (such as Olson in his early work). Most recently, the potential for reaching diverse conclusions from public choice methods has been demonstrated by the growth of analytical Marxism whose key exponents use rational choice techniques to clarify, extend and revise the central tenets of Marxist theory. Much of this work is first principles analysis (for example, Roemer, 1986; Elster, 1985, and see O'Leary, 1987a). But there are also important contributions to institutional public choice, especially in explaining the behaviour of trade unions, labour movements and socialist parties (Wallerstein, 1989; Przeworski, 1985; Przeworski and Sprague, 1986).

My own view is that the political values previously associated with public choice theory were only contingently linked to the models developed, in many cases on the basis of mistaken or unanalyzed assumptions. Despite the problems which beset the application of economic concepts and methods in political contexts, the rational choice approach is too powerful an analytical tool-kit to neglect or abandon. Instead, the most interesting intellectual challenge is selectively to remove or alter contestable premises in rational actor accounts and to examine the implications of replacing them with acceptable assumptions. The new or reconstructed models thus developed

5

remain within the boundaries of a public choice approach, but yield radically different explanations of political phenomena.

To highlight the contestable and partial quality of these revised accounts, I describe them as instrumental models – indicating that they start from assumptions of individually self-interested behaviour. Instrumental models of this kind will never capture the whole of social behaviour adequately. They can only be sensibly used as theory-advancing and information-economizing devices, to see how far we can go with relatively parsimonious and deductively constructed theories before needing to shift gear to a more inclusive or descriptively compelling form of analysis.

The individualistic basis of public choice

Outside critics frequently allege that the individualism of public choice presents a fundamental intellectual obstacle to any effort at reconstruction of the type made here. On this view rational actor premises are inherently individualistic, and incapable of including structural pressures and constraints on people's actions. Yet, as the Austrian school of political economy has never ceased to complain, individual actors in conventional neo-classical economics are presented simply as disembodied bearers of preferences whose decision-making behaviour is strikingly homogeneous once we can ascertain what their preferences are.

> Conventional economics is not about choice, but about acting according to necessity. Economic man obeys the *dictates* of reason, follows the *logic of choice*. To call this conduct choice is surely to misuse words, when we suppose that to him the ends among which he can select, and the criteria of selection are given, and the means to each end are known. . . . Choice in such a theory is empty. (Shackle, 1969, pp. 272–3)

Indeed, public choice theory, as much as conventional micro-economics, is the opposite of individualistic in brooking no diversity in the decision procedures followed by actors. 'In the neo-classical system agents are treated as if they are mindless automata who respond in a fully programmed fashion to external stimuli such as price and quantity signals' (Jackson, 1982, p. 87). Hence reconstructed public choice models can be produced which are perfectly consistent with a structuralist view of the determination of social behaviour (see Blau and Merton, 1981).

The instrumental accounts of group-joining, party competition, bureaucratic operations and sub-national government developed in the rest of the book are also radical models. They are based on realist and critical values and perceptions which stress the continuing inequalities of contemporary capitalist societies and the limitations and imperfections of liberal democracies. These radical accounts are intended to confront or contest key elements of new right and pluralist thinking based upon public choice methods. They also lead to conclusions sympathetic to democratic socialist positions in practical politics. Theory construction cannot take place in a vacuum, but the political values which provided the initial basis for these models need not limit their applicability or appeal. The arguments set out here are themselves open to being reconstructed as well as empirically falsified. And if they help to stimulate a broader, better informed, more open, or more theoretically diversified debate within and about institutional public choice they will have served a useful purpose.

THE STRUCTURE OF THE BOOK

The first part of the book deals with the political input processes which are most distinctive of liberal democracies – interest groups and party competitive elections. The second part analyzes the key supply-side institutions, government bureaucracies in central governments, hived-off agencies and sub-national governments. Throughout the book chapters or chapter sections which set out existing public choice approaches alternate with a rival or reconstructed radical view of the same institutions and political processes.

Part I starts by considering how collective action by citizens has been explained by four theoretical positions: pluralism, corporatism, Olson's original public choice analysis and new right views. Although public choice approaches are the main focus of this analysis, the political science perspectives contain important insights and approaches which economic views cannot afford to ignore. Variations in the way that the interest group process has been analyzed affect not only the basic assumptions of different theories, but also how they characterize the internal structures and organization of interest groups, their leaderships' characteristic strategies, and the 'universe' of groups which results.

Chapter 3 then sets out to reconstruct a public choice theory of groups which can integrate a wider range of phenomena within the scope of the analysis. First I 'surface' some of the implied public choice views about why people do not join collective actions, and then I examine how people come to perceive groups as relevant for their interests. The notion of a group identity is introduced to denote the perception of an interest shared with others. The reasons why rational actors join groups are complex: properly analyzed they offer little support for the simple faith of public choice accounts that large groups will be more difficult to organize than smaller ones. A typology of exogenous and endogenous groups is developed to explain the key non-size influences upon a group's effectiveness. In addition, the group identity approach can successfully explain the importance of internal group democracy in a way which conventional public choice accounts cannot.

The electoral process is the focus for the rest of Part I. Chapter 4 first shows how the analysis of collective action already developed can also illuminate the paradox of why rational actors vote at all. It then queries the typical public choice assumption that voters' preferences are exogenously fixed and examines the case for relaxing it. Political parties do not compete at elections simply to win a golden challenge cup, but in order to gain access to government and hence control some key levers of state power. Chapter 5 explores the implications of partisan control of state power in a situation where voters' preferences are endogenously determined and capable of being influenced or partly restructured by the exercise of state and party power. Conventional public choice, and pluralist, accounts picture politicians as simply accommodating voters' preferences. I argue, by contrast, that rational party leaders have multiple incentives to adopt preference-shaping strategies, trying to change the distributions of voters' preferences in ways which are favourable for them.

In Part II the focus of concern becomes the characteristic ways in which government bureaucracies operate. Chapter 6 presents a summary comparison of two key public choice works, Anthony Downs' pluralist treatment in *Inside Bureaucracy* (1967) and William Niskanen's subsequent new right text, *Bureaucracy and Representative Government* (1971), which includes an influential model of how all rational public officials seek to maximize their agency's budget. The common failings of these otherwise different texts highlight some deep-rooted problems inherent in existing economic accounts of bureaucracy.

Chapter 7 sets out a radically different public choice model in which rationally self-interested top officials have few incentives to maximize their budgets. Instead, they pursue bureau-shaping strategies, that is, they remodel their agencies as small, élite, staff organizations devoid of direct line responsibilities. The categories of agency suggested by this bureau-shaping model are applied empirically in examples drawn from the contemporary US federal government and British central departments. I argue that strong variations in the strength of budget-maximizing and bureau-shaping motivations occur.

Since the plausibility of any model can best be assessed by comparing it with alternative frameworks, Chapter 8 begins by examining the available empirical literature on bureaucratic behaviour, arguing that budget-maximizing models have been strikingly unconfirmed by empirical evidence in the last two decades. By contrast, although not yet subject to rigorous testing, the bureau-shaping account seems strongly consistent with existing knowledge. The second half of the chapter compares budget-maximizing and bureau-shaping explanations of two large-scale changes in administrative organization in the United States and Britain over the last twenty years: privatization and deinstitutionalization. Privatization of administrative services involves contracting them out, or introducing competitive tendering. Deinstitutionalization strategies involve closing down large-scale manpower-intensive formal organizations (such as children's homes, old people's homes, and long-stay mental hospitals) and replacing them with less institutionalized forms of care.

Finally, Chapter 9 shows how the instrumental models developed here share a similar orientation by querying conventional public choice assumptions of perfect information, exogenously fixed preferences, unitary supply-side actors and decision-makers with single maximizing courses of action. Size manipulation strategies used by interest groups to attract members; preference-shaping strategies used by political parties to win voters' support; and bureau-shaping strategies used by officials to remodel their agencies, all these models share common features. They each explore political behaviour in an environment of limited information; where consumer preferences are malleable and reshaped by élite actions; and where political supply-side organizations have complex internal structures and confront choice dilemmas between alternative maximizing strategies.

The literature on public choice is now so vast that no one text could realistically cover it all, and by distinguishing between first principles and institutional analysis I have aimed to achieve a more manageable and coherent focus. However, for readers new to public choice it may be worthwhile briefly to make clear in some more detail the areas of liberal political economy not covered in the following chapters.

A large literature which applies game theory to modelling political behaviour has not been described, since it falls into the first principles category. This book includes occasional side-references to some fundamental game theory results, especially work on prisoner's dilemma and 'chicken' games, and on the circumstances in which voluntary co-operation between actors will tend to emerge. But abstract discussions of voting paradoxes and procedures are mostly ignored, since little progress has been made in developing the translation rules to connect this mainly algebraic literature with empirical analysis.

Nor have I systematically reviewed the work on how governments manage their macro-economic policies to fit in with their electoral timetables, whether this creates political-business cycles and what differences to public policy or welfare state development are made by the election of different parties into government (Castles, 1982). Although this literature is discussed a little in Chapter 5, much of it still treats government as a black box, mapping inputs and outputs but not studying institutional processes inside the political system itself.

Discussion of international political economy (Frey, 1984) and public choice models of relations between states are also omitted, partly for reasons of space, and partly because these accounts normally treat national governments as unitary, rational actors (Allison, 1971, pp. 10–38). In some contexts this academic fiction is legitimate, but it is not one which meshes easily with the institutional orientation here. Similar reasons preclude discussion of the interesting macro-theoretical models of the relations between states (and their rulers) and the rest of civil society developed by North (1981), Bates (1981), Levi (1988) and others. Again, government is treated as a unitary actor in these accounts. None the less much work in both these areas can be seen as falling within institutional public choice because it makes role-specific assumptions about what it is that political actors want (see Chapter 9).

Finally, I have not discussed or criticized prescriptive public choice theory, except in so far as its recommendations have been adopted by new right governments and hence can be analyzed as empirical strategies. Normative public choice work in welfare economics and public finance does not contribute much to our understanding of how actually existing political systems operate. Its relevance to empirical analysis derives chiefly from the influence it exerts on the behaviour of governments and political parties – and this role should be studied as an ideology like other policy-relevant belief systems.

PART I

DEMOCRACY

Chapter 2

INTEREST GROUPS AND
COLLECTIVE ACTION

In an immensely influential book, *The Logic of Collective Action* (1965),
Mancur Olson attacked conventional pluralist accounts of the interest
group process, which had formed the optimistic orthodoxy of American
liberalism for over half a century. 'It is characteristic of the traditional
theory in all its forms that it assumes that participation in voluntary
associations is virtually universal' (Olson, 1978, p. 20). Olson argued by
contrast that since groups organize around collective goals, it is often not
rational for self-interested individuals to join in such activity; they can
better pursue their interests by free-riding on other people's efforts. Hence
large groups especially are often chronically under-organized. People
should reason that their individual participation will make little or no
difference to a group's success or failure, and they will gain the same level of
collective benefits whether they participate or not.

However:

Olson proclaimed the impossibility of collective action for large
groups (just as Daniel Bell proclaimed the 'end of ideology') at the
precise moment [the mid-1960s] when the Western world was about
to be engulfed by an unprecedented wave of public movements,
marches, protests, strikes and ideologies. . . . It seems to me
conceivable that the success of Olson's book *owes* something to its
having been contradicted by the subsequently evolving events. Once
the latter had safely run their course, the many people who found
them deeply upsetting could go back to *The Logic of Collective
Action* and find in it good and reassuring reasons why those collective
actions of the sixties should never have happened in the first place,
were perhaps less real than they seemed, and were most unlikely ever
to recur. (Hirschman, 1985, p. 79)

The basic problem this experience poses for institutional public choice theory has not diminished in subsequent years. Rational actor models of interest groups or pressure groups (the terms are virtually interchangeable) explain why many groups should be under-organized, but not why large-scale collective actions occur. By contrast, pluralist writers (mostly political scientists) have refined their approach to sidestep Olson's critique of over-optimism, and to offer a more differentiated picture of participation in interest groups.

Two more recent approaches have qualified the contrast between the older positions, however. A new right view has been developed by economists, arguing on theoretical grounds that since action around collective goals is otherwise inexplicable, Olson's public choice account needs to be rewritten to take account of 'vested interests' organizing around semi-private goods. And a good deal of political science work since the 1970s has focused on corporatism, the mechanisms by which major interest groups and governments co-operatively shape economic and social policies in some Western countries.

This chapter examines all four existing accounts of interest groups – pluralism, corporatism, the logic of collective action model and the new right view. For each approach I explore its basic assumptions; how it interprets groups' internal organization; its account of group strategies; and its expectations about the 'group universe' or overall interest group system. I hope to show that none of these accounts can adequately explain the variety of interest group behaviour, while each contains some useful insights for the more inclusive rational choice explanation which I develop in Chapter 3.

THE PLURALIST APPROACH

Basic assumptions

Pluralist authors more or less defined interest groups as a focus of academic study, showing how they constitute some of the largest, longest-lasting and most active forms of political participation in liberal democracies (Bentley, 1967; Trueman, 1951). Their widely accepted definition (Wootton, 1970, Chapters 1–2) stresses that four features set interest groups apart from other forms of social organization:

1. *Multi-member organizations.* Interest groups associate various types of actors (individuals, firms, other organizations) and mobilize them to undertake some form of collective action (that is, simultaneous, joint activity). 'Peak associations' organize lower-tier interest groups, as when a central labour movement co-ordinates the activities of individual trade unions.

2. *Voluntary membership.* Interest group members cannot formally be prohibited from leaving, nor have contractual restrictions imposed on them. Members delegate fewer issues to a leadership than other forms of social organization. And outside the small leadership sub-set, the vast bulk of members have equal standing in group decisions – there is no extended hierarchy of roles. Hence interest groups' internal organizational patterns are more congruent with the formal political equality of liberal democracies than those of private corporations or public sector bureaucracies.

3. *Dependence on member involvement.* The effectiveness of groups depends on members first joining and then actively supporting their activities. In economic terms, the role of group members is unusual because they are 'involved in both the supply and demand sides, in both production and consumption of the organization's output' (Hirschman, 1970, p. 100). This is unlike commercial firms and their customers where there is a clear division between supply-side and demand-side actors. In addition, group members usually retain much more responsibility for directing their own activity (both formally and in practice).

4. *A narrow focus of concerns.* Interest groups mobilize around single issues or restricted areas of social life and public policy. They do not normally contest elections or seek to form a government. Hence they differ radically from political parties (which also share the characteristics above in liberal democracies). Parties bundle up multiple issues into packages, thereby simplifying electoral choices for voters. ⊁

Pluralist accounts emphasize that there is an enormous diversity of interest groups, with widely varying social bases, disparate objectives and sharply contrasting modes of operation. The interests and beliefs which lead people to form or join organizations, and lobby politicians, parties or governments for symbolic or material concessions, cannot be easily classified. Various typologies or schema have been sketched, such as the distinction between 'sectional groups' pursuing the collective self-interest of people in similar economic or social locations, and 'cause groups' whose members' involvement seems other-regarding, perhaps ideological and frequently altruistic (Richardson and Jordan, 1979, p. 17). But the fundamental pluralist position remains a stress on motivational diversity, the capacity of humanity to behave in ways which stubbornly resist explanation in a narrowly rational manner – for example by acting altruistically against their own apparent self-interest, or by supporting lost causes and joining willingly in certain defeats.

Motivational diversity goes along with and is underpinned by the ease of organizing groups. Resources for group-forming – such as basic organizational skills, financial help from a wide range of patrons (Walker, 1983), access to the mass media and legitimacy in the eyes of elected representatives and state officials – are readily available in advanced industrial

15

societies. The 'civic culture' of the most stable liberal democracies such as the United States and Britain fosters in citizens a conviction of their personal efficacy in the political realm, and presents group-forming as a key means of redressing grievances (Almond and Verba, 1963). Media attitudes reinforce this dominant ethos so long as groups use legitimate tactics. These factors mean that there is an immense variety of interest groups, and that few if any significant social interests remain chronically unorganized.

The internal organization of groups

Pluralists expect grass roots members of interest groups to maintain control over their leaderships for five reasons.

1. Information

Workers in trade unions, farmers supporting agricultural lobby groups, businessmen involved in trade associations, or members of professional societies, all have extensive daily experience of their group's concerns. Grass roots members may not appreciate the finer points of national strategies. But they are much more likely to have developed views on group policies than voters trying to decide between rival parties' economic strategies. Direct knowledge of the issues may be less extensive amongst cause groups pursuing altruistic goals or ideological positions. But since only people with strong personal motivations join such groups in the first place, members are likely to insist on retaining control over group policy.

2. Dependence on membership activism

Interest groups rely on their members being willing to bear the financial and time costs both of joining and of actively supporting their lobbying and campaigning. A sample of US interest groups found that membership fees and activities account for 75 per cent of occupational or economic groups' total incomes, and for 47 per cent of citizen or cause groups' income (Walker, 1983, p. 400). Most groups' small professional staffs can run only a few specialized, national-level activities and rely on voluntary, unpaid labour and special contributions from members for local organizing and campaigning. For example, trade unions need shop-floor representatives in each workplace they organize. And to undertake industrial action, unions need their ordinary members to vote for the costs and risks involved in a strike or overtime ban. Group members only meet such costs if they feel strongly about an issue. As a corollary, group leaders must carry their members with them if they want to move policy into new pathways.

3. Exit options

Members who become dissatisfied with group policies, services or effectiveness have three basic choices. They can leave the group – the 'exit' option;

or they can stay in and use their 'voice' option to try and change the group's performance, e.g. by campaigning for new policies or a new leadership. Alternatively, dissatisfied members may opt for the 'loyalty' option, remaining within the group and keeping quiet about their dissatisfactions (Hirschman, 1970). Economists have seen exit as the normal response, since consumers typically desert firms with declining products for alternative suppliers. Political scientists have been preoccupied with voice options and until the 1980s paid little systematic attention to the implications of exiting for organizational control.

In fact most cases of organizational decline trigger a mixture of exit and voice responses, depending upon how sensitive demand for the organization's outputs is to declines in quality (Figure 2.1). The top graph here shows this quality (in this case, the group's effectiveness) declining as we move up the vertical axis, while the horizontal axis shows the number of people consuming the outputs. As quality falls from W to V, so the people consuming outputs falls from A to B. The degree to which this change will affect the organization can be gauged from the bottom graph where outputs are diagrammed against the unit price of outputs (in this case the membership fee), which is assumed to be static here since we are modelling only a quality decline. The hatched area on this bottom graph is the 'exit' rectangle – the larger it becomes the more notice management will take of people leaving. On the top graph the rectangle WRSV represents the scale of any 'voice' reaction, which will be larger, according to Hirschman, the more people still stay with the group and consume the organization's output, and the greater the decline in quality which has taken place. In Hirschman's original schema the sensitivity of demand to quality declines is the key variable determining the relative influence of voice or exit reactions on the organizational leadership. In Figure 2.1 quite a small quality decline triggers a large loss of demand for the organization's outputs, so that exit reactions are more important than voice protests. In Figure 2.2, by contrast, demand is very insensitive (inelastic) with respect to quality, so that exit is less influential than voice, as shown by the relative sizes of the two shaded rectangles.

Political scientists have extended Hirschman's typology to capture better the multiple options open to voluntary group members (Barry, 1974; Birch, 1975), particularly by allowing for people to use *both* the exit and voice options to express dissatisfaction (see Figure 2.3). Unhappy group members who first protest and then leave will have more impact within the group than those who simply renounce their allegiance without publicizing their reasons for leaving. Exit can also take several forms. People may *defect* to a rival group, for example leaving one trade union for a direct competitor. If no viable rival exists people may *transfer concerns* to another issue completely, for example by giving up campaigning for nuclear disarmament in favour of animal liberation. Finally, dissatisfied interest group members

17

Democracy, Bureaucracy and Public Choice

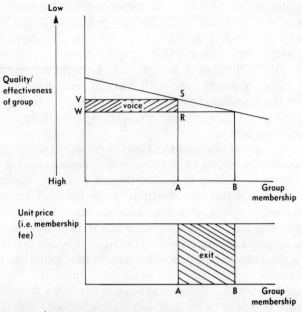

Source: Hirschman (1970), p. 130, Figure 2.

Figure 2.1 **The relative significance of exit and voice for an interest group – demand elastic with respect to quality**

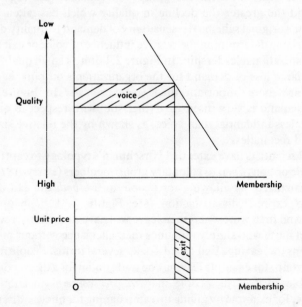

Figure 2.2 **Exit and voice with inelastic demand**

Interest groups and collective action

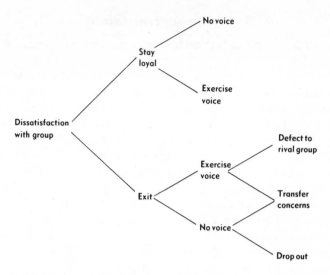

Figure 2.3 **Varieties of exit and voice options open to dissatisfied group members**

may *drop out* of activism altogether, reverting to more privatized or individualized concerns (Hirschman, 1985). Hence group leaderships cannot afford lightly to alienate their members, nor can they easily suffer a gradual seepage of members to other groups or causes through mildly unpopular polices. To keep their rank and file involved they must closely monitor their performance and adjust their policies.

4. Internal democracy

Most groups operate in a basically democratic fashion, partly because of the factors already discussed. Of course, some groups regularly display quite passive reactions by members (such as low participation in trade union elections in many Western countries), with leadership initiatives being uniformly adopted. However, the 'rule of anticipated reactions' argues that this situation can arise either because leaders are so powerful that members cannot gainsay them, or because leaders take care only to propose what members will accept. In addition, dissatisfied members may simply exit, or choose a more appropriate group in the first place. Hence grass roots passivity or minimal participation within democratic structures normally reflects basic satisfaction with the leadership's policies. Group participation is like a deep pool where the existing pattern of surface ripples involves relatively few members. But if leaders mishandle an issue or get out of touch, members can quickly become involved in large numbers, creating a wave of discontent that produces sweeping changes in group policies or top personnel.

19

5. Legitimacy constraints

No group leader can publicly claim to represent members' interests without regular and open procedures for gauging their views. Even groups where numerical representation is inappropriate (e.g. business trade associations covering large and small firms) have adopted procedures with a democratic façade (such as policy-making conferences) in search of external legitimacy. Internal democracy legitimates the group's advocacy to government by providing authentic evidence of its members' preference intensities, and it is critical for the group's public image with the potentially sceptical mass media and public. One study of influences on American public opinion suggests that: 'Groups and individuals representing various special interests, taken together, tend to have a negative effect on public opinion. In many instances they seem actively to have antagonized the public and created a genuine adverse effect' (Page et al., 1987, p. 37). While some groups influenced public opinion positively, the activity of others had negative impacts. Clearly, democratic legitimacy is critical in achieving a successful public stance for a group, as well as demonstrating that group interests are in line with a broader public interest. In the United States, protest movements and demonstrations, ethnic groups without organizational structures and business corporations seem not to be widely seen as 'credible or legitimate sources of opinion leadership' (Page et al., 1987, p. 37).

Interest group strategies

Groups promote their goals in three main ways. A first requirement is to *demonstrate preference intensities* using a series of progressively more costly actions as a thermometer of members' feelings on an issue:

Low-cost actions	Responding to routine consultations.
	Petitions.
	Lobbying elected representatives.
	Mass media publicity.
	Testifying before the legislature or other hearings.
	Commissioning research.
	Continuous involvement in consultations.
	Public campaigns.
	Demonstrations.
	Attempts to obstruct policy implementation.
	Non-co-operation with government.
	Boycotts or non-compliance.
	Strikes/industrial action.
High-cost actions	Civil disobedience.

Group members will only incur particular costs if they feel strongly enough about an issue. The graduated continuum of more costly actions means that group leaders cannot easily misrepresent their members' preference intensities. Few other political input processes are so focused or provide reliable information about preference intensities. For instance, voting or opinion poll answers are almost costless, hence people may vote strategically or dissimulate about their feelings in such surveys. Since most issues directly touch the interests only of small parts of society, 'the steady appeasement of relatively small groups' (Dahl, 1961, p. 145) allows politicians to reweight policy-making somewhat towards the interests of intense minorities.

A second key strategy is to *routinize the group's influence*, boosting the ratio of influence achieved per unit cost incurred by members. Key activities here include fund-raising, better organization, regular lobbying, systematic public monitoring and consultation with government and legislators. Group leaders want to be able to influence decision-making in its earliest, formative stages, before key political actors have adopted fixed public positions. Group leaders also want to increase their own freedom of manoeuvre by lowering costs to members of a given level of group effectiveness. Hence they strive to secure an 'insider' position with government agencies and the legislature, cultivating a responsible image. Their efforts coincide with the anxiety of politicians to keep on the right side of major groups which establish a track record of effectively influencing the legislature or public opinion about government proposals – thereby drastically reducing groups' need to resort to public campaigning or high-cost obstructionist tactics in future. The difficulty of advocating some 'special interest' claims in public debate (noted above, page 20) increases group leaders' preference for insider access. Hence success on one round of an issue normally becomes a resource for further rounds of the same issue, conferring procedural advantages on the group as well as building it a reputation for having influence.

However, pluralists argue that winning one issue will not translate into success on otherwise unrelated issues because the government system in liberal democracies is highly fragmented. Agencies handle only a few closely connected issues, while committees of the legislature usually follow departmental boundaries. In addition, mass media coverage and public attitudes both vary greatly from issue to issue. So no group can be an insider in all policy networks simultaneously. Thus a farmer's lobby may successfully persuade one agency to curb foreign food imports, have some modest influence over another in securing property tax exemptions and yet completely fail to convince a third agency that hormone drugs for cattle do not represent a health risk.

The third group strategy is *directly influencing majority opinion* in favourable ways. For the group process to work well, the underlying structure of social cleavages must be favourable. In benign configurations conflicting interests do not run too deep, can be compromised easily, or are 'tradeable'. For example, with 'partisan mutual adjustment' people with divergent views need not agree on any single compromise, but modify their claims and counter-claims so as to minimize mutual losses and decision-making costs. With tradeable interest cleavages (such as most economic issues) outcomes supported by large majorities can normally be constructed. But the conflicts between races, ethnic groups, linguistic affiliations, and nationalist/regionalist movements are often non-negotiable. Status quo policies – such as the maintenance of racial superiority, the social dominance of one ethnic group, or an official monopoly for one language – often load costs onto minorities, who in turn can embrace objectives incompatible with the existing system, such as a demand for complete self-government or the right to secede from the state. Conflicts of this kind are unlikely to permit any effective compromise between the two (or more) sides involved.

The pattern of multiple cleavages can have considerable importance, especially on less tradeable issues. Cross-cutting cleavages allow a minority adversely affected by policy proposals to appeal to sections of the majority (Lipset, 1959; Dahl, 1956 and 1971, pp. 105–24). For example, if union organization cuts across social class lines, the minority of unionized manual workers in Western societies can make twin appeals, across the class divide to unionized non-manual people, and across the organizational divide to non-unionized workers, with a correspondingly better change of influencing majority views. Cumulative cleavages are the least benign, for here multiple lines of social division bisect the social structure in almost the same place. For example, if union organization runs on strictly class lines, with almost all manual workers being members while the non-manual majority is wholly non-union, there is no basis for dialogue across the class-plus-union divide.

The group universe

Pluralists acknowledge the obvious fact that interest groups have widely varying levels of political influence. But they insist that it is legitimate and desirable for democratically elected politicians to take account of four factors, which empirically determine the relative influence of groups over policy-making:

- *Absolute size.* Other things being equal, larger groups carry more weight than smaller ones, because they control more votes at election time.
- *Rates of mobilization.* This factor is defined as a group's actual membership divided by its potential membership. Holding other factors constant, groups which clearly command majority support in a defined sector of the population are more influential than those which are weakly mobilized in another sector.
- *Preference intensities.* Other things being equal, the groups whose members feel strongly about something are more influential than those whose members are relatively apathetic.

22

- *Pivotal position.* Again when everything else is held constant, groups occupying a social or political position marginal between two alternative majority coalitions are more influential than those which fall in the main body of these coalitions. Pivotal groups can swing behind different positions, whereas the mainstream groups in social coalitions are normally locked into fixed positions.

Combining these variables yields the following general equation:

$$E = aS + bM + cI + dP$$

where E stands for group effectiveness, S for size, M for the rate of mobilization, I for the intensity of members' preferences and P for an index of the group's pivotality; and a, b, c and d are unknown variables which vary across countries and time periods. An influential group need not score highly on S, M, I and P simultaneously. Politicians may well discount a large group's protests if they think its members are not concerned or organized enough to change their votes over an issue, or if the group is already firmly committed to supporting or opposing them. But a small, relatively non-aligned group, incensed over a key question, really might sway more votes – because its members feel so strongly, are sufficiently organized to make their vote-switching count and form part of the floating voter population politicians need to attract. More generally, of course, politicians want to avoid public controversy where they appear as unpopular or attract damaging publicity.

To see how the pluralist model can cope with starkly unequal interest group influence, consider two British examples of contrasting behaviour by the same politicians. In 1984–5 Margaret Thatcher's Conservative government resolutely held out against a year-long protest strike by the reputedly powerful British coal miners' union. A year later, however, the government suffered a very rare defeat in the legislature following a protest campaign against a publicly announced law allowing shops to trade freely on Sundays. The National Union of Mineworkers (NUM) lost because it was small, decimated by redundancies in the period since its previously successful strikes in the early 1970s. In addition, the NUM was affiliated to the Labour party, which most miners firmly supported – so that defying the strike would hardly lose the Conservatives any votes. More critically the NUM's membership divided for and against the strike. Two-thirds of miners took action to prevent further job losses in the industry; but the remaining third worked normally, and eventually seceded from the NUM to form a breakaway trade union. These factors more than offset the obviously intense preferences of a majority of miners, who sacrificed a year's pay in the struggle. By contrast, the coalition of interests who successfully blocked Sunday trading was quite large and broadly based, including the shopworkers' union (and hence the labour movement generally) plus the Christian churches. Although diverse in make-up, these groups were able to unite in defence of the status quo and in opposition to the government's market-oriented law. And although the shop workers and Christians prepared to change their vote on the issue were less numerous than the consumers who could benefit from Sunday trading, the protest coalition spanned many previous government supporters dissatisfied with the Conservatives' apparently 'unheeding' approach to policy-making. This minority's strong opposition persuaded far more Conservative MPs to vote against their government than the apathetic support of a largely passive majority opinion. The only groups enthusiastically in favour of Sunday trading were businessmen and shopkeepers, virtually certain to vote Conservative anyway, whatever the government did.

Pluralists expect many diverse interest groups continuously to lobby government, legislators and parties. Patterns of group influence vary widely across issues and time periods. Because start-up costs for new groups are low in liberal democracies, and access to decision-makers relatively easy, the composition of the group universe is in constant flux. Studies of US national interest groups suggest that the period since the late 1950s has seen a relatively concentrated burst of new group formations, by citizens' groups and political action committees, and in the 1980s by business groups (Walker, 1983, pp. 394–5; Wilson, 1981). Competition between groups is vigorous, and winning alliances tend to be unstable over time, breaking down and re-forming in new configurations. Even where the group universe shows a very stable pattern of mobilization, the potential for new configurations is always present if currently quiescent people feel their interests under threat, and become 'sporadic interventionists' (Dowse and Hughes, 1977). A small change in the proportion of politically active citizens can radically reconstruct existing influences, and group leaders exert influence over politicians partly because of their ability to mobilize their members to turn out and vote (Uhlaner, 1989). Policy-makers must constantly adjust their decisions to reflect not only observable inequalities of influence between mobilized groups, but also the balance of electoral forces amongst currently less active voters.

Pluralists admit that chronic inequalities of influence can arise, reinforced if favoured groups achieve a clear insider status or political inequalities reinforce those in economic markets. Yet they remain optimistic that stark influence imbalances will create systems of *countervailing powers* (Galbraith, 1953). In generally competitive economic markets, corporations or trade unions which achieve monopoly power can earn super-normal profits for a time. But these exceptional rewards also create strong incentives for other economic actors to enter the relevant market, and to compete for a share of the action. This effect does not mean that an initially unorganized group will suddenly be able to organize against a monopoly interest. It only requires that one concentration of influence should tend to provoke the growth of some competitor. For example, in the present century a tiny handful of national companies have dominated the British newspaper market. Yet this corporate control was qualified principally by a parallel growth of union power in the industry, and later by the emergence of alternative power centres controlling the broadcasting media.

A strong public choice version of this argument rationalizes existing patterns of public policy as an equilibrium outcome struck between groups pressuring for more state subsidies, and those seeking lower taxes (Becker, 1985). Since total subsidies cannot exceed total taxes (including taxes on future generations and hidden taxes such as inflation), the sum of all interest group influences is zero (Becker, 1983, p. 395). However, different subsidy and tax arrangements have varying effects on aggregate social welfare, some increasing efficiency while others create 'deadweight costs'. There is an important asymmetry favouring taxpayers here: more efficient taxes will be supported by groups pressing for both more subsidies and lower taxes, since it will reduce taxation costs for taxpayers but also cut political organization costs for subsidy-seekers. But more efficient subsidies will not be welcomed by taxpayer groups: subsidy-seekers' political efforts will become more worthwhile, causing their activism to rise and thereby imposing greater costs on taxpayers.

Over many rounds of this conflict, influence from both types of group will favour the emergence of more efficient public policies, especially those which maximize aggregate welfare – where overall gainers could in principle compensate overall losers, even if no such direct compensation in fact takes place:

> The condemnation of special interest groups is excessive because competition among these groups contributes to the survival of policies that raise output: favourably affected groups tend to lobby more for these policies than unfavourably affected groups against. Indeed, no policy that lowered social output would survive if all groups were equally large and skillful at producing political influence, for the opposition would always exert more influence than proponents. (Becker, 1985, p. 344)

By picturing political life as an economic terrain fought over by multiple well-organized groups, Becker's model reproduces Galbraith's original countervailing powers argument: any group which acquires monopoly influence and differential subsidies or freedom from taxation will trigger rival groups to invade its policy space in search of a share of its excess benefits, or produce greater mobilization by taxpayers to secure reduced payouts. The general pattern is likely to be one of many groups receiving relatively small subsidies, and a complex pattern of 'cross-hauling' produced by multiple taxes and subsidy schemes. The only exceptions, reaping substantial net benefits, are likely to be relatively small groups (such as farmers in the United States and Britain) who are differentially

25

efficient at organizing themselves and whose benefits end up being funded by many different taxpaying groups (Wilson, 1973, Chapter 16). Underpinning this argument again there remains a general pluralist optimism that 'democracies have political competition among groups with relatively equal political strength' (Becker, 1985, p. 344).

Finally, pluralists do not perceive any significant trend towards the creation of 'corporatist' relations between government and major interest blocs. For politicians ballot box signals count most. Where closed relations between government and insider interest groups develop, it is chiefly on discrete issue areas and involves relatively low-level agencies – as with agriculture ministries in many liberal democracies. But these departments are often overridden by legislatures, cabinets and elected chief executives who recognize that unorganized interests also need protection and control more votes.

The massing of similar interest groups into peak associations, such as labour union congresses or federations of business associations, poses more problems for pluralists, especially if governments regularly negotiate with these organizations on issues such as the management of inflation. But in many countries peak associations are quite weak bodies, with few coercive powers over member interest groups, who retain the capacity to make autonomous decisions on issues which are critical for their members. Constituent interest groups can usually withdraw from peak associations with little damage to their basic operations – especially if more than one peak association claims to represent the overarching interests of business/ employers or (less commonly) of labour. Labour unions or business associations maintain more or less united fronts for public relations purposes. But conflicts of interest between firms, industries and sectors are often mirrored inside trade union and business organizations, making their common platforms fragile and susceptible to internal dissent. Alternatively, peak associations represent lowest common denominator interests or stress consensual themes – making them unlikely to exercise any overweening power over government policy, whatever their apparently privileged role in policy consultations.

Stable and powerful corporatist arrangements are not usual in liberal democracies, outside small states in vulnerable positions in world markets, where internal social interests have especially strong incentives to co-operate in a turbulent world economic environment (Katzenstein, 1985). In larger countries, most government/peak association co-ordination amounts only to a weak *tripartism*. In crises, governments have tried to persuade labour movements to hold down wage claims or pressured business leaders to moderate price increases, especially in the late 1970s when both President Carter in the United States (with wage and price guidelines) and the Labour government in Britain (with a formalized 'social contract') followed different versions of this strategy. Yet when such efforts at tripartism break down (as they did in the US recession of 1980 and in the British 'winter of discontent' of 1978–9), previous anti-inflation gains may be offset and interventionist policies abandoned. Later political leaders often renounce anything resembling corporatist arrangements – as both Reagan and Thatcher did from 1980 onwards.

Such sharp swings in government/peak association relations reflect the considerable dissensus in many liberal democracies about the legitimacy or advisability of government negotiating policy implementation with 'the big battalions'. Co-opting the labour movement into policy-making is opposed by right-wing parties and market liberals, who see trade unions as vested interests constraining competition in free markets. Outside North America, strong socialist parties are equally critical of government–big business linkages. Pluralists argue that long-term partisan controversy over the legitimacy of tripartite arrangements decisively refutes claims that advanced industrial societies are ineluctably developing towards corporatism.

THE CORPORATIST APPROACH

Basic assumptions

Exponents of corporatism acknowledge that much routine policy-making in Western democracies operates on pluralist lines. But strategic interrelationships between government and major interest organizations are qualitatively different from the conventional interest group process (Lehmbruch and Schmitter, 1982; Schmitter and Lehmbruch, 1979). Key economic interests – trade unions, big business trade associations and the professions – play a disproportionate role in social development for four reasons:

1. *Class basis.* The key groups express the economic interests of large social classes or class fractions. Differences between occupational or social classes are a basic social division. Economic struggles between these interest blocs (e.g. between unions for wage increments and capital for higher profits) largely determine the pace and direction of economic development.

2. *Control of resources.* Major groups exercise collective power over resources which are vital for overall economic activity; professions claim to control access to socially indispensable knowledge; business corporations determine the scale, location and timing of capital movements and investments; and an effective trade union movement can withdraw labour, even in vital public utilities or services. Structural variations in resource endowments are critical in explaining cross-national differences in the way that the same interest groups are organized. For example, Wallerstein (1989) argues that trade union densities are over 90 per cent in Sweden but under 20 per cent in the United States chiefly as a function of labour market size. In Sweden's small labour market of less than 4 million people it is much easier for trade unions to ensure that few if any workers can be

27

brought in by employers to replace those who have gone on strike. Saturation levels of unionization are hence cost effective, and the value of union membership increases accordingly. By contrast, in the US's 93–million-strong labour market, the largest by far of any liberal democracy, it would be prohibitively expensive in organizing costs for trade unions to pursue any similar objective. US unions' equilibrium level of organization is much lower, hence fresh labour can fairly easily be substituted for strikers by employers, and the effectiveness of the unions' basic resource (the strike weapon) is significantly less than in Sweden.

3. *Ideological distinctiveness.* Major socio-economic groups generate and maintain ideologies which command widespread support, and extensively condition how their members interpret social issues. The integral relationship between trade unions and socialist/social democratic parties in most West European countries demonstrates the strength of this ideological development. Business linkages with political parties are usually less formally institutionalized, but in practical terms business support for one party or a party bloc is just as apparent in most liberal democracies. Some professions (such as medicine and law) develop ideologies claiming to be socially impartial, to 'stand outside' class conflicts and to be neutral in their professional work about political controversies (Johnson, 1972). But even in these cases, professional ideologies powerfully influence a wide range of their members' social attitudes and behaviour, usually in a socially conservative direction (Wilding, 1982).

4. *Solidaristic group loyalties.* For all these reasons people's social identities are partly constituted by membership of a trade union or profession, or holding a managerial post in a large corporation. Because these roles condition how people interpret their own interests and those of other social groups, members of major functional groups tend to behave and respond fairly cohesively in the political system. And this in turn reinforces the pressure for groups to mass together into powerful inclusive peak associations, which formulate some policies across the board. Clearly, however, feelings of 'solidarism' are considerably diluted in larger social blocs of this kind, with major conflicts of interest arising inside peak associations as well as between them.

Interest groups' internal organization

Major interest blocs are not internally organized on pluralist lines. Group leaders' discretion in policy-making is limited, but chiefly by pressures to maintain consistency with past organizational policy, to sustain organizational resources and to safeguard the group's ideology from erosion. Group leaders do respond to large-scale movements of opinion amongst their mass membership. But such shifts are relatively rare. Most of the time, group leaders are insulated from detailed control by their members, and need not respond in a fine-grained way to small-scale variations in rank-and-file views.

Group leaders and grass roots members are bound together by power–dependency relations. On the one hand, pluralists are right to stress that members have considerable resources, and some groups depend heavily on mass participation. On the other hand, members also rely extensively on group leaders for information about national issues and feasible policy options. Leaders run their organizations so as to conserve their autonomy, deploying centrally-held resources in local or specific conflicts, and monopolizing the group's external relations with other interest groups and with government.

In addition, leaders of corporate groups (trade unions, the professions and business associations) try to limit members' exit options or make them costly to implement. Peak associations reflect the common interest of similar group leaders in limiting their competition for members – as in the 1928 agreement by Trade Union Congress unions in Britain to eliminate poaching of one union's members by another. Union leaders wanted a 'rational' pattern with as far as possible a single dominant union organizing each trade, or at least an orderly oligarchy. Moreover, closed-shop rules make a particular union card a condition of employment. Together with defined territories for unions, the closed shop implies that those workers who dissent from their union's national policies confront insuperable difficulties in leaving or exercising 'voice' inside their current union (Hemingway, 1978). Similarly, in many professions, membership of or qualification by the professional body is a key criterion for employment or advancement, making any challenge to organization policies difficult.

Group strategies

Pluralist accounts picture a one-way flow of representation from interest groups to government, but corporatist exponents see instead a two-way representation/control relationship. Group leaders undertake to control their members' behaviour on behalf of government, in return for concessions on other issues affecting the group leadership. 'Responsible' pay bargaining in Sweden or Austria is achieved at top levels by governments consulting labour movement leaders on a wide range of social and economic issues, often remote from the concerns of grass roots trade unionists.

The development of dual control/representation systems restructures inter-group relations. There is no constant flux of groups but a pyramiding of key economic interests into strong, hierarchical and stable interest blocs. Group leaders are partly organizational *apparatchiks*, prepared to sublimate some of their group's autonomy in a wider and more powerful collective organization, and interested in achieving political influence well outside their nominal area of concern.

The group universe

A fluid and variable interest group process operates only at the 'middle levels of power' in modern democracies. The pressures for corporatist decision-making arise at a different level involving strategic issues for economic and social development – control of inflation, management of international economic competitiveness, shaping technological development and setting economic priorities. In all these cases policy is set by conflicts or co-operation between functional interest groups themselves, and with government, relegating conventional representative politics to the sidelines. Patterns of corporatism vary considerably. In some cases (such as post-war Japan or France under de Gaulle), strong links are forged between central government departments and giant industrial corporations to shape national economic development. In Austria and most of Scandinavia more balanced three-way corporatist practices have developed, formally involving both labour union and business organizations in the determination of wide areas of public policy. Professions are typically integrated into the mass of supporting branches which spread out the corporatist net below top-level national planning or 'concertation' institutions, a set of institutions sometimes called 'meso-corporatism' (Cawson, 1985).

The corporatist model of government–interest group relations is an immanent trend, an 'ideal type' situation not necessarily always approximated in practice. Swings against previous corporatist intermediation may well occur. Liberal democratic governments can always try to manage the economy without the active support of major interest blocs. The costs of regaining government autonomy in this manner are likely to be prohibitive, however. For example, when the Thatcher government in 1979–82 controlled British inflation by monetary means alone, their strategy tripled mass unemployment and decimated manufacturing industry. Cushioned at the time by the windfall benefits of North Sea oil the economy could get by, while the Falklands War provided an extraneous political boost for the government. Yet long-term inflationary pressures and acute balance-of-payments problems reappeared in Britain by the end of the decade (Whiteley, 1990). For corporatists Britain in the 1980s demonstrated only that political parties and leaders retained the freedom to embark on objectively damaging policies for ideological reasons. But normally 'anti-corporatism in one country' is an unsustainable stance both economically and electorally.

THE LOGIC OF COLLECTIVE ACTION MODEL

Basic assumptions

Olson's starting point is the claim that individuals or organizations only join together to form interest groups when they are trying to achieve *collective benefits* which, once they are provided for some people, accrue to everyone else in a particular social category. Examples are union members campaigning for a wage increase benefiting all workers in their workplace whether union members or not, or a trade association lobbying for a tariff helping all firms in a particular industry, some of whom may not join the association.

In fact, Olson's original text made a narrower argument than this summary. He claimed that all interest groups pursue objectives which are 'public goods', defined by Samuelson (1954) as benefits which are *indivisible* (so that once produced for one person they are available for a wider group as well, or even for everyone in some relevant social category) and are also *non-excludable* (so that the supply of the good in question cannot be restricted to those people who organized to ensure its provision). In practice, public goods are hard to define precisely because of multiple criteria for inclusion, and the same problem also plagues Olson's model:

> Very few of the goals or goods that groups seek can accurately be
> described as pure public goods [in Samuelson's terms]. [So] it is
> probably best not to confuse the analysis of collective action by
> treating it as a problem in the provision of public goods. [Interest
> group] goods need to be collective only in the sense that they are
> collectively provided . . . Olson's analysis of collective action depends
> only . . . on *de facto* infeasibility of exclusion. (Hardin, 1982, p. 19)

Because all interest groups exist to provide collective goods, they confront the same central problem – how to persuade people to contribute. A public choice model must assume that all actors are rational utility maximizers, who join any group only if the benefits of membership exceed the costs. Each actor should:

1. Establish her individual welfare gain if the group exists and is successful.
2. Multiply (or discount) this net benefit by the likelihood that her personal contribution to the group will be decisive in achieving its objectives.
3. Compare this discounted net benefit with the undiscounted costs of joining up.

There is a key asymmetry here. While the potential benefits from group success may be substantial, the likelihood that any one individual's contribution will be decisive in securing these gains will decrease the larger the group. Yet participation costs (membership fees, time and resources involved in being active in the organization, and any risks or disadvantages of membership) will accrue to everyone who joins, however negligible their contribution to overall group success. In most circumstances then, rational actors should free-ride – that is, let other people incur the costs of collective action, while still receiving the same level of non-excludable goods.

Collective action around common objectives will only be spontaneously forthcoming in 'privileged' groups where *either* the number of potential members is small, *or* where the benefits of group activity are unequally distributed between members. In small groups one individual's non-participation may visibly reduce the group's viability. So long as group members can interact they will also develop ways of fostering mutual contributions, such as a 'tit for tat' strategy, refusing to help non-joiners while rewarding those who behave co-operatively (Axelrod, 1984). In larger groups, however, defectors make little difference to outcomes and become less visible. Sizeable privileged groups may still exist if some actors in the group stand to gain disproportionately from its success, and hence are willing to shoulder a large share of the organizing costs – Olson's example is NATO, where the United States shouldered a disproportionately large share of the costs of the post-war military alliance. By contrast with privileged groups, Olson argues, larger groups campaigning for collective benefits always remain under-mobilized or even completely latent unless they can develop some means of combating free-rider problems.

Group strategies

The essential task for group leaders therefore is to develop private membership benefits, that is, either rewards restricted to those who join the group, or sanctions against non-joiners. Because these 'selective incentives' can be administered so as to discriminate between members and outsiders there is no rationale for free-riding. Potential members know for sure that they cannot receive private benefits without joining the group, or that sanctions will probably be applied to them. Hence they compare these benefits (or absence of sanctions) directly with membership costs – whereas collective benefits are discounted by the probability that the individual member's contribution will be decisive in securing them.

Positive selective incentives (benefits of membership) can include the intrinsic interest of group activities, and 'rewards created by the act of associating' (Hansen, 1985, p. 81), such as friendship and a sense of belonging. However, Olson envisaged a primary role for more materialistic incentives, almost all of which commercial organizations could also provide. For example, trade unions or professions can offer their members specialized insurance services, or legal aid in disputes with employers, in addition to the collective benefits of solidarity. Or membership benefits might be unrelated to the group's collective goals – as when unions offer shopping discount cards or cheaper holiday travel. A classic example is a joint group, the National Retired Teachers Association and the American Association of Retired Persons:

> In 1965 the combined membership of NRTA/AARP stood at approximately 750,000 and by 1979 it had grown to 13 million members, making it one of the largest voluntary associations in the world. The secret of this phenomenal growth, however, was not the

attractiveness of the policies being advocated by the group; rather it was the special medical insurance policies available to older persons through membership, the tours and vacations conducted by the groups with the special needs of the elderly in mind, the commercial discounts and the many useful personal services available for retired persons through membership. . . . These two groups grew because of their ability to provide selective material benefits for their members, not because of the devotion of their members to the common interests of the elderly. (Walker, 1983, p. 396)

Negative selective incentives against non-members played a key part in the historical development of trade unions in all Western countries. Union ideologies stigmatize strike-breakers as 'scabs' and 'blacklegs', and legitimize boycotts on speaking to or working with non-members. These measures were often backed up in earlier periods by extensive physical intimidation. Manual trade unions also pushed for all-union workplaces, thereby obviating the free-rider problem and converting initially collective goods of organization into private benefits of union membership. Refusing to join industrial action in such a 'closed shop' could precipitate loss of membership, followed by loss of employment.

The group-joining decision which Olson envisages can be summed up in a simple inequality (Hansen, 1985). People will join a group only where:

$$(G_j * p_j) + I_j - C_j > R_j$$

Here G_j stands for individual j's net gain if the group realizes collective benefits; p_j indicates the probability that the individual's decision to join will determine whether the collective good is provided; I_j stands for the private benefits of group membership to the individual; and C_j stands for the costs of membership. On the other side of the inequality, R_j stands for the optimum pay-off which the individual could get in some alternative way by investing C_j amount of money, time or other resources. To specify the equation a bit mort, assume for the moment that $p_j = P/N$, where P is the group's overall probability of achieving its aims and N is its potential membership, and the actor has no alternative use for C_j amount of resources. Then:

$$(G_j * P/N) + I_j > C_j$$

In any reasonably large group collective benefits, however substantial, are so discounted that they have little influence on the decision to join or not: instead the balance of I_j and C_j is crucial. The greater the alternative uses for resources, the more selective incentives must exceed membership costs. More generally, as the opportunity costs of participation rise, so must I.

In addition, membership costs are incurred before benefits are received, and normally involve different types of assets (such as cash for membership dues, or spare time for activism). Even if group membership produces a net welfare gain, these assets are usually not directly replaced. Hence to join the group, people must have Cj amount of spare resources. Passing this threshold is easier for the well-off, while poorer people will have more pressing demands upon their marginal resources. Hence group participation rates should be class-biased – as they are in most Western democracies with involvement in groups rising broadly in line with people's incomes.

The internal organization of groups

Because selective incentives are vital in overcoming free-rider problems, interest groups are highly unlikely to be internally democratic, whatever their formal organization charts may proclaim. Developing positive incentives for group-joining requires special skills in identifying opportunities for new goods or suppliers, organizing production and devising marketing campaigns. And applying negative sanctions to non-members normally demands high levels of group discipline, especially in an unfavourable legal or social environment. In public choice accounts group leaders are seen as political entrepreneurs on a par with profit-maximizing businessmen: self-interested risk-takers who seize a chance to make good by providing goods or services to others. But political entrepreneurs operate in basically non-market contexts, dominated by collective goods production (Frohlich *et al.*, 1971). Their key role is to link up collective goals with selective incentives, so that large- and medium-sized groups can overcome free-rider problems. 'The successful entrepreneur in the large group case . . . is above all an innovator with selective incentives' (Olson, 1978, p. 177).

When a group is just forming, a political entrepreneur must invest in subsidizing its activities to keep membership costs down and overcome teething problems until it becomes independently viable. Once the group achieves critical mass using selective incentives, it acquires political influence and the leadership can deliver additional collective benefits to group members as a by-product. But unless an appropriate structure of private benefits is first created to make joining worthwhile, large groups never reach this stage. Hence group members are fundamentally dependent upon leaders to provide the entrepreneurial skills and initial subsidies.

For this system to work, group leaders' individual utilities must correspond in some key respects with those of the membership. Leadership incomes, perks, influence, patronage and social prestige all tend to increase with group size and effectiveness, other things being equal. The higher the group's rate of mobilization (its ability to recruit potential members in its chosen market), the more secure leaders become against competing entrepreneurs or new group entrants in their market, and the more they can raise the rate at which they charge group members for their services. Super-normal incomes for leaders require an insulated market, high member dependency and few exit possibilities. Higher rates of mobilization also boost the group's effectiveness and leaders' income if it is performance-related. Even if leaders are paid on a flat-rate basis, interest groups become easier to manage as they get more successful and established. These incentives should ensure that group size, effectiveness and leaders' welfare all go up simultaneously.

Group leaders want a centralized organization, capable of responding flexibly to external threats. They always act to increase their autonomy from control by the membership, to enhance their discretionary authority and to raise or maintain group members' dependence upon them. At the limit, interest groups' internal organization may resemble the hierarchical patterns of business corporations, rather than the democratic idyll perceived by pluralists. Other things being equal, members might want a more democratic organization, committed to consulting them on policy issues. But of course other things never are equal, so members by and large passively accept leadership initiatives.

However, Olson's model has more difficulty in explaining the behaviour of grass roots activists, who in many interest groups carry the workload of local campaigning and meetings. One possible explanation of activism argues backwards from evidence of their strong involvement to the claim that they derive stronger selective incentives from their participation, for example, in local patronage powers or status. A second tack (used in the 'adversary politics' model of party activists) is to picture group activists as strongly committed ideologically, unwilling to tolerate any policy changes which qualify the pursuit of collective benefits (see page 133). On either interpretation some significant conflicts may arise between leaders and activists.

The group universe

Public choice analysis contradicts pluralist optimism about the role of groups in policy-making for three reasons. First, patterns of interest group activity reveal very little about underlying preference intensities in society. Group mobilization is a by-product of the ability of entrepreneurs to develop selective incentives, and the distribution of such opportunities bears no relation to how strongly people feel about shared goals. Collective action problems keep many medium- and large-sized groups 'latent' or chronically under-mobilized, despite potential members' strong preference intensities. For example, public interest in consumer affairs is high but consumer organizations remain weakly developed in most Western countries. By contrast, other groups which are easy to organize may be highly effective in representing their members' moderately strong feelings within the political system.

Second, groups acquire sharply unequal levels of influence over policy-making which once established persist for long periods. The interest group universe is stable over time, with little evidence of the constant flux of influence or changing alliances that pluralists claim to find. Only radical shifts in social or economic conditions, or the advent of new entrepreneurs, create new groups. There is no basis for expecting countervailing powers to develop, indeed quite the contrary: successful groups will strengthen over time, while under-mobilized groups will remain latent.

Third, governments, legislators and public bureaucrats are all aware that the pattern of interest group activity gives little or no worthwhile or reliable information about the social distribution of preference intensities. Hence they are free to act arbitrarily, according influence to some groups they want to encourage and denying it to others. Policy-makers of course use the pluralist rhetoric of consulting all legitimate interests as a useful ideological cover. In practice, they defer to well-mobilized groups controlling powerful economic resources, or those which are important for the governing party's electoral support. This discretionary ability explains why many Western European social democratic governments accord primary influence to trade unions, while right-wing governments exclude the unions from influence and defer instead to business organizations. Governments' ability to legitimate some interests and ignore others creates a clear distinction between 'insider' and 'outsider' groups, further undermining the openness or permeability of the system.

THE NEW RIGHT MODEL

Basic assumptions

More recent public choice work on interest groups retains the rational actor model, but parts company fundamentally with Olson by denying that the central objectives of groups involve non-excludable public goods. Some groups do seek genuinely or intrinsically indivisible benefits. But most groups campaign for benefits which could be supplied as divisible and excludable goods through normal market mechanisms. Their objectives only involve 'collective benefits' because the group wages a political struggle to obtain them from government. The state apparatus can supply almost any private good in a collective form simply by exercising coercive powers to requisition the social resources necessary, or by funding service provision out of general taxation.

In Western legal systems, government provision must not be overtly discriminatory (e.g. by subsidizing named persons): rule-of-law constraints are the primary reason why government-provided goods are not as excludable or divisible as those provided in markets. Virtually all welfare state benefits (health care, employment insurance, education, public housing, state-subsidized transport) *could* be delivered as private goods;

identical services are successfully marketed in the same societies. Of course, some social welfare benefits can accrue when government accedes to demands to subsidize or organize consumption of various 'worthy' goods of this kind, as when universal free health care reduces communicable diseases. But the new right believe that similar benefits accrue with private provision of these services, or could themselves be marketed more cheaply (e.g by buying inoculations against communicable diseases). Nor is most regulation any more 'inherently' concerned with public goods. Product safety requirements, rent controls in housing, or tariff barriers for particular industries are all disguised means of subsidizing some kinds of people while invisibly loading costs onto others. For the new right only a tiny proportion of the products and services supplied by government are genuine public goods – such as national defence or provisions which safeguard the legal basis for society.

Where group objectives involve securing government provision of basically private goods, or ensuring that indivisible but excludable goods are produced on the state budget, Olson's stress on free-rider problems in interest groups is inappropriate. Group leaders try to realize their private goods objectives in a form where they can influence the flow of benefits, making them excludable – for example, by 'colonizing' the agency providing the funding or regulation, winning over the agency's personnel by offering perks (such as lucrative post-retirement jobs for senior agency officials) or political and legislative support for the agency. Since senior bureaucrats want to maximize their agency's budget (see page 154 below), groups are pushing at an open door. Long-term relations between major groups, government agencies and (in some countries like the United States) the relevant committees of the legislature create 'iron triangles', single-mindedly pursuing the growth of sectional interest budgets or regulation. Many groups even receive government start-up subsidies or ongoing support, and reciprocate by expressing enhanced demands for state intervention (Walker, 1983, p. 402).

Closed or corporatist arrangements take further the creation of vested interests which are symbiotically linked to government agencies, with key groups integrated into the implementation process. At its simplest the group becomes a vital intermediary interpreting complex regulations to firms or citizens entitled to transfers. In more developed cases, rule-of-law constraints requiring the impartial application of regulations or disbursement of subsidies are by-passed so that something akin to a closed shop is created, and government help or subsidies are only effectively available to interest group members.

> For example, certain [American] trade associations sponsor the creation of codes meant to govern the specifications of goods produced by their industry. Uniform sizes of components or safety standards

established in these private codes are often accepted by government or private purchasing agents as minimum requirements and may sometimes be written directly into state or local statutes, thus taking on the force of law. . . . Similarly many associations of professionals in both the public and private sectors have managed to gain significant influence over licensing procedures, and several serve as accrediting agencies for educational programmes in their professional specialities. Until a decision by the Supreme Court in 1978 prevented the practice, many associations required any person wishing certification in the field to hold membership in the group – a direct form of coercion – but even now this practice has been made illegal, many professionals apparently regard membership in their professional society as a hedge against decertification. (Walker, 1983, p. 397)

In other cases, group leaders may succeed in regulating entry to their activity sector: for example, acreage restrictions in some American farm markets make it hard for new competitors to start up, while 'the US Civil Aeronautics Board did not certify a single new trunk airline between 1938 and 1976' (Becker, 1985, p. 100). Group leaders may also favour long-term subsidies because of the ability they confer to identify and penalize free-riders. As in other areas, the more fixed and stable group membership is, the greater the capacity for leaders to develop effective sanctions against non-joiners in an iterated game. Consequently, even large interest groups do not confront severe free-riding or collective action problems.

Group activity is essentially an organized effort by sectional interests to exploit government, artificially enlarging its budget and its tax demands. State growth imposes diffuse costs on interest group members, but because inequalities in group organization are so large and so long-lasting, successful groups can secure far more concentrated benefits from favourable government subsidies or regulation. Of course, group members may not gain striking *net* benefits because of the cumulation of deadweight costs impairing societal efficiency. And group leaders may recognize Becker's (1983) point that the sum of group influences must be zero since taxes and subsidies even out in the long run. But both members and leaders of individual groups continue to believe that larger sectional gains are possible. In addition, some government action may transfer subsidies directly between groups, without going through formal tax-raising, as with rent controls in private housing (Block and Olsen, 1981). And opting out of the competitive struggle for political influence over government would simply mean that the state machinery is captured by other groups which would impose additional costs upon the rest of society. Groups may be able to agree on some measures to constrain their joint costs of political organization (for example, limiting election campaign contributions), but this kind of collective action is likely to be minimal and fragile.

The internal organization of groups

New right accounts go further than Olson in stressing that political entrepreneurs can insulate themselves from control by interest group members. The position of group leaders is strengthened by their influence over a flow of benefits from government, and by their ability to capture regulatory agencies and get involved in public policy implementation. The more a group's leadership gain monopoly control over excludable benefits, the more costly it becomes for grass roots members to risk challenging their policies. An extreme example of the lack of internal democracy occurs when 'altruistic' élite groups acquire influential positions intermediating between welfare state agencies and their poorest client groups, whose voices are never heard directly and who have few means of controlling what is advocated in their name. 'Poverty professionals' (such as social workers, lawyers and middle-class cause groups demanding more welfare spending) shape policy implementation so as to maximize their own role in the process and to perpetuate and increase poor people's dependence upon them. They share a common interest with welfare bureaucrats in maintaining (perhaps even increasing) the numbers and types of social security payments, or the complexity and impenetrability of the rules which govern entitlements.

Group strategies

The fundamental group strategy is to build alliances by vote-trading with other interests organizing around different objectives. Group A agrees to support group B's priority concerns if B agree to vote in turn for A's key issue. *Log-rolling* in this fashion chains together interests which are objectively quite separate because the preferences of groups who vote-trade with each other cannot directly conflict. It is an especially successful 'coalition of minorities' strategy: groups which cannot command majority support individually can none the less become part of a winning majority. For example, Table 2.1 shows a society with five equally-sized and equally influential groups, where each group's priority demand benefits only

Table 2.1 *The initial configuration for log-rolling in a five-person society*

Group	Priority project	Project cost ($)	$ Pay-offs to:		Tax share (%)
			Group	Society	
Industrialists	Tariff	900	1,500	600	50
Motorists	New road	500	700	200	15
Pensioners	Elderly housing	500	800	300	5
Animal lovers	Vivisection ban	100	300	200	10
Parents	Better schools	100	200	200	20

themselves. Assuming equal political influence (e.g. equal voting power in elections or referenda) simplifies discussions: later on I relax this assumption. If project proposals are debated one by one, then with equal group voting power every proposal is defeated by four sets of votes to one, since no group has any incentive to approve any project except their own. Yet suppose that (somehow) the groups representing industrialists, motorists and animal lovers get together and agree to vote for each other's proposals, creating a package costing $1,500, with total benefits of $2,700 and favourable net pay-offs for all three participants. By contrast, the parents and pensioners incur net losses:

Group	Pay-off from total package	Share of total package costs	Net benefit
Industrialists	1,500	750	750
Motorists	700	225	475
Animal lovers	300	150	150
Parents	0	300	−300
Pensioners	0	75	−75
Society totals	*2,500*	*1,500*	*1,000*

The winning coalition secures three sets of votes against two for its package, whose net benefits handsomely exceed its social costs. Here vote-trading has clearly boosted social welfare, even though the losing minority are worse off.

Changing the pay-offs to make the package a welfare-reducing one does not rule out log-rolling however. If the pay-offs to the industrialists' and motorists' groups are cut to $850 and $300 dollars respectively, then the tariff and road programme cost respectively $50 and $200 more to implement than the benefits they yield. Yet the same package including both projects can still get voted through as a result of log-rolling, with revised costs and pay-offs as follows:

Group	Pay-off from total package	Share of total package costs	Net benefit
Industrialists	850	750	100
Motorists	300	225	75
Animal lovers	200	150	50
Parents	0	300	−300
Pensioners	0	75	75
Society totals	*1,350*	*1,500*	*−150*

Although two of the package elements decrease the social welfare and lower overall pay-offs, industrialists, motorists and animal lovers all still receive net benefits because some of the aggregate costs are distributed onto pensioners and parents. Because log-rolling can exploit minorities while actively reducing the social welfare, the political culture of liberal democracies typically frowns on explicit vote-trading.

The group universe

When a new democracy is set up, the interest group universe will characteristically appear very unstable. The search by group leaders for an optimal alliance may initially produce a rapid turnover of different majority coalitions on each issue. In Table 2.1 I did not explain why the groups representing industrialists, motorists and animal lovers could get together to vote through their package as opposed to some other grouping, nor why their alliance should persist. Suppose, for example, that the groups representing pensioners and parents offer the animal lovers' group an extra inducement (say, a side payment of $60 to go towards better animal care) to join up with them instead. The distribution of costs and benefits from the new package of elderly housing, better schooling and a ban on vivisection, plus the $60 side-payment, is now:

Group	Pay-off from total package	Share of total package costs	Net benefit
Animal lovers	360	70	290
Parents	200	170	30
Pensioners	800	65	735
Industrialists	0	350	−350
Motorists	0	105	−105
Society totals	*1,360*	*760*	*600*

So long as large majority coalitions cannot realize any greater benefits for their members than smaller coalitions, 'minimum winning coalitions' should emerge – where the smallest feasible majority offers each of its member interest groups the maximum opportunity for exploiting the excluded minority (Riker, 1962; Taylor and Laver, 1973). For example, in the five-group society considered above, coalitions of three groups should emerge, rather than four-group majorities.

The simple examples discussed so far explicitly assume equally-sized and equally influential groups. But in practice interest groups vary greatly in their political influence and voting power, thereby introducing a major complication into coalition theory. The new right argue that it is common to find situations where large groups with polarized interests compete to attract smaller marginal groups who can switch either way to create a majority. These pivotal or strategically advantaged minorities are *median groups*, needed to attain 51 per cent support; they typically attract benefits disproportionate to their electoral strength or numerical size. At elections or inside legislatures, where each participant counts for one, minimum winning coalitions involve the smallest feasible number of actors. Where group sizes are uneven, the coalition should consist of a mix of groups just able to secure a majority or to control policy-making.

Unlike other forms of alliance-building, minimum winning coalitions should be stable, an equilibrium outcome, which once achieved will not be disturbed unless one of the multiple system parameters shifts (for example, because of a new intake in legislatures). Alliances between groups become more stable as they bargain over successive rounds of decisions. The longer a liberal democracy lasts undisturbed, the more the interest group universe settles into a fixed pattern of mobilizations and alliances. The group system is further stabilized because public agencies and the legislature's committee system are 'colonized' by the major interest groups in each issue area.

Over time the group process raises the rate of exploitation of the government budget to meet sectional interests. Public expenditure and coercive taxation rise until an equilibrium point is reached where citizens no longer believe in the illusion that further enlargement of the state budget will deliver benefits to them net of its tax costs. The fragmentation of policy influence between multiple well-mobilized 'veto groups' converts the group universe into a structure frustrating the implementation of social changes. Since the most general and the most salient form of social change is economic growth, stable democracies tend to have slower rates of increase in their GDPs, a position adopted by Olson in *The Rise and Decline of Nations* (1982). Evidence cited for Olson's revised new-right position points to the United States and Great Britain as long-lasting, stable democracies where an established system of interest group mobilizations has matured and ossified, and where economic growth rates have tapered off to modest levels. By contrast, societies such as Japan, Germany and Italy (where liberal democratic systems were overthrown in the 1920s and 1930s and then refounded after 1945), or France (where an established democratic system was disrupted by wartime defeats and occupation), have lesser levels of interest group activity and higher rates of economic growth.

Conclusion

Because political science is an inherently multi-theoretical discipline (Dunleavy and O'Leary, 1987; Alford and Friedland, 1985), it is not surprising to find fundamentally different interpretations of the interest group process. More interesting perhaps is the extent to which both the political science approaches (pluralism and corporatism) and public choice approaches (the logic of collective action model and new right views) are internally bifurcated about the likely extent of interest group organization. Some political scientists are uncomfortable with evidence of such deep disagreements, searching instead for some unitary model which can encompass disparate theories and evidence. The danger here is that over-inclusive and non-parsimonious accounts are constructed, which only redescribe complex social phenomena without explaining them. But in looking at the literature on interest groups, it is hard to escape the feeling that each model has captured only part of the phenomena to be explained.

The central problem for pluralist accounts remains the ungrounded character of their prevailing optimism about the group process. Their approach contains no effective counter to Olson's fundamental point that because of the difficulties of organizing collective action, the pattern of group mobilization may have little or no correlation with preference intensities. Oddly enough, the new right model falls prey to a similar difficulty. In their anxiety to identify large welfare state clienteles as sources of pressure behind state growth, the new right skate over the full implications of collective action problems for large groups. For example, their account makes a none-too-plausible effort to cope with free-riding caused by groups organizing around non-excludable goods. But it says nothing about the parallel problem of free-riding by individuals who know that their contribution is negligible in determining whether their interest group realizes its semi-collective benefits or not. Corporatism's difficulties remain primarily empirical – the fact that many large liberal democracies fit poorly with the immanent trend it identifies.

The logic of collective action account in many ways remains the central model of interest group politics, cited as much by conventional political scientists as by public choice theorists: 'Olson's theory appears unassailable, [so] the question of the role of lobbies and pressure groups in the political process must be analysed anew' (Breton, 1974, p. 79). The critical importance of group size in determining whether groups become mobilized or remain latent has been accepted even by writers on the left (Offe and Wiesenthal, 1985; Crouch, 1982). Yet a central difficulty remains. Year in and year out huge numbers of people do join large interest groups, and engage in even more risky forms of collective action (such as violent demonstrations, riots or direct action against repressive governments). On the logic of collective action model it is virtually impossible to escape the conclusion that such behaviour is (formally, economically) irrational, just as public choice theories of voting cannot easily explain turning out at elections as rational behaviour. Many bolt-on modifications to Olson's model have been suggested in the last two decades, but have failed to keep its core propositions intact while simultaneously accounting for large-scale collective action.

43

In the next chapter, I suggest a revised instrumental model which can better meet the twin demands of explaining the difficulties of group mobilization and how they are so extensively overcome. In the process I also draw on the many valuable insights about the group process contained in corporatist, new right and especially pluralist approaches. This revised account is deliberately not an inclusive model: for example, it starts from the eminently contestable premiss that people join groups for hard-edged instrumental reasons. But it aims to provide a more articulated, integrated and coherent analysis than the literature reviewed in this chapter.

Chapter 3

RECONSTRUCTING THE THEORY
OF GROUPS

To better understand interest groups I first explore why the objective size of groups is a much less important influence on participation decisions than the public choice literature suggests, and the implications of large size are more ambiguous. Second, similarly sized interest groups often confront very different levels of collective action problem, so that a systematic account is needed of how other (non-size) influences shape a group's capacity to mobilize. Third, while the existing public choice literature unanimously predicts that interest groups are run by their leaders, an adequate instrumental explanation of interest groups must explain why maintaining internal group democracy is so pervasive a strategy for leaders and members.

WHY PEOPLE JOIN GROUPS

Against the rather general accounts of group-joining discussed in Chapter 2, I argue that:

- in public choice accounts there are multiple reasons for people to free-ride, and several different indices of group size;
- when information is imperfect, there are a number of conceptually distinct stages which people must go through in order to recognize that a group pursues their interests, well before a group-joining or free-riding decision can be made;
- group-joining decisions are not straightforward but involve multiple assessments of a group's aims, actual and potential membership, and chances of success.

45

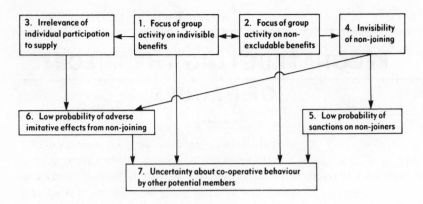

Figure 3.1 **Constraints on group participation**

Constraints on participation

The public choice literature offers a number of different accounts of why people should free-ride rather than join medium-sized or large interest groups. Sifting through the arguments about whether groups pursue genuine public goods or simply lower grade collective benefits suggests that there are four separate primary constraints which discourage people from participating in groups, as shown in Figure 3.1:

1. *The focus of group activity on indivisible benefits.* Where a group aims to secure benefits which are hard to split up (for inherent or technical reasons), it will matter less whether a marginal individual joins the group or free-rides. Where goods are 'lumpy' (that is, they cannot be realized piecemeal or incrementally but only in large chunks or on an all-or-nothing basis), marginal variations in participation are especially unlikely to affect the group's ability to supply the good.

2. *The focus of group activity on non-excludable benefits* which cannot be confined to their own memberships but become available to everyone in a given section of society. Olson assumed that non-excludability is technically or naturally inherent in the kinds of benefits which groups want to secure. But goals of this kind are quite hard to identify; in many cases private goods exist which are close substitutes for non-excludable benefits. Most of the time the new right are correct to argue that liberal democratic governments are prevented from explicitly targeting benefits on interest group members not by features of the goods themselves but by the general operations of the rule of law, or public perceptions of such a stance as illegitimate. Whatever the genesis of this constraint, for a group to focus on non-excludable benefits encourages rational free-riding, since non-members in that section

of society can enjoy the products of group activity without bearing any costs. Because members largely produce as well as consume an interest group's outputs, non-joining directly lowers its organizational viability.

3. *The irrelevance of individual participation to supply.* Potential and existing members of large or medium-sized groups know that their individual participation will negligibly affect the group's ability to achieve its goals. Because groups are multi-member bodies with a restricted division of labour, most individual contributions are equally irrelevant to aggregate group efficacy. With indivisible public goods, individual pay-offs derive directly from the group's overall effectiveness, so the numerical irrelevance of individual participation to aggregate supply also implies its irrelevance to individual supply. However, if a group is finely poised close to a success threshold (as when an American trade union has just under 50 per cent support in a union recognition ballot), then securing a few extra members may be very important. In addition, where a group's objectives can be realized in a graduated way individual irrelevance to supply may be reduced somewhat. A strong example is provided by some branches of the women's movement and some environmentalist groups which stress that the social changes they advocate can only be achieved by individual people changing their own lifestyles and aspirations, and trying to convince their personal contacts to do likewise (Offe, 1985). Rather like early Christianity, individual participation is seen as the only viable pathway to realizing social change. Collective goods are hence seen as *constituted* by individual participation. Hirschman (1985, pp. 82–91) re-expresses this point in a strong way by arguing that some factors which economists typically count on the *cost* side of the people's group-joining equation in fact reappear on the benefit side for many kinds of public affairs activity.

4. *The invisibility of non-joining.* People who free-ride from a medium-sized or large group, or who first join but then drop out, cannot be easily identified by existing members or other potential members. If interest groups pursued pure 'public goods' (however we define this concept), then the invisibility of non-joining would be a strictly secondary factor. But in practice most interest groups have very mixed bundles of 'public' and 'private' objectives. Here rational individuals considering not joining a group will be encouraged if they can conceal their decision from other people.

These four basic participation constraints have the following three derived or secondary implications.

5. *A low probability of sanctions for non-joining.* If non-joiners are invisible to members, groups cannot develop sanctions or negative selective incentives against those who free-ride. Groups cannot develop 'stick and carrot' strategies fostering conditional co-operation among potential members, such as 'tit for tat' tactics of rewarding participants but withdrawing group contacts from non-joiners, for two reasons. The group controls few if

any excludable benefits to provide the 'carrot' ingredients, and cannot identify non-joiners to wield a 'stick' against them.

6. *Few adverse imitative effects from non-joining.* Even if one individual's decision to stay out of a group has no direct effect in reducing its viability, her decision could still be damaging if many other people see her behaviour and imitate it. One non-joiner could then become the 'thin end of the wedge', triggering larger-scale free-riding. Where such multiplier effects occur, both group members and free-riders experience a worsened supply of collective benefits as the group's effectiveness declines. However, the less visible non-joining behaviour becomes, the more free-riders can be confident that their individual decisions will not be noticed by other actual or potential group members.

7. *Uncertainty about co-operative behaviour by other potential members.* Because of the features above people may also fear that even if they contribute to group activity similarly placed people making simultaneous decisions will not, so that the group is ineffective, and their own contribution becomes pointless. The greater the turnover of group members, the more evidence any individual will notice to support this concern. Uncertainty and high turnover also raise the rate at which potential group members discount future outcomes (that is, any excludable benefits from joining, and any costs of being sanctioned by the group) compared with the present costs of joining. A higher discount rate further undermines the group's ability to develop conditional co-operation strategies.

How can these multiple constraints be overcome? The existing public choice literature offers only a thin account of the full range of interest group participation (see page 30). When his perfectly general account of collective action was criticized for not explaining 'cause' groups, Olson disingenuously asserted that it was limited to economic contexts (hence all his examples relate to trade associations, professions and labour unions). According to this 'cop-out' position, the model is unsuitable for explaining areas of social behaviour characterized by 'altruism' or ideology (Olson, 1978, Chapters 3 and 6; Simms, 1990, pp. 6–8). In addition, Olson treats all participation constraints as immovable, exogenously fixed by factors beyond group leaders' control.

By contrast, the new right concentrate only on what group leaders can do to convert collective objectives into private benefits (see page 36); and corporatism stresses that leaders make alliances with rival group leaderships to restrict members' exit options (see page 29). Financial muscle and organizational skills may help to advertise group activities and membership, and to persuade waverers. Solidaristic ideologies may be developed to stigmatize non-joiners or defectors, to broaden the range of social sanctions available for use against free-riders, to legitimize the use of such sanctions and to reduce uncertainty about co-operative behaviour. But group resources provide only secondary solutions to the problem of participation constraints. They help explain the differential recruiting ability of existing interest groups, but do not help us understand how the fundamental constraints on participation are first overcome and a group set up.

A third group of public choice authors have reacted to difficulties in explaining the full range and extent of group participation by importing altruism into their models. For example, Margolis (1982) supposes that individuals should be analyzed as split personalities, with self-interested and group-oriented personas battling for supremacy. Such mixed models could not conceivably be falsified under experimental conditions, and should be rejected on these grounds alone. But neither do they explain away all of the constraints on participation discussed above. If individual participation is objectively irrelevant to the supply of collective benefits, and people are perfectly informed about this situation, then even the most group-oriented or altruistic individuals should still decide rationally not to participate in collective action.

> Each [altruistic] maximizer of group utility would reason as follows. Regardless of whether I contribute or not, either enough others will contribute or they won't. If the former then my costs of contribution would do no good, while constituting a subtraction from the utility the group gains from the collective benefit. If the latter, then my costs of contribution are again a subtraction from the group's utility. So [either way] maximizing group utility requires that I be a free-rider. (Buchanan, 1979, p. 65)

In addition, of course, those contraints which relate to sanctions would still be relevant to the non-altruistic parts of group-joiners' decision-making.

So in existing public choice accounts, differences in group sizes must remain the key determinant of how severe participation constraints are, although the impacts of size are rarely discussed systematically. In fact the concept of group size in public choice accounts is ambiguous. In deciding whether or not to join a group, individuals need to be able to estimate three important variables: the number of *potential members* of the group; its *actual membership*; and its *rate of mobilization* (that is, actual members divided by potential members). Table 3.1 shows how changes in these size variables affect the seven participation constraints above. The extent to which a group's activity focuses upon indivisible goods or upon non-excludable benefits is constant whatever the number of its potential or actual members. However, as mobilization increases, the group's focus upon collective benefits should decline somewhat, because well-mobilized groups can find more ways to confine the benefits of collective action to their members. If a group's viability is a linear function of its size then the irrelevance of individual participation to supply obviously increases with both potential

Table 3.1 *The impact of increasing size variables on the importance of participation constraints**

Participation constraint	Increasing size variable		
	Potential members	Actual members	Group mobilization
1. Focus of group activity on indivisible benefits	Static	Static	Static
2. Focus of group activity on non-excludable benefits	Static	Static	Goes down
3. Irrelevance of individual participation to supply	Goes up (if no threshold effects)	Goes up (if no threshold effects)	Goes up
4. Invisibility of non-joining	Goes up	Goes up, then down	Goes down
5. Probability of escaping sanctions for non-joining	Goes up	Goes up	Goes down
6. Probability of avoiding adverse imitative effects from non-joining	Goes up	Goes up	Goes up
7. Uncertainty about co-operative behaviour by other potential members	Goes up	Goes down	Goes down

Note: *Cell entries here show whether the importance of each participation constraint goes up, remains static, or goes down with increases in a group's potential membership, actual membership, or rate of mobilization.

and actual group membership; and in better mobilized groups marginal contributions are also less significant. However, as I noted above, a group may be operating near an effectiveness threshold, as when a trade union has to win majority support in a workplace ballot in order to win recognition from the employer. In such circumstances, recruiting a few more members is often disproportionately important to the group's effectiveness. More generally, whenever aggregate group effectiveness increases *more* rapidly than membership size, any individuals' proportionate influence share also increases (Dahl and Tufte, 1974). Hence it seems best to regard irrelevance to supply as strictly indeterminate with respect to size variables, although it will generally tend to increase with group size.

The larger a group's potential membership becomes, the more invisible non-joiners are. And in general the larger a group's actual membership, the more invisible an individual non-joiner will be. However, where a group has a very large actual membership (including most people in the relevant section of society), this invisibility declines – the small minority of people who stay out of the group become noticeable as exceptions to the predominant practice. So long as invisibility goes up less slowly with actual than with potential membership, it may decline when high rates of mobilization are attained. Hence the probability of escaping sanctions for non-joining also increases with potential membership, increases more slowly with actual membership, but declines with greater group mobilization. On the other hand, the likelihood of avoiding adverse imitative effects from non-joining goes up with all three indices. Better mobilized groups (able to identify and impose sanctions on non-joiners) can more effectively dissuade others from following a bad example. Finally, uncertainty about co-operative behaviour by other potential members obviously increases (other things being equal) the larger a group's potential membership. But it goes down dramatically the more the group's actual membership and rate of mobilization expand.

Overall, groups with larger potential memberships should face greater constraints on five out of the seven factors listed in Table 3.1. Larger actual memberships have a more ambiguous effect. They make it harder for groups to apply sanctions, increase individuals' irrelevance to supply (in the absence of threshold effects), and reduce the risk of adverse imitative effects from non-joining. But people deciding whether to join a large membership group confront much less uncertainty about whether other people will behave co-operatively. Finally (as pluralists argue), boosting group mobilization clearly reduces some constraints on individual participation. Well-mobilized groups focus less on non-excludable benefits; can identify non-joiners more easily and have a better chance of applying sanctions; and can radically reduce uncertainty about other people's co-operative behaviour. Unless threshold effects are present, larger well-mobilized groups still cannot offset individuals' irrelevance to supply. Even if other people imitate my free-riding, the effectiveness of a well-mobilized group is not significantly impaired.

A root cause of the variable relationship between impediments to participation and indices of group size is that two of these size indices themselves are often negatively correlated, namely the number of people which a group could recruit and its rate of mobilization. 'A negative relationship between number of potential members and density of membership should exist for [all] organizations for whom the benefits depend on the proportion who have been recruited while costs depend on number being recruited' (Wallerstein, 1989, p. 494). Thus unionization rates are much lower in large labour markets (see page 27), and cartels are less effective in competitive industries with many firms.

Group joining and information

How do people become aware that groups exist, are relevant to their interests, and are worth joining? Existing public choice uses four assumptions to skate over these micro-level questions.

1. People know their own preferences

Like neo-classical economics, public choice theory eschews any investigation of the origins or variability of preferences (see page 98). So objective interests cannot be attributed to people distinct from their wants, and changes in preferences as a result of political participation are also ignored.

2. It is obvious that some goals require collective action

This assumption is smuggled into the existing public choice literature in two ways. First, Olson's insistence that economic interest groups organize around public goods implies that the indivisibility and non-excludability of some preferences is inherent, and perceived as such. However, 'pure' public goods are very hard to find and few group objectives meet Samuelson's criteria. As the new right argue, successful political mobilization to supply a given benefit from the state budget is by itself a sufficient condition for converting almost any technically 'private' commodity into a collective benefit for the group concerned.

Second, public choice studies often assume 'that interest groups exist, that they supply incentives at some cost, and that some of the benefits supplied are political' (Hansen, 1985, p. 85). The premiss underpins empirical studies, such as Hansen's longitudinal analysis of membership trends in three major US interest groups (the American Farm Bureau Federation, the League of Women Voters and the National Association of Home Builders). He concluded that participation levels go up when an established supply of collective benefits is under threat, because the same change in welfare weighs more heavily with people when it is presented as a loss than as a gain (Quattrone and Tversky, 1988); when members' disposable resources of income and time are growing, because they can more easily meet the resource costs of membership; and when their levels of information increase.

However, if a large, established group already exists, it becomes legitimate to assume widespread 'automatic' recognition for it. And questions about how groups ever became organized disappear from view:

> It makes little difference whether or not members of large groups respond to collective incentives if associations representing large groups never come into being; that is, for individuals to respond to political incentives (or to any incentives) they first must exist.
> (Hansen, 1985, p. 93)

Hansen excuses this limitation by positing a 'Say's law of interest groups: supply creates its own demand' (p. 94). Yet if we assume an established interest group already provides collective benefits which all potential group members are aware of, it is inevitable that interest groups' origins end up being explained axiomatically from within an untested model as the product of 'subsidization . . . by entrepreneurs, by other groups or by government'. Empirical evidence of such initial subsidization is much rarer for economic and occupational groups than citizens' groups (see p. 69).

3. Plentiful, low-cost information on group-joining

People simply inspect their already formed preferences, and act on unambiguous estimations of the eventualities of joining or staying out of a group. Olson's index records no references at all to information costs and deficiencies. No scope is left for difficulties in assessing the effectiveness of interest groups in securing collective benefits. Few authors query whether a public choice analysis of group formation based on 'objective' benefits, costs and probabilities is methodologically acceptable.

> It is assumed that people know their own interests perfectly (or that there is no other sense of 'knowing interests' than what people say them to be). . . . But that is not the same as having perfect information about how best to pursue their interests. There is no reason why public choice models must assume perfect information there; it is true that they tend to, just for ease of modelling. But that is always regarded as a complication (like air friction in Newtonian mechanics) that can be added later when the basic arguments have been laid out. (R. E. Goodin, personal communication)

However, even in sophisticated studies, information is presented in highly simplified fashion. The more information an individual has, the closer the fit becomes between the objective levels and subjective estimations of four variables: collective benefits generated by group activity; the probability of individual membership decisions influencing group effectiveness; the costs of membership; and the level of selective incentives. Increased information always increases the objectivity of people's perceptions (Hansen, 1985, p. 80). As Downs put it in relation to electoral competition:

> For the purposes of our present analysis, we make a simplifying assumption about information: no false information is provided by any sources. Th[is] does not mean that facts cannot be manipulated so as to give false impressions; it only means that *all factual statements can be accepted as correct without further checking*, although their significance may be equivocal. (Downs, 1957, p. 208, my emphasis)

Even this revised approach seems unsustainable. The effectiveness of most interest groups is far from self-evident, but bitterly contested. For example, trade union claims to advance their members' living standards relative to non-union workers are highly controversial in all liberal democracies. Academic surveys conclude only that 'unions do influence relative wages and that the magnitude of the union/non-union differential is in the region of *0 to 40 per cent*' (Mulvey, 1978, pp. 105–17, my emphasis). The notion that in such situations all information helps people to appreciate the 'actual' level of such critical choice variables as benefits, costs and probabilities is simply a vain effort to disguise the extreme difficulty in practice of determining these objective levels.

4. Group-joining as a one-off problem

How do people select between multiple groups competing for their attention? Public choice accounts normally discuss only decisions to join particular (already established) groups. Presumably, people must periodically rank prospective groups' discounted collective benefits, private benefits and costs, before distributing their resources down the ranking until a resource constraint applies or a cut-off level of welfare gain is no longer satisfied. Substantial decision costs seem to be involved, because information-economizing devices (such as reading a partisan newspaper before deciding how to vote) may be harder in handling the group universe.

And unlike elections (where voters need consider very few parties) in the group universe extended multi-way comparisons are needed. There are no reliable estimates of the number of groups active at any government level, because of differences in defining what is to count. American studies of the early 1980s, using narrow definitions and focusing solely on Washington-based lobbying organizations, put the number of groups active at the federal level at 1,300; other sources identified nearly 1,000 voluntary associations, excluding trade unions, not-for-profit companies and business corporations (Walker, 1983, pp. 391–2, 394). Yet Newton (1976, Chapters 3–4), adopting a broader definition counted 4,000 groups active in a single British city, Birmingham – suggesting that the US figures seriously understate the number of groups vying for attention. Of course, only some of this total are relevant for any individual, but members of this sub-set are always bound to be numerous.

Group identities

To help devise a better account of interest groups, I want to introduce two new concepts. The first is an ideal-type distinction between exogenous and endogenous groups, which is the focus of the next section but needs to be briefly introduced here to underpin the discussion of group joiners' information requirements.

Exogenous groups have an 'identity set', the ensemble of all the individuals who can join the group, delimited by external factors. An exogenous group's potential members are not randomly scattered in society but share a common situation defined outside their individual or collective control. For example, a group representing the interests of families whose children suffer from drug-induced birth defects has an identity set consisting of all parents of such children, only a fraction of whom become actual members. This identity set is crucial for group activities, but its size and composition are fixed beyond the group's control. Four main factors define exogenous groups' identity sets: nature and chance, which lie outside human agency altogether; history, the structural influence of past actions constraining present choices; and power, the use of current social or organizational capacities to define the social situation of others. In all societies the capacity to reshape the identity sets of other groups is highly concentrated in the hands of some social interests at the expense of others. Under capitalism, capital owners and associated management strata have a discretionary capacity to fragment and reshape the identities of employees by restructuring work organization (Offe and Wiesenthal, 1985). And in some markets product design and advertising can be used successfully to mould consumers' identities (Galbraith, 1969) – hence the phenomenon of people developing strong loyalties to their particular type of car, personal computer, newspaper, or health care system. Similarly, in a patriarchal society men (as a gender and within each household) can very extensively reshape the social situation of women.

Endogenous groups are formed simply by the coming together of like-minded people. Only the actors involved determine what is common to an endogenous group's potential members (or identity set). At an individual level the motivation for joining the group is self-selected. And collectively members can control what the group stands for, without being abnormally constrained by external factors such as history or power. 'Cause groups' (such as those advocating an end to animal vivisection, or the scrapping of nuclear weapons) are fairly pure endogenous groups, but many different lobbies share some of these characteristics.

The second concept introduced here is that of a *group identity*. If people consider collective benefits at all in deciding whether to join a group, then simply inspecting their preferences or recognizing a subjective interest in a particular goal is not enough to make them participate. The group identity concept captures the 'something more' that is required. Basically, unless a rational actor accepts that she has a subjective interest which is shared with others, she has no basis for contributing to the group's activities because of its collective benefits. Of course, people might join groups completely without reference to the collective benefits of membership, but solely because the balance of private benefits and costs makes it worthwhile given their social situation or personal values. I assume that such 'privatized' decisions are both unproblematic and (contra Olson) very untypical of most people's group-joining calculus.

Table 3.2   *Perceptual, acceptance and efficacy constraints on group joining*

	General constraints		Individual constraints
	Does the actor perceive that:		
Perceptual constraints	1. Identity set Y exists	2. Group X represents people in set Y	3. She falls within set Y
	Does the actor accept that:		
Acceptance constraints	4. People in set Y share interest I	5. Group X promotes interest I	6. She also shares interest I
	Does the actor have confidence that:		
Efficacy constraints		7. Group X is a viable group in promoting this interest	8. Her participation in group X will enhance her benefits from interest I

Looking first at exogenous groups, three levels of information constraints can influence an actor's decisions about joining: perceptual, acceptance and efficacy constraints (see Table 3.2).

At the perceptual or informational level

1. The actor must *recognize that the identity set for the exogenous group exists.* For example, if a trade union bases its appeal upon a claim to organize and represent 'craftsmen', potential members need to know what this category means and who is included in it.

2. The actor must *know that a given group claims to organize people who fall into a given identity set.* People may perceive a group's activities without accurately appreciating the identity set to which it appeals.

3. The actor must *recognize that she herself falls within the group's identity set.* Even if people perceive the interrelationship between an exogenous group and its identity set they will not join unless they see themselves in the category of potential members. That someone is included in a given identity set need not be obvious to that person – for this recognition must compete with multiple social identifications based on other aspects of the actor's social situation or personal values.

Ascribing interests to oneself or others involves more complex judgements. In liberal democracies individuals may always reach idiosyncratic or 'oddball' conclusions at variance with conventional judgements or those of existing group members. Hence:

At the level of acceptance

4. The actor must *recognize that people in the exogenous group's identity set share a given interest*. Even if someone perceives the identity set, she need not recognize any common interest, instead seeing the set as defined by 'natural', chance or historical influences with no implications for current social interests. Equally, unless individuals in the identity set are already well mobilized and expressing common demands, the actor may deny that the group members or leaders know what is in the best interests of the identity set.

5. The actor must then *accept that the group actually promotes the shared interest of people in the identity set*. People who have passed all the other thresholds can still withhold this acceptance, perhaps interpreting the group's activities as benefiting only its leaders or a minority within the identity set.

6. An actor who accepts that the group serves a shared interest of the identity set must also *accept that she shares this interest*. For many reasons people may feel that their individual situation offsets or negates any personal stake in the collective benefit promoted by the group.

Since endogenous groups are not shaped by external factors but self-defined by the group membership, they may not have an observable identity set (potential membership) distinct from the group membership itself. So steps 1 to 4 in Table 3.2 dealing with recognizing identity sets are not relevant to people considering whether to join an endogenous group. However, steps 5 and 6 are equally salient. Before joining an actor must recognize that the endogenous group exists and promotes a given interest; and she must accept that she shares that interest. Without the underpinning provided by the earlier steps, however, the perceptual thresholds that potential members of endogenous groups must surmount are characteristically higher than for exogenous groups.

Because of their importance in all group joining I use the 'group identity' label to denote steps 5 and 6, the recognition of a subjective interest shared with others who are organized in a group. Since group identities are subjective individual perceptions of a collective interest, they are a sub-set of subjective interests. Yet they include far more information than ordinary subjective interests in three ways: they tag a particular set of people as relevant to the actor's interests; they specify the collective stake involved; and they indicate how it relates to the individual's unique interests. The group identity concept does not weaken the fundamental presumption of self-interested behaviour which is necessary to preserve public choice accounts from tautology. By specifying the notion of subjective interests more precisely the group identity concept actually sustains an instrumental model which otherwise cannot explain the full range of observable interest group behaviour.

For both exogenous and endogenous groups, the group identity provides a crucial foundation for two further steps concerned with whether joining would be a worthwhile activity.

At the level of efficacy

7. The actor must *be confident that her prospective group is viable*, or (reasonably) effective in promoting the interests which she shares with group members.

> Whatever the reason why a person may attach himself to a cause, more enthusiasm for its pursuit is likely to be elicited if it looks as if it has a chance of succeeding than if it appears to be a forlorn hope. Nobody likes to feel that he is wasting his time, and that feeling may be induced by contributing to a campaign that never looks as if it has a chance. (Barry, 1978, p. 30)

A group's viability is its probability of successfully mobilizing people (in its identity set, if it is an exogenous group), maintaining itself in an organizationally effective manner, and achieving its collective objectives. The group must be able to acquire political influence and retain and activate its own members against strong competition for resources and political/ media attention from multiple other groups, and often in the face of directly countervailing mobilizations by opposing interests, or by rival groups seeking to organize the same identity set (Downs, 1972).

8. The actor *must be convinced of the efficacy of her own contribution to the group* in advancing the individual interest which she shares with other group

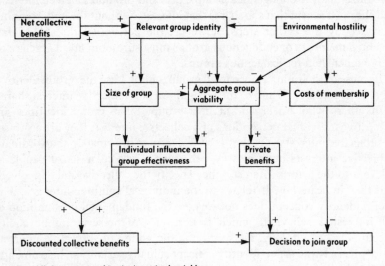

Note: All elements are subjective/perceived variables.

Figure 3.2 **Why people join groups**

58

members. The decision choice analyzed by Olson, about whether it is rational to make an individual contribution or to free ride, only arises if the actor already believes that the group is in some way a viable means of promoting her shared interest.

To recap, there are four informational prerequisites for a rational actor considering joining *any* kind of group wholly or partly because of the collective benefits of membership. The actor must recognize a group identity (steps 5 and 6), believe in the group's viability (step 7) and be convinced of the efficacy of her own contribution (step 8). For exogenous groups alone, recognizing a group identity also entails that the actor has the concept of the identity set (step 1), sees that the group involved represents the identity set (step 2), perceives that she falls within the identity set (step 3) and accepts that people in the identity set share an interest (step 4). Once these informational requirements have been surmounted, the actor of course still confronts resource constraints in deciding whether she can afford to participate in the group under consideration, given her available time and money budgets and her other interests and priorities.

The decision to join a group

The key factors in why people join groups can now be pictured as in Figure 3.2, where all the variables included are subjective perceptions (for example, 'size of group' means that perceived by the individual concerned). Starting in the top left-hand corner of the diagram, there is a two-way flow between perceiving a stake in a group's success and accepting that it promotes a given interest. Self-interest makes people notice groups more. But recognizing a group identity also increases people's assessment of what they will gain from the group's success. For any individual, the choice of how to represent their interests is a complex matter. The group identity short-circuits the information problems in coping with many different interest groups vying for attention. And group identities compete with multiple social identifications based on other aspects of people's social situation or personal values remote from the group process. For example, a trade union identity has to offset the demobilizing effects of alternative identifications encouraged by the employer – such as loyalty to the firm, or being 'mission committed' to making its products. Employers often use divide-and-rule strategies to inhibit union identities: encouraging the fragmentation of the workforce by gender, skill status, functional categorizations, departmentalism, and ethnic identifications. Companies may also create directly rival identities to sap the appeal of trade unions, as with 'company unions' in Japanese industry or the personnel packages offered by non-union corporations in the United States. A successful union identity must be strongly developed to survive such competition.

The key role of group identities, however, is in conveying information about the group's size and viability. As in Olson's model, if a group is perceived as a large one potential members always see a lower probability that their individual contribution can be decisive for group success. But to make an estimate of the group's size people must know that it exists and represents a particular interest, the first component of recognizing a group identity. For pure endogenous groups (matching the ideal type sketched above) the relevant size variable is the actual membership – since it may be impossible to define any finite identity set of potential members, or estimate any meaningful level of group mobilization. But for pure exogenous groups it may be as important to know how many people are included in the identity set and what their rate of mobilization is, as it is to know the group's actual membership level. Again, a group identity provides the information needed for rational decision-making.

Recognizing a group identity also provides a crucial foundation for estimating how viable or effective a group is likely to be. By focusing an actor's attention on one among many competing bases for identifying her interests, a group identity normally boosts her estimates of the group's organizational resources, the skills of its leadership, the preference intensities of group members, and other internal factors determining how effective the group can be in pursuing its objectives.

Again, there is a two-way relationship between perceptions of the group's size and viability, which may substantially offset the effect of larger size in reducing people's confidence that their own contribution to the group will advance their interests. A group must be seen as viable if potential members are to rate their own contributions as helping to produce collective benefits (Figure 3.2). The strength of this important interrelationship varies from one person or group to another. A priori it is impossible to say how size and viability considerations are related in individual subjective estimations. Other things being equal, the larger a group's actual size and rate of mobilization, the more likely people will be to perceive it as viable. This effect is especially strong where there are high effectiveness thresholds which must be surmounted before the group achieves any collective benefits at all, or where there is counter-mobilization by a powerful opposing group. Large size is also a critical determinant of viability wherever a group's ability to deliver collective benefits depends on numbers at the ballot box. In addition, bigger groups may be able to exploit economies of scale in establishing and maintaining awareness of their activities, and in recruiting and retaining members. They can certainly create a greater pool of organizational resources to be flexibly deployed in conflict situations, as well as attracting better leadership personnel.

Of course, other influences from the political and organizational environment upon how potential members perceive group viability must be incorporated (Hansen, 1985). For group X these include: rival groups (competing for membership in X's identity set); opposing groups (espousing a conflicting interest); groups whose memberships, finances, or effectiveness are ecologically linked with X's in some way; mass media attitudes and coverage; and the reactions of political parties, decision-makers and public opinion towards X's policies and campaigning. In a more hostile environment, potential members are less likely to recognize a group identity; and even if they do, they will estimate group viability more conservatively. Environmental favourability also conditions people's perceptions of the costs of joining a group. If the political environment suddenly becomes more favourable for the group, a cumulation of influences may trigger a 'bandwagon' surge in membership. Contrasting momentum effects occur if the general climate moves in an unfavourable direction, such as the 'spiral of silence' in which members of an unpopular group respond to hostile media and personal interaction messages by staying silent about their affiliation, thereby diminishing the group's public visibility and political viability even further (Noelle-Newman, 1984).

Potential members also pay attention (at some level) to the private benefits and costs of joining the group. More viable groups usually have lower perceived membership costs, especially where multi-level activism is important to group strategies. For example, trade unions rely on their members not just for union dues but also for grass roots organization, solidarity against employers' attacks and support during industrial actions. Similarly wherever 'rewards created by the act of associating' are an important selective incentive, then more viable groups will be more congenial and offer greater private benefits than less successful or declining organizations (Hansen, 1985, p. 81). Expanding groups can also create more easily the organizational and resource bases needed to deliver enhanced quasi-commercial benefits.

Overall, Figure 3.2 demonstrates that the decision to join a group is a complex and multivalent one, in which perceptions of group size play a structurally ambivalent role. *Ceteris paribus*, people recognize that their individual contribution to group effectiveness is lower in large groups, but they also perceive the group as more viable. So a public choice model cannot offer any specific conclusion about how increasing interest group size affects participation levels. Only if potential members have perfect information about a group's size and are already convinced of its overall effectiveness will Olson's analysis of the inherent difficulties of organizing large groups be appropriate. The record of strikes, social movements and revolutions repeatedly demonstrates that improvements in a group's viability can swamp people's awareness that any individual's contribution is objectively irrelevant in achieving collective benefits.

Group identities also provide a strong basis for the development of other beliefs which sustain group mobilization. The competition between alternative identities explains why groups develop distinctive ideologies stressing both an ethical duty on potential members to participate and not free ride, and the empirically widespread belief in the 'unity principle' – which holds that 'the participation of *everyone* [in the identity set] is necessary to have a chance of obtaining the [group's] public good' (Finkel *et al.*, 1989, p. 888). In addition, Sen argues that 'groups intermediate between oneself and all, such as class and community, provide the focus of many actions involving commitment', where commitment is defined 'in terms of a person choosing an act that he believes will yield a lower level of personal welfare to him than an alternative that is also available to him' (Sen, 1977, pp. 327, 344). Although the analysis given here is strictly in terms of people's subjectively perceived personal welfare, it also provides a key foundation for exploring political behaviour without the deliberate simplifying assumption that personal welfare determines people's political (or other) choices.

EXPLAINING VARIATIONS IN GROUP EFFECTIVENESS

Why are some interest groups easier and others harder to organize? Olson recognized the importance of this problem, for he redescribed it in the terminology of 'privileged', 'intermediate' and 'latent' groups – without shedding much new light on the origins of variation (Olson, 1978, pp. 43–52). Only the idea of members of 'privileged' groups deriving uneven benefits from group success, so that some members are differentially prepared to bear the costs of organization, really differentiates this typology from simple size influences. Most public choice authors assume that fluctuations in the level of interest group organization reflect differences in the availability of selective incentives to group leaders, or differences in the skills and competences of leaders themselves. While group leaderships basically maximize their memberships (by analogy with profit-maximizing firms), some run more efficient organizations and are better at combating free-riding than others (Becker, 1983, 1985). However, empirical tests of these propositions are not common, and they can easily be abused as indiscriminate equation-fillers.

A few writers speculate vaguely about why some types of group find it easier to develop selective incentives than others:

> Producer groups were more likely than consumer to call forth
> entrepreneurs willing to bear initial costs [of organizing a group].
> Miller *et al.* (1981) have documented the importance of group
> identification in predicting other forms of participation. Part of the
> advantage of producer groups over diffuse groups, then, was *more
> natural identification* with the former and hence greater responsiveness
> to intrinsic, group-centred rewards such as solidary and expressive
> benefits. (Hansen, 1985, p.94, my emphasis)

However, these hints are never codified or expressed systematically, perhaps because the supply-side factors mentioned above can always be wheeled in. Alternatively, public choice theorists argue that variations in ease of group organization simply reflect the changing nature of people's preferences across different identity sets – which places it outside their area of explanation on the basis that 'there's no accounting for tastes' (see page 98).

The theory of groups is severely limited by these constraints. Not enquiring into the origins of preferences makes it impossible to examine the size of potential memberships or the impact of group mobilization (that is, actual members divided by potential members) on participation decisions. Attributing all variations in effectiveness to leadership qualities ignores the evidence (hinted at by Hansen) that there are some broad structural determinants of group organization about which generalizations can be made.

By contrast, the group identities approach argues that if we want to understand why some groups (of a given size) are relatively successful and others are not, we need to analyze how their potential members are defined, and the implications of variations in identity sets for their ease of organization. I briefly described above the basic difference between exogenous and endogenous groups in these terms. These ideal types are very useful also in systematizing propositions about the complex non-size influences on groups' ease of organization.

Exogenous groups

Where a group's identity set is shaped by external forces, one or more of the following first-order implications usually holds true as well (Figure 3.3).

1. *The identity set is compact.* It is restricted to people in only some social situations, and specifies a finite potential membership for the group. 'Compactness' is an analytically separate characteristic from size. Some large groups may have very compact identity sets, some small groups may have very diffuse identity sets.

2. *Inclusion in the identity set is intrinsic to a given role*, or effectively involuntary for the individuals concerned, especially where the group identity is based on or linked with ascriptive characteristics (such as race, ethnicity, gender, or age). It follows that turnover in the identity set is small, confined to the normal process of population replacement in society.

3. In many cases, *inclusion in the identity set is associated with social stigmata*, defined as 'any characteristic of a group of persons that is easily identifiable by others in their society' (Rogowski, 1974, p. 71). Identifiable characteristics are not necessarily obvious physical features, such as gender or skin colour. They may encompass many behaviour patterns, manner-isms, social clues and signals by which we place our everyday personal

63

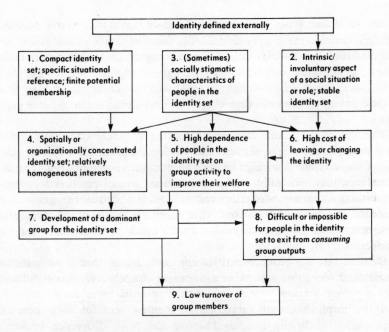

Figure 3.3 **The characteristics of exogenous groups**

contacts. In conflict-ridden societies, people's abilities and concern to determine affiliations can become highly developed, as in the ability of Catholics and Protestants in Northern Ireland, or Muslims and Christians in the Lebanon, to tell each other apart.

There are three second-order implications of these characteristics:

4. *People in the identity set are concentrated in particular spatial or organizational locations*, making them relatively easy to contact and mobilize. Economies of scale are better exploited and 'critical mass' thresholds more simply overcome. Potential group members tend to have similar interests and perceptions in several areas of social life simultaneously. Because the potential membership is finite, visible, contactable, and has extensive common interests supplementary to the group identity itself, private benefits relating to a broader social situation can be more easily devised and marketed even against strong competition from commercial firms, hostile groups, or state agency services. In addition, sanctions can more easily be used against non-joiners.

5. *Potential members depend heavily on collective efforts to improve their situation.* If people in the identity set share obvious characteristics and a given social situation, they cannot easily boost their welfare by individual-level action. For example, rank-and-file workers in large-scale manufacturing plants cannot easily influence their personal income level; and ethnic

minorities in a racist society may find their career avenues severely limited. Where people's choices are so limited by collective constraints or disadvantages, difficulties in finding resources for contributions to a relevant interest group can be significantly reduced.

6. *High costs of leaving or changing an exogenous identity reinforce reliance on collective action* (Rogowski, 1974, p. 85). People in the identity set cannot easily exit or adopt a different group identity because the implications of belonging to their current identity set affect their whole lives. As a result exogenous groups frequently have three associated features:

7. *One group may develop a monopoly position in producing collective benefits for an identity set* – usually boosting its effectiveness. Even if rival groups initially exist, there are strong pressures to create a single exogenous group at the most inclusive level: to raise the group mobilization rate, to match the scale of opposing groups, and to co-ordinate collective actions where grass roots members interact extensively anyway. The less choice of groups is available to people in the identity set, the more dependent they are on the dominant group to improve their welfare, so that aggregate participation rates may rise.

8. With many (but not all) exogenous groups, *people in the identity set have to consume the group's output*. In these cases:

> The output or quality of the organization *matters to one even after exit*. In other words, *full exit [from the group] is impossible*; in some sense, one remains a consumer of the article [i.e. the good] in spite of the decision not to buy it any longer, and a member of the organization in spite of formal exit. . . . If I disagree with an organization, say, a political party, I can resign as a member, but generally I cannot stop being a member of the society in which the objectionable party functions.
> . . . [The individual] can stop being producer, but cannot stop being consumer. (Hirschman, 1970, pp. 100, 102)

Continued consumption of a group's output skews the exit vs voice decision in favour of remaining put. People become 'quality-makers' who 'care about the consequences of [their] exit on the quality of the organization, to the point where the prospective decline in quality would keep [them] from exiting' (Hirschman, 1970, p. 100). In an identity set with a dominant group, people who leave sacrifice voice influence over its policies, without avoiding the costs of its deteriorating output.

9. *Relatively low turnover in group membership* follows from previous features, especially a stable set of potential members, the absence of rival groups, and the difficulty of exiting fully. Members who know that they will stay in a group for a long period will be prepared to invest more in recruitment and organization-building, incurring present costs to strengthen its future position (Wallerstein, 1989, p. 488).

Endogenous groups

An identity which is defined by potential members themselves has three first-order implications (Figure 3.4).

1. *The identity set is characteristically a diffuse one*, unrelated to any specific social situation or clear target profile. Even with relatively small groups, potential members are not 'bunched'. In principle, some large endogenous groups, such as the Campaign for Nuclear Disarmament in Britain, can include almost anyone in a society (Byrne, 1988; Mattausch, 1989; Day and Robbins, 1987). A small but growing assortment of cause groups (such as Greenpeace) are explicitly transnational in their appeal.

2. *Potential members of an endogenous group are often socially invisible.* What separates people in the identity set from those outside are private mental states (values, perceptions, preferences or judgements), which by definition are non-observable. Of course, committed members of endogenous groups often adopt deliberately public forms of demonstrating their views – such as wearing distinctive clothes or badges, putting up posters or adopting easily recognizable lifestyles. But most people in the identity set who do not join the group, and even many who do, commonly do none of these things. Hence they can choose to remain invisible to others inside or outside the group's identity set.

3. *Identity sets are unstable.* The potential memberships of endogenous groups fluctuate sharply over time. The turnover of people in a given group's identity set is relatively high, because the shape of a diffuse set can

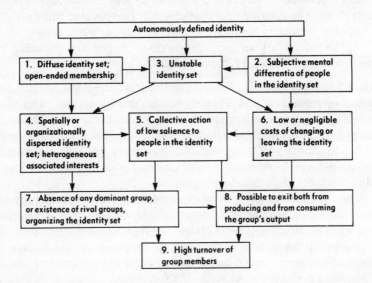

Figure 3.4 **The characteristics of endogenous groups**

shift more radically than a compact one, and because mental differentia are inherently more changeable than social roles.

Three second-order implications follow in turn:

4. *The potential members of endogenous groups are generally dispersed across many different spatial or organizational locations.* They have heterogeneous interests and perceptions apart from the shared group identity itself, making it hard to develop selective incentives or to capitalize on economies of scale, whatever the group's size. Because people in the identity set turn over a lot, potential members apply a high discount rate to future benefits, making conditional co-operation strategies hard to develop. Endogenous groups' private benefits often rely on associative benefits (friendship, or the entertainment value of taking part in group activities) which can only influence potential defectors, since non-joiners never experience them. Leaders and members have few if any sanctions against non-joiners.

5. Because the identity is self-selected and defined only by mental differentia, *collective action is less important for the welfare of potential group members.* Potential group members can enhance their welfare via individual action in multiple ways. Or they may simply alter their values and preferences, ignoring or adapting to a state of affairs which they previously found unacceptable.

6. *The costs of leaving the identity set of an endogenous group are low,* since people need only change their attitudes or preferences. Because potential memberships fluctuate anyway, exit costs are small, while adopting a new group identity is also relatively easy.

Three associated features of endogenous groups frequently follow:

7. *Several rival groups may compete to organize a given identity set,* appealing to different sorts of potential member or associated interests. Where no group emerges as dominant within the identity set, people's dependence on a given organization is reduced. If existing group members become dissatisfied, they can thus defect to a rival group tapping the same identity. With exogenously defined identity sets multiple rival groups lower overall participation levels by impairing each other's viability. But with endogenous groups, trying to create one organization for the whole identity set is often infeasible and counter-productive. Rival endogenous groups can maximize overall participation levels within the relevant identity set. For example, in the United States and Britain there are numerous charities in the social welfare field, each pursuing slightly different objectives and types of funding, and apparently imposing high information costs on donors, members and recipients of aid (Ware, 1989). But this high level of brand differentiation is justified by its defenders in terms of tapping more diverse sources of voluntary labour and finance than could a streamlined cluster of very large charities.

8. *People can exit fully,* both from producing and from consuming an endogenous group's output – because they can change or abandon the group

identity, improve their welfare by individual means, and are not dependent upon a dominant group.

9. *Turnover of group members is high*, because of an unstable set of potential members, low exit costs, the possibility of full exit and competition from rival groups or alternative group identities. If members are unlikely to stay in the group long, they are less willing to incur current recruitment or organizing costs in order to strengthen the group's future position: equilibrium levels of mobilization activity are thus lower (Wallerstein, 1989, p. 488).

The presence of dominant or rival groups, the ability to exit from consuming a group's output, and differing rates of membership turnover are all associated rather than necessary or defining features of these ideal types. This important caveat means that any endogenous group which can monopolize a salient identity, erect exit barriers and retain a stable membership over a long period creates dependence and compromises endogeneity – with increasing effects the longer the group is established and the greater the structural costs of trying to replace it or dispense with it. For example, most trade unions originated as endogeneous groups bridging across multiple exogenous group identities defined by the work process, which inhibited joint action. As unions became established, some of these features (such as job grading, apprenticeships, recruitment, bargaining arrangements, etc.) were successfully reshaped to support the central group identity. As participation increased so unions amalgamated, with dominant unions emerging in many industries (later strengthened by no-poaching deals), defining long-run identities, stabilizing their memberships, and creating strong dependency effects among potential members. Over time, trade unions' identity sets became less dependent on individual ideological commitments and more on the established dominance of the union organization.

Clearly this account implies that exogenous groups are always easier to organize than endogenous groups, after controlling for group size, environmental hostility, and so on. Exogenous groups attract 'solidaristic' participation because their group identity is grounded in people's social situation. By contrast people who join endogenous groups solely because of their collective benefits will have 'expressive' motivations, grounded in their personal values. But these motivational differences are consequences, not causes, of the relationship between the group membership, the group's identity set and the rest of society.

For *pure endogenous groups* it may not be feasible to distinguish empirically a class of 'free riders', that is, potential members who benefit from group activity without joining. With no observable basis for identifying the group's potential members except some degree of participation in its organization, there are only two classes of people: those who join the group, and those untouched by its activities (for whom they are presumably irrelevant). An amorphous set of 'sympathizers' may also exist, but they cannot be usefully labelled as 'free riders', nor easily targeted by leadership strategies. Hence non-joiners parasitic upon group members' efforts are effectively undetectable or unsanctionable, many people who do join leave quickly, group leadership strategies are more constrained, group discipline is weak, and under-organization prevalent. Endogenous groups may also rely heavily on the intense preferences of an activist minority prepared to incur disproportionate organizing costs. They should also depend more than exogenous groups on attracting financial support from 'patrons', wealthy individuals, philanthropic foundations, corporations or government agencies. Research on a national sample of 545 US interest groups operating in Washington supports this claim (Table 3.3). Here occupationally-based economic or professional groups (but excluding trade unions) are generally exogenous in my terms, while citizens groups are generally endogenous. Walker (1983, p. 404) concludes that dependence on outside support is critical for 'groups that speak for newly emerging elements of society and promote new legislative agendas and social values', which are also likely to meet many of the criteria for endogenous groups set out above.

Wealthy individuals and private foundations often take the lead in promoting groups designed to mobilize large segments of the public in support of controversial causes. Without the influence of patrons of political action, the flourishing system of interest groups in the United States would be much smaller and would include very few groups seeking to obtain broad collective or public goods.

The identity sets of endogenous groups (including 'sympathizers' along with members) are so diffuse and invisible that it can be impossible for prospective members to make meaningful calculations of their potential size, rate of mobilization, or even what they do or what kind of organization they actually are. Hence a programme of group activity is critical in making contact with both members and sympathizers, creating and sustaining an

Table 3.3   *The reliance of US interest groups on external funding*

	Occupational groups	Citizens' groups
Percentage of groups receiving outside finance at start-up	49	89
Average percentage of current revenue from outside finance	15	42

Source: Computed from Walker (1983), Tables 2 and 5, pp. 398, 400.

69

identity set out of an otherwise undifferentiated public. Good US examples are the League of Women Voters which stresses interpersonal interaction in decentralized groups as a method of retaining and recruiting members (Hansen, 1985, pp. 88–90), and the more issue-specific and centralized group Common Cause which contacts its members by mail and 'phone, and potential members via advertising. A detailed study of why a high proportion of Common Cause recruits quit the organization stresses (in line with the previous section) that people with only imperfect information often join groups as part of an 'experiential search procedure' (Rothenberg, 1988, p. 1147). Particularly for endogenous groups:

> Individuals join an organization about which they are largely uninformed. They have a rough idea about what it stands for, but they lack the detailed knowledge needed to decide whether this is the best association for them. [People who leave a group] are as informed about politics, as educated and as wealthy as long-time members. But they lack organization-specific information, which is best gained experientially. (Rothenberg, 1988, p. 1147)

Pure exogenous groups pose a clear contrast. To begin with there are always four main classes of people involved: group members; individuals in the identity set who have not joined the group because of perceptual or acceptance constraints; people in the identity set who are consciously free-riding; and the rest of society who cannot join the group, and are hence mostly indifferent to or oppose the group's activities. For example, consider a lobby representing families hit by drug-induced birth defects, such as thalidomide children. The group recruits some parents of deformed children, but other affected parents are unaware of its existence, or do not accept that it serves their interests. Some affected parents who are well informed consciously free-ride on the group's efforts. The rest of society (without deformed children) are not members of the relevant identity set – they can neither join nor free-ride, although they may sympathize with or help the group. Because exogenous groups can identify a relatively specific identity set beyond their existing members, they can achieve broadly based mobilizations with a lesser degree of prior organization. And successful activity which attracts increased participation observably improves an exogenous group's rate of mobilization.

Finally, the differences between exogenous and endogenous groups open up a crucial variation in leaders' strategies for influencing members' and potential members' perceptions of the group's size. In addition to trying to raise their membership levels, group leaderships may want to control the size of their identity sets. Olson made a distinction between 'inclusive' groups, which try to maximize their membership in pursuit of an open-ended supply of public goods, and 'exclusive' groups, which seek to restrict new entrants because they face a fixed supply of public goods

(Olson, 1978, pp. 36–43). In fact his usage is based on a confusion. All the 'exclusive' groups which he cites are trying to *restrict the size of their identity set*, not the group membership itself. Because they have a distinct identity set, exogenous groups pursue a quite general first strategy of restricting their potential membership. But once a compact and manageable identity set exists, all groups want to maximize their membership levels and mobilization rates. For example, trade unions often seek to limit entry into a particular craft or workplace by enforcing restrictive apprenticeship rules, while simultaneously maximizing their membership amongst those already in work. Endogenous groups usually cannot attempt this particular form of size manipulation because their identity sets are too indeterminate, too invisible or too diffuse.

EXPLAINING INTEREST GROUP DEMOCRACY

Existing public choice models portray interest groups as quasi-commercial bodies, run on hierarchical lines by entrepreneurial leaders maximizing membership (Frohlich *et al.*, 1971). Group members depend on leaders for start-up subsidies, and skills in packaging selective incentives, attracting outside finance, creating organizational resources, and bargaining with other groups or government. As a result, internal dissent is minimal. Yet in practice, most interest groups are much less hierarchical than business organizations. Indeed, their commonest formal structure is some type of imperfect democracy, a type of arrangement used in few other social organizations. Leaders are often directly elected (and re-elected) by grass roots members, who also vote on key policy decisions, often accompanied by decentralization down to local level not just in organizing activities but also in policy-making. The substantial costs of these arrangements are worth elucidating before examining their rationale for groups.

Paradoxes of democratic control

The maintenance of internal democracy in interest groups poses four explanatory problems for Olson and the new right.

1. *Reduced leadership discretion in setting group policies.* In a democratic organization if leaders do not respect grass roots opinion then their decisions can be reversed or not obeyed, and they risk losing their elective positions. Group activists may well have more fixed ideological preferences and generally possess more limited information than leaders. They often dissent from leaders' priorities or judgements when these involve compromising on the organization's collective goods objectives, with which activists identify most. Internal democracy also places a heavier burden on

71

the group's *discipline* – defined as any factor (such as trust or the threat of negative sanctions) which can bridge the gap in perceptions and expectations between leaders and the rank and file, or between members and their representatives in highly democratic groups (Crouch, 1982, pp. 148–54). Group leaderships can insulate themselves in various ways from effective control by the mass of members, but to the extent that such strategies widen the perception/preference gap to be bridged by discipline they are double-edged weapons.

2. *Enhanced collective action problems.* Internal democracy creates a multi-tiered collective action problem for group leaders trying to persuade their members to make the translation from lower-cost forms of participation to higher-cost campaigning. For example, to raise wage levels in a factory, a trade union must get a majority of workers first to join the union and achieve recognition and then vote for industrial action if collective bargaining breaks down. Next, members and non-members have to be encouraged to comply with the majority decision, and persuaded to maintain this stance as the costs of industrial action mount. At each stage, democratic self-government combined with reliance on voluntary activism introduce additional uncertainties into the group's policy-making. They magnify the scope for free-riding, and increase members' worries that other people will not bear their share of the costs of collective action.

3. *Public disclosure of internal dissent.* A democratic group negotiating with a hierarchically organized firm or the government, is placed at a serious disadvantage by its internal organization, because evidence of internal disunity or lack of support for group policy can so easily emerge in conflict situations (Offe and Wiesenthal, 1985, pp. 184–91). For example, if union leaders negotiating with employers threaten industrial action they must first be sure that they will win a strike ballot, otherwise the employers will actively force a vote in order to humiliate them. Even in the general competition for political influence, a democratic group is disadvantaged because its internal affairs are relatively open for inspection whereas other types of organizations can restrict the outflow of information. Group leaders' ability to dissimulate about their expectations, objectives and preference intensities is greatly constrained – so that they find it much harder to engage in agenda-setting behaviour in negotiations.

4. *Reduced organizational efficiency.* Organization theorists suggest that in small groups a simple hierarchy (leader and led) outperforms communities with no designated leader by economizing on information flows (Williamson, 1975, Chapter 2). Of course, few if any large interest groups are organized as simple hierarchies, let alone as self-governing communities. Groups' professional staffs are usually conventional rank-structured hierarchies. But retaining members' democratic control over top officials and key decisions, together with elected representatives overseeing bureaucrats, more than offsets these arrangements. The extra information

and decision-processing costs involved in democratic controls should mean that groups are slower, less efficient and indecisive when compared with the business or government organizations.

How then can existing public choice models explain the persistence and prevalence of interest group democracy? Only two tactics seem open, neither of them plausible. The first approach described in Chapter 2 is to impugn the quality of group democracy. Such arguments often have force in particular instances, and it is even possible to point to successful groups which are run very much like firms. But these exceptions do not alter the *general* picture of groups as differentially more democratic than other forms of social organization. The second approach is to argue that democratic procedures have been imposed on interest groups from outside – by government, legislators, the law courts, employers, the mass media, etc. Again this has some truth – witness the ballot procedures legally imposed on trade unions in many liberal democracies. But interest group democracy originated before such provisions; and laws often strengthen democracy in organizations which espouse it in their rule books, rather than imposing it afresh. Unlike 'shareholder democracy' inside companies, there is no possibility for group voting to be controlled by a few vote-owners, who have amassed large resources: group members cannot legally sell their votes on to others. And far more groups adhere to basically democratic procedures than are covered by regulations. Finally, where laws clearly do impose new levels of interest group democracy they often reflect efforts by policy-makers to reduce the target group's effectiveness, as with the Thatcher government's tightening of trade union laws and funding of strike ballots in Britain during the 1980s (Crouch, 1990). Hence for existing public choice work interest group democracy remains a puzzling anomaly, a problematic deviation from rationality.

However, one corner of the problem has been addressed by Bendor and Mookherjee (1987) whose sophisticated game theory analysis offers a formal proof that ongoing collective action can be more easily maintained in a large group which adopts a two-tier structure. In conditions of complete certainty a purely decentralized organization with fairly small local branches fosters the most conditional co-operation (where people participate as a result of stick-and-carrot incentives, co-operation from other members if they contribute but sanctions if they do not). However, with any realistic degree of uncertainty in monitoring other members' behaviour this 'solution' degrades rapidly. Instead, a centralized unit has to be added to develop and administer selective incentives, and to make all local branches conform with organizational policy. The greatest level of collective action is achieved where hierarchical control is *combined* with local branches, rather than displacing them, because 'the smallest sub-units provide a natural breeding ground for decentralized conditional cooperation':

Empirically, of course, nested structures are the rule. Among

73

[American] interest groups, it is virtually impossible to find a single one of any substantial size that does not exhibit a 'Chinese box' form. Trade associations are built out of firms, themselves hierarchic systems; the American Medical Association has well-organized state associations; the AFL-CIO is nested many layers deep, with member unions organized into locals. (Bendor and Mookherjee, 1987, p. 145)

So functional decentralization rather than complete hierarchy offers interest groups a rational strategy of institutional design (under very limiting game theoretic assumptions). Yet this analysis also assumes a completely hierarchic central unit in the group, and takes no account of the substantial costs of democratic control at both central and local levels. Hence the problem of group democracy remains mostly unexplained.

Internal democracy and size manipulation strategies

The approach developed here explains the internal democracy of groups in terms of a different instrumental logic where group identities play the key role. Fused with the functional decentralization of power down to smaller groups of members, internal democracy allows interest groups to develop *size manipulation strategies* which communicate partially contradictory messages about the group's size and viability to members. In attracting potential members interest groups stress that they are large, viable, nationally organized and worth joining. Yet simultaneously potential members are told that the group is small and local enough for their participation to make a difference; or at least their non-participation will be visible and noticeably impair group effectiveness. Thus internal democracy plus decentralization allow large groups to manipulate partially contradictory group identities in order to maximize levels of participation.

People are more likely to support an apparently powerful and effective organization, so to achieve this image groups stress their aggregate membership size – and leaders maximize membership numbers, within the limits set by their basic identity set. This entrepreneurial search for members also pushes leaders to diversify the group's fields of activity, so long as they are consistent with its established identity – an especially intense search if the size of the identity set is declining. Similarly, leaders try to take over or merge with rival groups (those trying to organize the same identity set), or with groups whose objectives and identity sets are congruent with their own existing activity. Environmental hostility often strongly pushes ahead scale increases in interest group organization, as when trade union aggregation matched the growth of business trade associations and large corporations in turn-of-the-century Britain (Pelling, 1987).

On Olson's model, all these strategies reduce incentives for participation, and therefore would be irrational behaviour for group leaderships. Of

Reconstructing the theory of groups

course, increases in group size could be offset by extra selective incentives to members, perhaps produced by economies of scale. Yet any slight gains larger groups make in organizing private benefits seem unlikely to match the disincentive effects of larger scale, and cannot automatically be assumed. On the group identity model, the leaders of expanding or larger groups offset their increased size by creating sections or local branches within which individual members' activities can continue to make an observable difference to group effectiveness. Multi-level activism is also encouraged by localized campaigns and by creating influential grass roots positions where the personal qualities of different individuals can make a real difference to the conduct of vital group activities. For example, in the period since 1918 when trade unions have become amongst the largest interest groups in Britain, there has also been a very considerable extension of their local level organization and activity, with a shift away from relying on branches based on large areas and towards local organization in all major workplaces, centring on the critical role of elected plant representatives, the shop stewards (Coates and Topham, 1988). Union militancy has also focused more on forms of industrial action specific to one firm or one workplace, and less on national or whole-industry strikes.

In principle, functional decentralization might be used on its own to encourage participation, without being linked to internal democracy. Leaders could devise 'work for idle hands', to keep their rank-and-file members busy without gaining any control over policy. This solution works well for the Conservative party in Britain where local branches mainly run social events and fund-raising, and offer uncritical public support for the leadership. But even in this case, branches do resolve major local decisions from time to time, and with a few exceptions genuinely decentralized patterns appear to be common in interest groups. A greater level of democratic control seems to be essential because leaderships have to operate in a competitive group environment, with a basically voluntary membership, non-excludable outputs, and a very much smaller battery of coercive or pecuniary mechanisms than can, say, business corporations. A transition to a more contract-based form of organization can occur only where commercial substitutes for membership activities are available and politically legitimate, which in most cases they are not. Only a few endogenous cause groups (such as Greenpeace) manage to survive on media publicity and arm's-length donations from sympathizers with no apparatus for democratic control and little by way of a local group network.

Internal democracy helps maximize participation in group activities for three reasons.

1. *Realizing collective benefits.* Grass roots controls over leaders help solve a key problem with Olson's 'by product' theory: according to which large groups only come into existence because their leaders can market selective incentives to members, thereby creating an organization able to begin

75

providing collective benefits as well. Laver (1981) points out that there is no reason to assume that an economically rational group leadership will *want* to produce collective benefits for their own sake. Why do the leaders not just convert any surplus raised from marketing selective incentives into perks or profits for themselves, since they will not lose any members by doing so? Take Olson's example

> of a trade union, which sells insurance to its members in order to induce them to join. . . . When it sells insurance, the trade union is an insurance broker engaged in private transactions. If these private transactions provide members with sufficient private surplus to justify their participation, they will participate whether or not a public good is provided by the union, since they are making a [private return] anyway. There is thus no reason to suppose that the public good will be provided. (Laver, 1981, p. 41)

Internal democracy means that group members can ensure that any surplus which leaders raise from selling selective incentives is actually devoted to producing more collective benefits. Oversight by rank-and-file members can stop the most entrepreneurial group leaders from simply boosting their own private welfare. Internal democracy also maximizes take-up by potential members, providing a guarantee of appropriate leadership behaviour in future. Its effect is similar to the professions' regulation and certification procedures which boost demand for doctors' or lawyers' services from consumers who are otherwise open to being exploited (Johnson, 1972). Particularly where groups compete with commercial firms in a market with standardized cost curves, internal group democracy confers a comparative advantage in attracting members.

2. *Altering voice payoffs.* By offering members a 'voice' option in setting group policy, internal democracy changes individuals' calculation of how their participation affects supply. Potential members may well want to influence the group's policy choices, especially where there are major disagreements or where people are locked into consuming a dominant group's outputs even if they free-ride (see page 65 above). For example, it may matter a great deal to trade union members who is elected to represent them in their workplace, creating an extra inducement to keep paying their dues. Voice capabilities (leadership elections, referenda on major policy changes, strike ballots, sending delegations to annual conferences, protests, etc.) can only be activated by members, and so are excludable benefits of participation. Within local branches, an individual's use of voice is far more influential than at national or regional level, especially if opinions are finely balanced. In addition, to the extent that an individual can influence group policy in what they perceive as a more effective direction, the subjective impact of their participation in realizing collective benefits increases.

3. *External legitimacy.* As pluralists argue (see page 20), a reputable system

for ascertaining the membership's views is important for a group's public position – especially where group activity imposes costs on the public at large.

Conclusion

Existing public choice accounts make a central mistake in assuming that instrumentally rational actors are overwhelmingly influenced by the objective size of an interest group in assessing whether their individual membership will enhance the supply of collective benefits which they receive. In fact, non-excludability (the fact that non-members also enjoy collective benefits) and irrelevance to supply (the fact that any individual makes a negligible contribution to group viability) are only two amongst several separate disincentives to rational participation. Most of these constraints on participation decline with increasing group mobilization rates, and even with rising actual group size. (It is the size of a group's potential membership which is most linked with disincentives to participation.) And given the complexity of the interest group universe, the crucial difficulties of recruiting members often do not concern free-riding but rather overcoming perceptual and acceptance constraints on group-joining.

If groups are to attract people because of the collective benefits which they promote, they need to make potential members aware that they share an interest with other people, and that a group exists which can cater effectively for this interest. Because a group's existence and its relation to individual interests are not perceived easily or automatically, group identities (perceptions of an interest shared with others and represented by a group) are conceptually separate variables from ordinary subjective interests. Identities also heavily influence perceptions of group size and viability. Because increasing size generally enhances a group's viability in a liberal democratic political system, it has an ambiguous impact on participation decisions.

Existing public choice accounts do not account for variations in the level of organization of similarly sized groups. By contrast, the group identity approach uses the ideal types of exogenous and endogenous groups to explain why non-size influences on participation decisions and ease of organization are more than capable of offsetting any simple tendency for participation to fall with increased group size.

Moreover, in conventional public choice accounts the distinctiveness of internally democratic interest group organizations compared with corporate or government bureaucracies is a puzzling anomaly. But for the group identity approach it emerges as a key means of shaping the identity of the group so as to maximize overall participation levels. Size manipulation strategies allow the leaders of large interest groups to assure their members both that the group is viable (because of its size) and that their own participation is important (because their efforts and voice would be missed at the local level).

Finally, the approach used here suggests a revised picture of interest group leaders. In previous public choice accounts, the leadership is pictured as a unitary actor, a single entrepreneur or a unified team, confronting a one-dimensional problem – of mobilizing a (somehow pre-defined) potential membership by devising appropriate selective incentives. Variations in the efficiency of this supply-side operation (chiefly in relation to group size) were seen as almost the only source of differing rates of mobilization. Only Olson's brief and mishandled discussion of 'inclusive' versus 'exclusive' groups breached this picture, and even here the source of variations in approach lay outside the control of group leaders.

By contrast, the group identity model reinstates the organizational structures and political processes inside interest groups as key influences on their strategies. Group leaders are only one set of actors in quite a complex internal picture, and they confront a wide range of decision choices in maximizing their group's effectiveness and size (within its identity set). Devising and maintaining a group identity; overcoming perceptual, acceptance and effectiveness barriers to participation; shaping identity sets; constructing selective incentives; managing (imperfectly) democratic internal group decision-making; and sustaining a delicate balance of contradictory images of the group's size and situation via size manipulation strategies – all of these tasks create multi-tiered decision choices for group leaders.

Chapter 4

ECONOMIC EXPLANATIONS OF VOTING BEHAVIOUR

with Hugh Ward

The public choice model of voting and party competition was created by Hotelling (1929) and Downs (1957) from the initial insight that parties or candidates could be seen as behaving analogously to firms and voters in much the same way as consumers. Parties alter their position in electoral space to attract the maximum number of votes, and voters choose the party closest to their personal position on key issues – just as ice-cream stalls position themselves on a beach to attract the maximum custom, and holiday-makers collect their ice-cream from the nearest stall. The most famous substantive proposition derived from the early public choice literature is median voter convergence. In a two-party race, the pressures of competition push party leaders to adopt policy platforms close to the position of the median voter – defined as someone with exactly as many people holding more left-wing views as there are people holding more right-wing attitudes. Converging on the median voter's views maximizes the pool of voters from whom either party or candidate in a competition may hope to draw support. Moving away from this position will throw the election and cede control of government to the rival party or candidate.

Of course, some people will not vote at all, and parties must take account of such decisions in deciding what policies to advocate. Just as some customers on a beach may not get up to buy ice-cream if it would take too long to walk to the sales points, so some citizens may find no party or candidate offering policy stances close enough to their position to motivate them to vote (Smithies, 1941). The market analogy breaks down on a different kind of abstention, however. If parties adopt almost identical positions, citizens as a whole will confront decreasing incentives to turn out and vote since whichever party wins will implement almost the same policies – citizens get identical results whether they vote or not. By contrast, in economic markets there is no tendency for consumers on the beach to consume less simply because they are served by two equally satisfactory

79

ice-cream stalls. If the pressures for citizens to abstain from alienation (no party is putting forward a viewpoint which they positively support) or from indifference (the parties are too close together) become strong enough then parties in a two-horse race may not converge on the median voter position.

There is now a large formal literature which explores how different circumstances and starting assumptions alter the early results, especially the presence of more parties and multiple-issue dimensions, both of which make it less likely that any stable equilibrium situation exists towards which parties can move their programmes. Many of these studies are simply theoretical elaborations of hypothetical situations and have not been translated to apply in detail to actual electoral competition. In the process of formalization, it is common for many of the starting assumptions of public choice accounts to disappear from view. The major work in the field still remains Anthony Downs's *An Economic Theory of Democracy* (1957) which stands out because of its exceptionally full and applied analysis of what rational action by voters would look like, and of the ways in which parties could be expected to behave. Downs's work provides the starting-point for both the main sections of this brief chapter, focusing on the demand-side of electoral competition, that is, voters' behaviour.

The first section applies the analysis of group-joining given in the previous chapter to a problem which has bedevilled public choice voting models from the outset. Unless someone's vote is going significantly to determine which party or candidate forms the next government, why should she cast a ballot at all – why not spend time in a more valuable way? The second section examines the assumptions about individual and aggregate preferences involved in public choice models, with special reference to the claim that preferences can be taken as exogenously determined.

THE DECISION TO VOTE

A key problem in the existing public choice accounts of voting behaviour is explaining why anyone bothers to vote. A rational voter should first work out her 'party differential' (the benefit she will receive if one party rather than its rivals wins the election). This stake is then multiplied by the likelihood that her own vote will be decisive in determining which party forms the government. This probability is almost always minute. So however large her party differential, a rational voter cannot receive discounted benefits sufficient to offset the costs of acquiring political information or travelling to the polling station to vote (Downs, 1957, Chapter 14). Hence rational citizens should abstain, letting others absorb the costs of participating – small though they may be in liberal democracies with secret ballots and free elections, and with extensive free mass media coverage of political life. Individual voters' irrelevance to supply should cripple public support for the electoral process. Since this clearly does not happen in most liberal democracies, how can a consistent public choice account of rational voting be offered? For the United States this question gains added significance because it is the leading liberal democracy where turnout has fallen significantly, from 63 per cent of registered voters in 1960 to 53 per cent by the 1980s. At the same time, empirical evidence suggests that geographical differences in turnout are relatively little affected by how American voters see the degree of closeness of presidential campaigns (especially in 1968, 1976 and 1980). 'The perceived probability of a tied election at the state level is not a powerful or reliable factor in explaining across-state variation in voter participation rates in presidential elections' (Foster, 1984, p. 688).

I briefly examine various efforts to evade the problems over rational voting in the existing literature, before comparing voting behaviour with group-joining, and then outlining how the group identity approach can be extended to explain rational turnout.

Attempts to explain away rational abstention

Downs argued that people might vote out of a concern to maintain the health of their democratic system. But a single voter's decision to participate is also very unlikely to affect the overall vitality of democracy. However large someone's interest in preserving democracy, it too must be discounted by the likelihood that their own vote will make any difference, which must be negligibly small (Barry, 1978, pp. 19–23). The same objection floors all accounts of rational voting in terms of altruistic motivations amongst voters. As I noted above (page 49), if someone's contribution to a collective action is irrelevant to the supply of collective benefits that results, then even an altruistic voter must conclude that her own participation only reduces the amount of welfare (Buchanan, 1979, pp. 65–6). Where some collective benefits are provided with her irrelevant participation, then overall welfare could be marginally improved by her abstention. And where no collective benefits are provided despite her participation, what point is served by contributing to a lost cause?

An approach taken seriously by some game theorists argues that voting can be explained by considering the interaction between one person's behaviour and others. Suppose actor A works out that it is not rational for her to vote, she will also appreciate that it is generally not rational for others to vote either. However, if many other people abstain then it would be rational for A to go to the polls after all, since her influence will be magnified by mass abstentions. In the abstract, the 'game' between A and other voters is characterized by uncertainty. It is possible that A will fail to vote when she could actually decide or at least significantly influence an election outcome.

81

If she would then experience regret at this missed opportunity, it could be rational for her to vote regularly simply as a form of low-cost insurance against this negatively valued outcome. But although a rational actor trying to anticipate the behaviour of other actors in the abstract game confronts significant uncertainty, in actually existing liberal democracies voters have a great deal more information about how others will behave. Past electoral behaviour and current opinion polls mean that most people will be certain that a majority of their fellow citizens will participate, and only the distribution of votes between parties may be hard to predict.

Another attempt to evade the rational abstention problem argues that citizens scale up the benefits of their own party differential to apply to everyone else involved in the election as well as themselves, creating a hugely magnified stake in the electoral outcome (McLean, 1987, pp. 48–9; Margolis, 1982, Chapter 7). If this net benefit estimate is multiplied by even a tiny probability of individual influence, it may now be sufficient to override the small costs of becoming informed about the election and of casting a ballot. One problem with this move is that it assumes that only positive-sum policy changes will be involved in voters' calculation of their party differential, i.e. policies which boost their social welfare without harming anyone else's. In fact, many voters support parties advocating zero-sum policies – for example, tax/welfare strategies which redistribute income from one social group to another. Even the most ideological voter obviously cannot consistently scale up gains of this kind across the electorate as a whole. The more fundamental objection, however, is that allowing people to ascribe their own party differential to all citizens converts voters from rationally self-interested actors into altruistic utilitarians, acting not to maximize their personal utilities but to increase the global amount of happiness in their society. Such a move should be resisted because it makes a public choice model completely unspecific and unfalsifiable. 'Soon all behaviour whatsoever becomes rational because it is a means to some end the actor values' (Downs, 1957, p. 276).

The same objection vitiates explanations of electoral participation in terms of either the psychic benefits of voting or a feeling of civic duty which impels people to go to the polls. An illuminating micro-economic theory of market behaviour could not be effectively developed in a society where people fixed prices not through the interplay of supply and demand but from religious convictions (Barry, 1978, p. 33). In a similar way, there can be little explanatory scope for a public choice model of political behaviour if we can simply invoke equation-filling ethical voting, or 'psychic benefits', or a pre-rational moral compulsion to vote, as ways out of difficult problems (see Mueller, 1987; Plott, 1987). If the decision to go to the polls is to be explained in such terms, then a public choice explanation of how people choose between parties cannot consistently exclude such factors as child-hood socialization into support for one party, or a desire to please one's

82

husband or wife, or a phobia about certain politicians' haircuts. Such an enlargement of the scope of admissible factors would render public choice explanations completely undistinctive.

A final dimension of the abstention problems concerns comparative turnout across different types of elections. If probabilities of influencing election outcomes are very influential in shaping voters' decision to participate, the proportion of people voting should be inversely related to the size of the electorate. In national elections, most people's party differentials are greater than in local or regional contests, but their individual probability of being decisive is drastically reduced – especially where the whole country constitutes a single constituency in national elections, as in French presidential contests or voting for the Israeli Parliament. Even with multi-constituency voting, turnout should be less at national than local or regional elections if irrelevance to supply is as critical as Downs suggests in the voting calculus. In practice, this pattern rarely occurs in liberal democracies. In some countries, such as West Germany and France (in the 1970s at least), turnout levels are high across all elections – with as many French voters participating in elections for small-scale rural communes with little power as in national contests (Becquart-Leclerc, 1976). In other countries, like the United States and Britain, there are major differences in turnout but the pattern of variation is the opposite of what a public choice approach suggests – turnout levels at local elections are often up to half those at national elections.

Comparing voting with group-joining

The problem of rational abstention in large-scale elections is not *sui generis*. It is a special case of a general paradox, according to which no one should join in a collective action unless their net utility from a favourable outcome, discounted by the probability that their individual participation influences the eventual outcome, exceeds the (non-discounted) costs incurred in taking the action. Chapter 3 outlined a particular solution of this paradox for group-joining activity which can be extended to explain why most citizens vote.

The constraints inhibiting turnout at elections are simpler than those affecting group-joining (see Figure 3.1, page 46). Clearly the policy stances adopted by political parties concern non-excludable and indivisible benefits (or costs) which accrue to citizens whether or not they vote for them. And most individual voting decisions are objectively irrelevant to the supply of collective benefits which results from the victory of the party closest to their personal optimum (or to the collective costs incurred if a less preferred party gains control of government). But citizens considering whether to support an established party can be much more certain that their fellow citizens will behave co-operatively than with group-joining. There are far fewer political parties than interest groups, and support for established parties is relatively stable from one election to the next in most liberal democracies. However, candidate-oriented elections, such as the primary contests for the presidential nomination in the US Democratic and Republican parties, present greater problems for citizens in evaluating diverse politicians.

The other three factors included in Figure 3.1 have little relevance for voting behaviour because the basic electoral arrangements in a democracy are designed to exclude them. The secret ballot guarantees that most non-voting is invisible. (However, in some countries parties still make a vigorous effort to monitor who goes to the polls on election day, in order to recanvass late in the day their declared supporters who have not yet voted.) Secret voting means that non-voters can also be certain that their personal non-participation will have no adverse imitative effects on their party's support. Lastly, the whole fabric of electoral law safeguards citizens from the threat of sanctions being applied to them because of their simple choice between parties– although other forms of political activism can be costly (see page 88 below).

The informational pre-requisites of choosing between parties are simpler than those for potential interest group members. With a very few parties or candidates in competition being accorded saturation coverage by the mass media, almost everyone is aware that the main parties exist and stand for some distinctive policies. However, the four elements of a group identity remain important. At the level of acceptance, rational voters must accept that party X promotes some set of interests I, and that they share these interests. At the level of efficacy, they must also see party X as a viable party promoting their interests, and believe that if they vote for party X it will enhance their benefits from the interest set I. These stages could be short-circuited most powerfully in the case of those interest group members who follow clear advice given by their group leaders and vote collectively for the candidate or party that is most successful in negotiating support from the group leaders. Turnout levels for members of solidaristic groups making endorsements should thus be greater, as they seem to be in recent US congressional elections (Uhlaner, 1989).

Having few, very well-known political parties may seem to imply that they resemble endogenous groups, that is, membership of the set of party supporters is self-selected, the group defines its own identity and there is virtually no identity set over and above actual members. The calculus for voting just outlined includes only the four stages relevant to endogenous groups. It should also be clear that some newly formed parties based on particular ideologies (rather than tapping a social cleavage) and still building up to become major electoral contenders, closely match the criteria for pure endogenous groups (see Figure 3.4, page 66). However, major parties progressively acquire the characteristics of exogenous groups. They

84

solidify an appeal to people in defined social locations, make alliances with corporatist interests, manipulate the electoral system to prevent new parties entering competition and establish themselves as the dominant party in one area of the political spectrum – hence creating strong dependence effects amongst voters. With no viable alternative to support, dissatisfied voters whose views fall in the relevant area can abstain but may still find that their welfare is closely reliant on the party's performance (Hirschman, 1970, p. 102). In Chapter 5 I explore further how party leaders may actively strengthen tendencies for parties to become exogenous groups. But some effects of this kind will operate even without a deliberate leadership strategy to encourage them.

A second key difference between group-joining and voting concerns resources. Voting is much cheaper than group-joining in terms of time, money, risk, etc. Rational participation in elections may require quite a lot of knowledge and information, but specialized mass media readily provide these to citizens. In addition, the vote itself is a highly valued resource, both historically in terms of political struggles to secure a universal franchise, and by contemporary public opinion in most liberal democracies. For example, in a recent study three-quarters of UK voters endorsed five or more attitudinal items supportive of the 'democratic creed', declaring voting worthwhile, a positive duty, an effective means of influence, etc. (Catt, 1989). Behind this consensus is the recognition that citizens might expect to use this resource only twelve to fifteen times in an average lifetime, in respect of US presidential elections or general elections in Britain. Choosing to abstain from voting is thus an odder decision than might appear at first sight. Because the vote is a resource which is non-transferable between persons or over time, it simply goes to waste when left unused.

Modelling the decision to vote

The group identity approach developed above suggests a reconstructed model of why people vote at elections, set out in Figure 4.1 in which all the variables are subjective perceptions. Starting in the top left-hand corner, the more definitely an individual's utility is likely to be served by one party's election (or harmed by the election of a rival party) the more likely she will be to accept that the party regularly promotes interests which she shares with others. I term this recognition a 'party identity' (analogous to the group identity in Chapter 3: the label also indicates that the concept is distinct from the conventional political science concept of 'party identification'). Forming a party identity means that the voter can abridge any close comparison of alternative party programmes or performance records, unless her personal situation changes drastically and she alters her preferences. Such a voter may also internalize a distinctive party ideology as a method of economizing on the costs of acquiring political information.

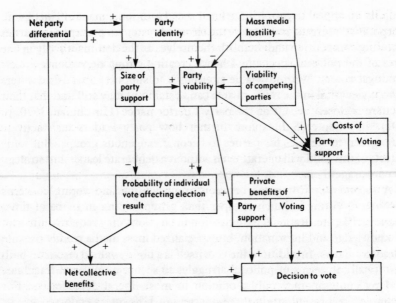

Figure 4.1 **The decision to vote**

This routinization of partisan perceptions of politics also increases voters' assessment of their party differential, their stake in the election of their preferred party. In US presidential elections since 1960, people are more likely to vote when they see a clear choice between candidates (that is, they are not indifferent between them) and when they see their personal position as reasonably close to that of one of the candidates (Zipp, 1985) – both views fostered by a party identity.

A party identity also positively conditions a voter's perceptions of that party's electoral viability. Far more clearly than in an interest group context, marginal increments of party support boost voters' perceptions of its viability since opinion polls provide frequent comparative rankings of parties' performance. If my preferred party noticeably increases its national support, my individual irrelevance to supply goes up infinitesimally (unless the party is brought closer to a key electoral threshold level). But the tiny incremental decline in my influence is always more than offset by the party's improved viability, so that the perceived probability of my vote successfully influencing the election outcome grows. In almost all cases people see their vote as more efficacious if their preferred party is going to win or perform strongly, even if it wins handsomely. In some situations, however, the probability of an individual vote affecting the election result may go down somewhat the more other people are going to vote the same way. If a party already has a clear lead, then evidence of a 'landslide' effect may convince some supporters that they no longer need to vote to be assured of victory.

The effects of increased party support in increasing individual irrelevance to supply but boosting estimates of the party's viability are mediated by the electoral system. These arrangements also determine whether a vote has a single meaning (as in the United States where a congressional election influences only who occupies a House or Senate seat, but not who occupies the presidency), or several meanings (as in the United Kingdom where constituency voting determines which party elects the local MP, but also which party forms the government and hence who becomes prime minister).

The other main determinants of how viable a party appears are environmental, especially the viability of competing parties and influence of the mass media. Elections are zero-sum games where one party's success entails another's loss of support. In two-party systems, of course, this trade-off hardly needs to be diagrammed separately: one party's gain in viability implies the other's loss. But with multiple parties in competition the interaction between different parties' blocs of support becomes more complex, especially where transfers of support between parties must take place through such devices as run-off elections or transferable second or third preference votes in proportional representation systems.

The mass media simplify and dramatize changes of party support. In many liberal democracies media systems manifest chronic partisan biases, with newspapers and to a lesser degree the broadcast media campaigning vigorously against particular candidates, parties or policy stances disliked by media proprietors or journalists. For example, in Britain in the 1980s over three-quarters of voters read solidly pro-Conservative and anti-Labour newspapers (Harrop, 1986), while analysis of the TV coverage of the 1987 general election showed a heavy bias in favour of the incumbent Conservative government (Miller *et al.*, 1990, Chapter 6). Because of the pooling of news values in any media system, the greater the level of mass media hostility towards a particular party the more voters are discouraged from forming a party identity or regular attachment to that party, and the more pessimistically they assess its viability.

A final qualification must be entered about the influence which voters see their vote as having in realizing collective benefits. What counts as 'influence' for different voters will vary widely, in ways which are not exclusive. For example, voters may be concerned only about winning outright nationally or in local constituency terms; or they may also consider parties' relative totals or 'headline votes', again at national or local levels (whether or not a candidate is elected at this level); or they may take into account quite extended consequences of elections, such as contributing to or eroding a parliamentary majority, making some kinds of governing coalitions feasible and preventing other formations, and limiting or accentuating the partisan distinctiveness of future legislative activity. Citizens will also try to use their votes in a bewildering variety of ways, to support a preferred party, to try to keep out a disliked party (which may involve tactical voting in a three-party or multiple-party system under plurality rule elections), to signal limited dissatisfaction to their preferred party leadership about current performance or policy stances, etc. The general critique of past voting studies which stresses a radically over-simplified focus on 'support voting' to the exclusion of these 'sophisticated voting' considerations (Catt, 1989) applies with particular force to previous public choice work.

Voters will also pay attention to the private benefits and costs of their decision, both of which need to be split into two headings: the benefits/costs of supporting a given party, and the benefits/costs of voting itself. In all democracies, the private benefits of supporting a party include associative benefits (being able to tell politically aligned friends, workmates or neighbours that you voted their way), plus the normal participation benefits surrounding spectator sports, such as backing a winner and accurately estimating parties' comparative performance. It is in this sense, too, that a rational choice account might legitimately incorporate the suggestion that people vote at elections despite minor costs, 'guided not so much by maximization of expected utility, but by something much simpler, viz, just a desire to record one's true preferences' (Sen, 1970, p. 195).

However, in many liberal democracies, and perhaps in some localities in all of them, these conventional and legitimate private benefits of party support are extended in various less legitimate ways by 'boss systems', clientelism, or political corruption. At the level of the individual voter, the scale of benefits involved is typically small – unlike the pay-offs available to those who finance parties' or candidates' election campaigns, or the leaders of large interest groups able to deliver sizeable blocs of support. But for ordinary voters, their gains from supporting a particular party – for example, job preferment possibilities, better access to social benefits, or getting your property connected to basic services – can still far outweigh the other factors considered so far. Obviously access to any of these benefits is likely to be heavily conditioned by a party's viability: only winners or members of a winning coalition can deliver the targeted goods. And supporting a losing or minority party can on occasion involve considerable private costs (see below), especially in clientelist or partially corrupt democratic systems. Of course, voters can in principle dissimulate about who they support and make private gains while using the secret ballot to express their real views. Yet where people's private gains from supporting one party are substantial, their collective benefits almost always run in the same direction.

In all liberal democracies the private costs of supporting a particular party can be significant (especially having to declare to politically aligned friends, workmates or neighbours that you voted another way). These costs increase if the viability of your preferred party goes down, seeming to back a certain loser – hence the 'spiral of silence' phenomenon (Noelle-Newman, 1984). Backing a much wider range of parties may carry costs where these choices are unpopular in particular countries, localities or time periods. As the barometers of mass or élite unpopularity, and the key means by which it is targeted, the mass media are again critically important (Page and Schapiro, 1983). Of course, so long as voting is truly secret people may always avoid these costs by not declaring or by publicly misdescribing their vote. But this approach may carry its own costs (for example, not taking part in political discussions or not going into partisan contexts), and obviously cannot be applied to any kind of political activity beyond the actual vote itself (such as going to meetings, putting up posters or wearing badges, expounding your views to the press, standing for election, etc.).

Where voting for particular parties is socially stigmatized much more serious costs are created. In many Western countries, overtly supporting communist or far-left socialist parties has carried considerable costs (such as attracting surveillance by intelligence agencies or social ostracism), sanctions less often applied to voters for far-right racist parties. Police or private investigation agencies often maintain blacklists of people who have done no more than publicly back a party judged 'extremist' by a consensus of public opinion or by people holding social power in that society. Inclusion in such blacklists can then result in such substantial costs as exclusion from public employment or lost job opportunities with private firms especially anxious to keep out left-wing 'troublemakers'.

The private benefits of the act of voting itself are normally slight, but they can be greater where elections are more of a social occasion. In Greece, for instance, people are registered as citizens in their place of birth, and must vote there even if they have since emigrated to another distant area; here elections are an important time for visits to the family home, with the main parties arranging trips back for their supporters.

In most countries the private costs of voting itself are also typically very small: travelling to the nearest polling station, being sufficiently informed to be able to make a rough choice and incurring the minimal costs of compulsory registration. However, in other countries such as the United States registering as a voter is not compulsory, and requires greater individual effort – despite the willingness of parties and some interest groups to facilitate registration (Harrop and Miller, 1987, pp. 44–5). In all countries, registering as a voter can be expensive for people who are mobile and miss regular registration procedures, those unequipped with citizenship papers because of illegal immigration, or anyone keen to avoid local taxes. The introduction of a substantial poll tax to finance local government in Britain in 1990 is expected to reduce voter registration, since would-be poll tax evaders clearly must remain anonymous to officialdom in general. Even so, significant registration costs are likely to be confined to small minorities of all potential voters, outside the US.

Overall, by focusing on the subjective variables which structure voters' 'party differential' and estimations of their individual influence, Figure 4.1 radically reduces any a priori reasons for expecting rational voters to abstain. In particular, although an increase in a preferred party's support somewhat reduces people's perception that their individual vote matters, this effect is likely to be more than offset by their assessment of the party's improved electoral viability. The balance of private benefits and costs in supporting particular parties also far outweighs the benefits and costs of actually voting itself, and may easily be decisive for people's partisan choices in some areas, countries or time periods.

EXOGENOUS VOTER PREFERENCES

A second fundamental problem for economic accounts of voting behaviour is explaining how voters come to have the views they have, and how shifts of public opinion take place. Before exploring this question in detail, I briefly consider public choice assumptions about individual voter's preferences and those of the electorate as a whole.

Individual and aggregate preferences

In order to build effective models of elections, public choice theorists make a series of very restrictive assumptions which it is easy to lose sight of. The first concerns the configuration of individual voters' *utility profiles* (their preferences). Figure 4.2a shows curves for the levels of utility (that is benefits net of costs measured along the vertical axis) which three individuals get from policy positions ordered along a single left/right political dimension (the horizontal axis). All three utility profiles are *single-peaked*, that is, the curves have one highest position. Many mathematical models also assume more restrictively that utility profiles are symmetrical, that is, they decline evenly on either side of the voter's optimum position, shown by the star points A and B in the Figure. In a two-dimensional electoral space – for example, one where left/right conflicts are supplemented by a cleavage between environmentalism and economic growth – we can draw contour lines to map voters' utility profiles (see Figure 4.2b). The single-peaked utility profile assumption requires that each voter has a single optimum position, shown by the points A and B in the Figure. Around the best point each roughly circular contour line shows combinations of equal utility to the voter. (These contour lines are also called *indifference curves*, since for that voter there is nothing to choose between one point or another on the line in utility terms.) Obviously, the further away each contour line is from the voter's optimum, the lower the level of utility shown. Again, the map for voter B shows symmetrical

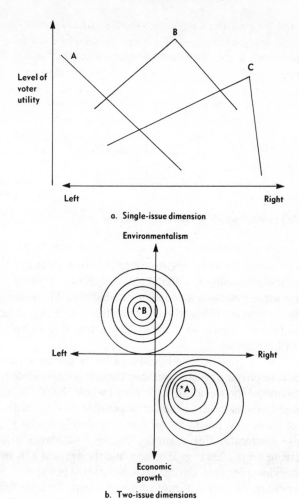

a. Single-issue dimension

b. Two-issue dimensions

Figure 4.2 **Single-peaked voter utility profiles**

single-peaked preferences, while that for voter A is asymmetric, declining steeply as policy positions move away in a centrist direction from the voter's personal right-wing optimum, but showing much greater tolerance of positions more right-wing than that optimum.

Single-peaked utility profiles, and even more symmetrical profiles, are often presented by the technical public choice literature as being unproblematic or widely accepted. They are not. Figure 4.3 shows examples of three utility profiles which are outlawed by the assumption but are highly likely to occur in practice. Here voter A has a single best optimum position, but also a subsidiary peak. Voter B has one left-wing peak and one right-wing peak, a configuration appropriate for someone who sees strong

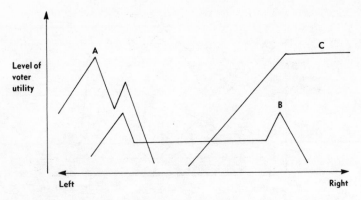

Figure 4.3 **Utility profiles which are not single-peaked**

conservatism or socialism as coherent strategies, but rejects intermediate 'fudge and mudge' alternatives. Voter C has a clear inclination to the right but accepts multiple positions as equally satisfactory. These supposedly unusual configurations are likely to occur quite frequently in practice. And there is absolutely no reason to suppose that a majority of voters have symmetrical utility profiles.

The assumption of single-peaked (and to a lesser degree symmetrical) utility profiles is important because without them it is impossible to create summary measures of the electorate's views as a whole. However, if we can take the assumptions as holding then it is possible to draw a frequency distribution of all voters' positions, an *aggregate distribution of preferences* (ADP) for the electorate. For example, Figure 4.4a shows a left/right political spectrum on the horizontal axis, while the vertical axis measures how many voters have personal optima at each left/right position. The shape of the ADP curve has important implications for party competition, with curves such as Figure 4.4a or Figure 4.4b very favourable for median voter convergence in a two-party system, even if we posit some abstentions due to alienation (parties being too far from voters to make it worth their while voting at all). The difference between the two situations is obviously that the median in Figure 4.4b is not at a centrist position on the left–right spectrum as it is in Figure 4.4a. Where most voters are bunched at each end of the ADP curve, as in Figure 4.4c, then much lower levels of abstention because of alienation are needed to prevent median voter convergence in a two-party system.

Obviously the ADP concept becomes much more complicated when there are multiple political dimensions: algebraic formulations rather than graphical representations become necessary with three or more dimensions. However, two-dimensional space can still be pictured diagrammatically as a surface rather than a line curve. In practical terms this may often be

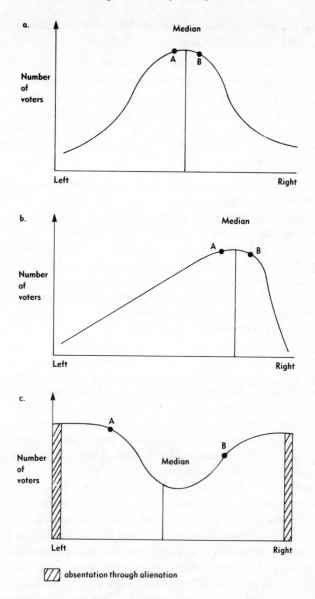

Figure 4.4 **Different configurations of the aggregate distribution of preferences**

sufficient to capture contemporary realities. In the United States, for example, although detailed issue attitudes show a complex picture of voter concerns, none the less the electorate *as a whole* reacted 'as if' it was ideologically consistent, operating on a Downsian 'political scale', in evaluating the 1980 presidential candidates, Carter and Reagan (Feld and Gofman, 1988). And for Britain:

> In nearly all studies, two dimensions recur. The first is a left/right factor covering government involvement in the economy and society, particularly for redistributive purposes. Nationalization [taking industries into public ownership] falls squarely into this factor. The second dimension is a 'tough–tender' factor covering such issues as law and order, capital punishment, immigration and race relations. (Harrop and Miller, 1987, p. 123)

It is important to stress that public choice models of elections directly make substantive assumptions about the shape of the aggregate distribution of preferences in the electorate. Certain premises about individual voters (such as single-peaked utility profiles) are necessary if the concept of a determinate ADP curve or surface is to make sense. But the shape of the aggregate distribution cannot be *derived from* individual-level assumptions. Downs at least did not lose sight of the fact that the empirical configuration of voters' views is critical: 'It is clear that the numerical distribution of voters along the political scale [that is, the ADP curve] determines to a great extent what kind of democracy will develop' (Downs, 1957, p. 121; and see also Dahl, 1956, pp. 90–102). By contrast, much of the technical public choice literature has downplayed the importance of this limitation, because it does not fit with their concerns to establish in formal models whether party equilibrium positions exist or not. These accounts of course acknowledge that: 'The existence of an election equilibrium and the corresponding Condorcet point [a point that is preferable for parties or candidates to all other points in pairwise comparisons] is sensitive to the exact distribution of preferences' (Ordeshook, 1986, p. 173). But this is very much a diversionary aside from the mainstream analysis.

Questions about the existence of equilibrium party competition points are intimately bound up with the number of ideological dimensions and the number of parties in competition. With three parties and a single electoral dimension median voter convergence is still likely: support for the middle party should be squeezed as the two 'outside' parties maximize votes by moving inwards. But four or more parties competing in a single dimension are likely to remain differentiated from each other, especially where the ADP configuration is flat or multi-peaked. Three parties competing in two dimensions will be unstable: even if median voter convergence is achieved one party is almost certain to be able to increase its support by moving away from that position (Tullock, 1967, pp. 54–5, and 1976, p. 23). In general, the more dimensions of competition exist the more likely it becomes that party positions are unstable over time, while the more parties are in competition, and the more easily new parties can enter the race and attract the votes of abstainers, the less likely it is that party positions will converge.

These general propositions hold so long as parties cannot leapfrog each other's positions: for example, an initially 'left' party is debarred from suddenly adopting more conservative, deflationary or libertarian positions than its 'right wing' rival (see Chapter 5 below).

Running through the whole public choice discussion of preferences there is the *proximity assumption* that voters always choose to support the party that is nearest to them. If everyone's utility profiles are single-peaked and symmetric, then being 'nearest' means the same thing for all voters: simple proximity in issue space. But if some people have asymmetric utility profiles, the nearest party or candidate for a voter is the one on an indifference curve closest to their optimum point – and if people have differently shaped indifference curve contours (as in Figure 4.2b) which party counts as nearest will vary from one individual to another. These conceptions of nearness are widely accepted in economic analysis, but they still remain controversial when applied to political life (Stokes, 1963) as a brief analysis can demonstrate.

Suppose that party competition involves two parties, and takes place in a space composed by two dimensions, one measuring attitudes for and against welfare state provision, and the other attitudes on environmental conservation vs economic growth (Figure 4.5). There are three voters in the society whose optimum positions are shown at A, B and C: this is obviously unrealistic, but helps keep the diagram simple (Chappell and Keech, 1986). Assume first that the three have well-developed public policy preferences; that all have symmetric, single-peaked utility profiles; and that they are perfectly informed about the parties' policy positions. The proximity assumption says that the further away a policy position is from any voter's optimum, the less attractive it is for them. If two parties start out competing for these voters' support, where will they locate? If party I notices that voters A and B are closest together in their views, it may locate at the point X_1 which is halfway between them. If the other party II starts out at another position (say, half way between B and C), they clearly lose the first election, and subsequently must choose a new competing position. By opting for Y_1 on the line between C and B, party II retain C's support but also attract B's vote: for both voters Y_1 is closer to their optimum positions than X_1. Party I can best attack this new winning coalition by shifting position radically from X_1 to Z_1 on the line from A to C, which retains A's vote but is closer to C's optimum. To break up this pattern, party II might shift to X_1, the position from which party I originally started out, indicating that a cycle has been set up. Over time, if we allow for more graduated competitive moves by the two parties, their policy stances are likely to shift unstably between positions on the heavily shaded stretches of line $X_1–X_2$, $Y_1–Y_2$ and $Z_1–Z_2$. Clearly, this is a non-equilibrium solution, but all three sets of policy positions are fairly centrist.

Now try dropping the proximity assumption, and substituting instead

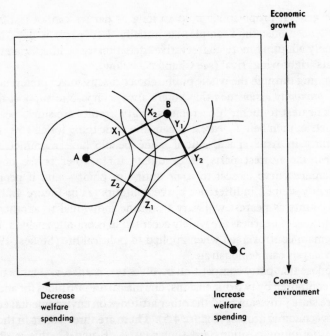

Figure 4.5 **Vote-cycling on the proximity assumption**

the empirical view of American voters' policy views offered by Rabinowitz and Macdonald (1989). They argue that most people have only a diffuse sense of 'direction' about political issues: they know roughly which side of the key issues they personally stand on, and which side parties or candidates stand on. If a party is on the same 'side' of the issue as voter A, this is a plus point for voter A; if the party is on the other side, this is a minus. How much of a plus or minus it is depends on how strongly the party advocates that issue: if the party makes a big thing of its issue stance, it will matter more to voters, whereas if the party says little about an issue it will matter less which side they are on. All of these judgements about sides are partly symbolic, triggering emotive reactions on the basis of little detailed information: and they use as a reference point a neutral position in two ideological dimensions, which are mapped onto the diagram in Figure 4.6. Here voters A, B and C are in exactly the same locations as in the previous diagram, but because we are following the 'directional model' and the voters are in separate quadrants, completely different patterns of party behaviour follow. No one will locate at the point X_1, for example. Although close to both A and B on the two issues, a party choosing X_1 would be so neutral and undistinctive that neither voter would have any incentive to support it. By contrast, party I might do well by locating at point T, taking a definite stance for welfare expansion while being basically neutral on economic

96

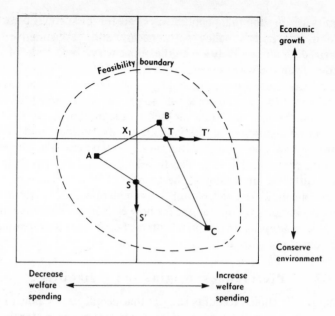

Figure 4.6 **Party divergence with 'directional' voting**

growth vs environmental conservation. This stance allows party I to appeal to the pro-welfare views of both B and C, while doing nothing to alienate them on the other issue. Similarly, party II might choose instead to locate itself at point S, de-emphasizing its welfare views, but stressing environmental conservation to attract support from C and A.

The 'directional model' goes further, however, arguing that voters respond to the strength of stimulus created by parties on an issue:

> The more intense a candidate is on an issue [without being seen as advocating extremist policies] the more the candidate generates intense support or opposition with regard to that issue. By taking clear, strong stands, candidates can make an issue central to judgements about themselves. (Rabinowitz and Macdonald, 1989, p. 98)

In other words, party I might be well advised to try to increase the salience of the welfare issue by pushing outwards from T to T', while for party II a rival tactic would be to push outwards from S to S', stressing environmentalism. These approaches of course run directly counter to the proximity assumption, yet they seem a familiar enough political tactic in everyday politics. Some empirical predictions from the model are plausibly supported by research on US presidential elections. At the least, then, the 'directional model' underscores the substantive, controversial quality of the proximity assumption that people always vote for the spatially closest party – even if that party's policy positions are dull, undistinctive, or de-emphasized, or alternatively are on the opposite symbolic 'side' of an issue altogether from the voter's views.

To sum up, there are considerable grounds for remaining aware of and sceptical about the normal apparatus of public choice models of electoral competition. Simplifying and contestable assumptions have to be made about the configuration of individual's utility profiles, and about the derivation of an aggregate distribution of preferences. The shape of the ADP curve or surface has to be directly assumed, and different shapes have radically different implications. The number of issue dimensions, number of parties or candidates, and assumptions about how they can move in issue space carry important implications for how electoral systems operate. And finally, the assumption that rational voters always vote on a proximity basis can reasonably be disputed.

Preferences: origins and variability

Existing public choice accounts suggest that people decide how to vote by inspecting already well-formed preferences before plumping for the closest party to their personal optimum. Critics respond that electoral choices are not simple preferences (like the preference for eating strawberries more than apples) which are known as soon as they are paid attention to (see Hare, 1952; and Kovesi, 1971 for some philosophical implications of this difference). Instead, electoral choices are 'volitions' or 'emergent acts of will' created only in the context of a campaign, and mixing together preference, empirical analysis and moral judgements (Lindblom, 1977, pp. 134–7). Similarly Plamenatz (1973, p. 150) complained of public choice accounts of democracy that:

> [They] take (individual) aims or goals for granted. They neither deny that men's values and institutions affect their aims nor enquire how they do. Indeed they are not much interested in the nature of . . . aims or goals. . . . When aims are political they describe them. But such aims as are not political, though political action is designed to achieve them, they take more or less in the abstract.

Downs set out the assumptional foundations of public choice theories of voting behaviour with characteristic frankness:

> [A major] problem is rooted in the very concept of a voter changing his mind about how to vote. . . . Every voter makes his voting decision by comparing various real and hypothetical streams of utility income. To decide what impact each government act has upon his [utility] income, he appraises it as good or bad in the light of his own view of 'the good society'. This procedure is rational because every citizen in

our model views government as a means to the achievement of the good society as he sees it.

Thus a man's evaluation of each party depends ultimately upon the information he has about its policies and the relation between those of its policies he knows about and his own conception of the good society. Once a voter has even provisionally decided how to vote, he can be persuaded to change his mind only if one of these two factors is altered. To simplify the analysis, *we assume that every citizen has a fixed conception of the good society* and has already related it to his knowledge of party policies in a consistent manner. Therefore only new information can persuade him to change his mind.

In essence we are assuming that citizens' political tastes are fixed. . . . In fact, fixed political tastes are more plausible to us than fixed consumption tastes, which are usually assumed in [micro-economic] demand studies. (Downs, 1957, pp. 46–7, my emphasis)

Viewing preferences as fixed externally to the choice process being analyzed is a key inheritance from conventional micro-economics. Only a few modern economists have examined ways of seeing changes in preferences as endogenous to the economic processes they analyze (for example, von Weizsacker, 1971). The rest of the literature treats the self-conscious concerns of Marshall and Jevons to specify 'an individual with his tight, impermeable, insulated equipment of desires and tastes' as now anachronistic 'logic-chopping' (Robinson, 1964, p. 51). Instead, it adopts what Arrow terms 'the standard view in economic theory':

Individuals in our society are free to choose, by varying their values [i.e. the wants underlying people's preferences or choices], among the alternatives available. . . . Individual values are taken as data and are not capable of being altered by the nature of the decision process itself. (Arrow, 1951, p. 7)

The economist's task is to trace the consequence of any given set of wants. . . . Economic theory proceeds largely to take wants as fixed. (Friedman, 1962, p. 13)

Since economists generally have had little to contribute, especially in recent times, to the understanding of how preferences are formed, preferences are assumed not to change substantially over time, nor to be very different between wealthy and poor persons, or even between persons in different societies and cultures. (Becker, 1966, p. 5)

On [the conventional] view, an explanation of economic phenomena that reaches a difference in tastes is abandoned *at this point* to whoever studies and explains tastes. (Stigler and Becker, 1977, p. 76)

The only alternative assumption propagated with any vigour by mainstream economists is the extreme claim, originating with the Scottish philosopher David Hume that 'Men are everywhere so alike' that their tastes for practical purposes can be assumed to be identical. The most influential modern version of this idea argues that 'all widespread and persistent behaviour' can be explained by supposing that everyone has *exactly the same underlying preferences* – irrespective of whether they are women or men, irrespective of age, and across all cultures, classes and time periods. On this view, differences in people's incomes and levels of information alone account for variations in their choices: 'One does not argue over tastes for the same reason that one does not argue over the Rocky Mountains – both are there, will be next year, and are the same for all men' (Stigler and Becker, 1977, p. 76). So far, public choice accounts of politics have refused to go this far down the road towards unrealism in assumptions, sticking to the claim that people's preferences are highly variable across individuals but are fixed outside the process of party or electoral competition.

This position is also retained because it fits closely with traditional liberal theories of democratic politics. In economics the consumer sovereignty doctrine emphasizes that people make up their own minds what to demand: they cannot have wants foisted upon them by corporation advertising or business manipulation of tastes. A similar axiom buttresses the pluralist and new right views of voters as making up their own minds without being influenced into changing their preferences by political parties' campaigning. Most of the public choice literature:

> insists on both moral and empirical grounds that a rational choice framework presupposes the existence of autonomous goals among all (or a vast majority of) electors, which are both necessary and sufficient for the independent evaluation of parties. Abandoning this point of view means adopting a highly elitist interpretation, contrary to normal justifications of representative democracy, in which parties shape electors' preferences. (Budge and Farlie, 1977, p. 383)

Public choice accounts can view preferences as immune to party competition in a number of different ways (Dunleavy and Ward, 1981, pp. 359–60). However, it is feasible to boil down these different forms of the fixed preference assumption into a simple algorithm, shown in Figure 4.7. The sequence of questions here focuses upon whether the aggregate distribution of preferences in the electorate will change in response to different kinds of stimuli. Four of the six endpoints shown are consistent with the existing public choice literature.

Box A is the view that voters' preferences never change at all, for any reason, so that the ADP curve (or ADP surface in multi-dimensional models) is completely fixed. Some mathematical public choice accounts say so little about preference changes that they seem implicitly to adopt this view, which is the equivalent in political analysis of Stigler and Becker's

Economic explanations of voting behaviour

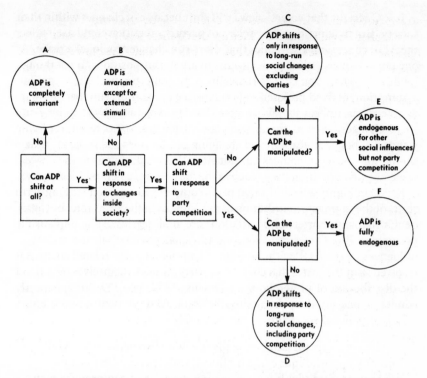

Figure 4.7 **Alternative views of whether the ADP curve responds to changes**

position in economics that tastes are absolutely invariant across people and over time.

Box B expresses the belief that the distribution of voters' views (and their relative rankings of issues in multi-dimensional models) change only in response to external events or stimuli, but not because of any internal developments in the political or social system being analyzed. For example, this position might argue that voters' attitudes in Western democracies are altered only by major world developments, such as the OPEC oil price hike in 1973 which was widely perceived as terminating the post-war era of cheap energy supplies. At a very macro-level of course public opinion configurations can be expected to show considerable continuity, as they do in the United States (Page and Schapiro, 1982). But more fine-grained analysis quickly demonstrates a wide variety of significant movements, both 'glacial, long-term shifts in public opinion that reflect major social, technological, and demographic changes', and medium-to-short-term fluctuations. One analysis of this latter group found significant (greater than 6 per cent) changes in American public opinion in nearly half of all issues analyzed (Page and Schapiro, 1983, pp. 25–6 and 38).

101

Box C accepts that voters' views will shift because of changes within their society. But it denies that the process of party competition could itself affect the ADP curve, and also denies that short-run changes could take place. At one point Downs (1957, p. 47) seems to argue this position: 'Even though [political] tastes often change radically in the long run, we believe that our assumption [of fixed preferences] is plausible in the short run, barring wars or other social upheavals.' What seems hard to explain is why some long-run social changes (such as changes in class structures, social mobility, living standards, better education, and changing gender roles and racial attitudes) should influence preferences but not alterations endogenous to the process of electoral competition itself (such as the founding of a new political party).

Box D in Figure 4.7 admits that party competition can produce long-term shifts of the aggregate distribution of preferences in the electorate, but again denies that any shorter-term variations are at all feasible. The implausible position in Box C of admitting long-run changes internal to a society as influences on the ADP with the single exception of party-related changes is resolved. But the cost is that changes of party strategy themselves may affect the distribution of preferences, as Downs (1957, pp. 129–30) apparently admits at one point in discussing different ADP configurations along a left/right political spectrum:

> Where voters are massed bimodally [i.e. with two peaks in the ADP curve] at opposite ends of the [political] scale, peaceful democratic government is difficult. . . . A faction desirous of compromise may grow up, thus altering the distribution [towards the centre]. . . . If this party grows as a result of continuous shifts of voters to the centre . . . eventually the centre has become preponderant.

Here Downs does not explicitly or precisely locate the reasons why 'a faction desirous of compromise' originates, except to imply on the lines of the adversary politics model (see below, page 133) that voters eventually realize that party competition and consequently government policy-making has become over-polarized. Equally, there are no clues about why there are 'continuous shifts of voters to the centre', but presumably a new centrist party would be an important influence in its own right. However, the quotation could also be read as restating Downs' formal position that preferences are exogenously fixed, and that parties simply respond to trends which they cannot themselves influence.

The remaining two endpoints in the algorithm in Figure 4.7 are not consistent with existing public choice assumptions. Box E accepts that the aggregate distribution of preferences can shift, even in the short term in significant ways, as a result of influences external and internal to the society. Yet anomalously only the process of party competition itself is excluded as a source of ADP shifts. Apparently changing his earlier view of invariant preferences in economic markets, Becker (1983, p. 392) adopts this odd stance in his account of the interest group process:

> I claim to have presented a theory of rational political behaviour, yet
> have hardly mentioned voting. This neglect is not accidental because I
> believe that voter preferences are frequently not a crucial *independent*
> force in political behaviour. These 'preferences' can be manipulated
> and created through the information and misinformation provided by
> interested pressure groups, who raise their political influence partly
> by changing the revealed 'preferences' of enough voters and
> politicians.

But if interest groups can reshape voters' views, why cannot parties and
political candidates with policy preferences do the same – a possibility dimly
admitted anyway within a few lines?

> The ignorance of voters also explains the importance of political form
> – including political rhetoric, the attachment to ideologies, endurance
> during long campaigns, and an 'honest' face – because voters with
> little direct knowledge about matters of substance must rely on crude
> proxies. (Becker, 1983, p. 393)

Various supplementary empirical arguments for the special ability of
groups to influence public opinion do not stand up to scrutiny. In US
national politics, interest groups' efforts overall seem to correlate negatively
with movements in public opinion, compared with very major mass media
effects (from commentators and 'experts'), and significant positive influences by statements from presidents and leading opposition politicians
(Page and Schapiro, 1983). Hence there seems no plausible basis on which
Box E might be defended.

Box F by contrast offers a simple and coherent position, which is
consistent with this evidence on what moves US public opinion, and similar
but much less systematic evidence for Britain (Dunleavy and Husbands,
1985, Chapters 5 and 7). The aggregate distribution of preferences is not
autonomous from the process of party competition, but may be influenced
by party strategies to some degree in both the short and long term, as well as
by a wide range of other factors external and internal to the society being
analyzed – especially mass media coverage and (as we shall see in Chapter 5)
government policy.

With characteristic frankness, Downs ended his own discussion of the
statics and dynamics of party competition by acknowledging the implausi-
bility of his starting assumption:

> What forces shape this important parameter [the ADP]? At the
> beginning of our study, we assumed that voters' tastes are fixed,
> which means that the voter distribution [along the political scale] is
> given. Thus we dodged the question just posed and have been evading
> it ever since. Even now we cannot answer, because the determinants

[of the ADP] are historic, cultural, and psychological, as well as economic; to attempt to analyse them would be to undertake a study vast beyond our scope.

All we can say is the following: (1) the distribution of voters is a crucial determinant moulding a nation's political life; (2) major changes in it are amongst the most important political events possible, and (3) though parties will move ideologically to adjust to the distribution under some circumstances, *they will also attempt to move voters towards their own locations, thus altering it.* (Downs, 1957, p. 140, my emphasis)

For Downs, however, the problem of starting from unrealistic assumptions was not a terribly significant one. He followed the basic methodological stance of micro-economics that making severe and possibly implausible-looking assumptions is defensible if substantive empirical hypotheses can be deduced from these assumptions and then submitted successfully to empirical testing (Friedman, 1962). 'Theoretical models should be tested primarily by the accuracy of their predictions rather than by the reality of their assumptions' (Downs, 1957, p. 21). Yet neither in micro-economics nor in public choice theory can the problems of the fixed preference assumption be so easily bypassed. Controversy about this issue has been rumbling on beneath the surface of neo-classical economics for over half a century (Blaug, 1980; Caldwell, 1984). Critics argue that the key implication of admitting changes of tastes into economic models is to render conventional methods of testing them ineffective:

It is crucial to understand that . . . the possibility of changes in tastes and preferences, which are not themselves susceptible to empirical test, vitiates any test of the rationality postulate, whether the result is a confirming or a disconfirming instance. Data that reveal transitive preference orderings [i.e., if someone prefers pears to apples, and apples to grapes, they also prefer pears to grapes] are usually taken to mean the consumer is rational. If the consumer's tastes were changing, however, revealed transitivities might reveal irrational behaviour. Similarly intransitivities can be interpreted [either] as due to changing tastes [thereby preserving a rational actor model] or [as] due to irrationality on the part of the consumer. Neither a confirming nor a disconfirming test result, then, is unambiguously interpretable. (Caldwell, 1984, p. 156)

Fixed preferences and empirical research

In public choice applications the fixed preference problem bedevils empirical work, since few authors have shared Downs's qualms about

Economic explanations of voting behaviour

assuming a completely stable ADP curve. To illustrate these difficulties consider David Robertson's serious effort to test a Downsian approach in *A Theory of Party Competition* (1976). He explores the strategies of the British Conservative and Labour parties over eleven general elections from 1924 to 1966 by coding every item in both parties' manifesto documents. Factor analysis was used to detect a structure of six basic-issue dimensions underlying the apparently variegated policy stances recorded over time. These dimensions were then mapped onto a single political spectrum representing party 'moderation' or 'extremism'. Of course, party election pledges are made on single issues, so that no party is located at a single point on any ideological dimension, but rather covers a range of positions.

The data on parties' moderation/extremism at each election were then correlated with the votes they received. British general elections have no fixed timetable beyond a maximum five-year term for any Parliament: they are normally called by the incumbent prime minister at a favourable moment, or more rarely forced on a minority government by a major defeat in Parliament. Election campaigns in the United Kingdom are very short – with polling occurring three to four weeks after an election is announced. Consequently, Robertson argues that election results should not be interpreted as consequences of party manifesto positions, but should instead be read as evidence of the party's level of support at the time when it produced its manifesto. Thus his study aims to show what kind of strategies parties pursue when they are riding high or falling behind in electoral terms. He shows convincingly that Labour's electoral successes were correlated with the adoption of moderate manifesto positions, while the Conservatives on the other hand put forward more extremist policies at times when they were performing well (Figure 4.8).

Robertson explains this finding using a modified Downsian account. In the 1924–66 period the Conservatives were favoured by inheriting large numbers of committed voters from the previous Conservative/Liberal two-party era. By contrast, Labour first campaigned nationwide only in 1918, and had far fewer committed voters. Labour could achieve a majority position *only* by moving towards the median voter position on the ADP curve showing overall moderation/extremism in the electorate. Because of their continuity with earlier periods, in all other circumstances the Conservatives would achieve majority support. This favourable situation in turn eased the constraints on the Conservative party leadership, who were able to respond to a favourable context (and a non-moderate Labour position) by adopting more extreme policies which gratified their party activists without losing them votes. Party leaders want to maximize votes when they are unsure about winning, but at some British elections in this period the Conservatives were certain to win anyway. At this juncture Conservative leaders adopted policies which solidified their positions inside their own party more than they piled up even larger majorities of voters.

(This hypothesis is supported by theoretical proofs about the behaviour of political candidates with policy attachments in conditions where they have some chance of winning an election for reasons other than their issue positions – for example, a successful performance in televised debates: 'So long as there is an a priori chance of winning, candidates will wish to offer policies closer to their own optima than to the opponent's' (Chappell and Keech, 1986, p. 895).)

For Robertson his explanation seems indubitable:

> One good reason for treating election results as indicators of the
> [parties'] popular support rather than being the results [of their
> manifesto strategies] is that it is otherwise impossible to produce a
> coherent account of why the Conservatives lose votes by becoming
> moderate and the Labour party gain them by a similar move. No
> existing theory of spatial competition, or indeed of rational or
> irrational voting, can do that. (Robertson, 1976, pp. 135–6)

Yet Robertson's 'finding' rests fundamentally on the assumption of exogenously fixed preferences. A correlation is shown between the Conservative and Labour parties' positions on the overall moderation/extremism dimension, and the size of the area under the ADP from which they attract voters' support as a result of their policy stance.

However, the period covered by this correlation is over forty years. In that time a great deal changed. A Conservative government survived a General Strike in 1926, whose failure sent the trade union movement into a long decline. The severe economic depression of the 1930s coincided with a 1931 split in the minority Labour government over public spending cuts, which brought about a decade of Conservative-dominated 'national' governments. The Second World War saw an all-party coalition government, and in its aftermath the first majority Labour government, which established a comprehensive welfare state and a large nationalized industry sector. The United Kingdom was forced out of or relinquished a series of overseas colonies and protectorates, dismantling the British Empire within two decades. The advent of the Cold War saw the establishment of a British nuclear deterrent. And in the post-war period a sustained period of historically rapid economic growth occurred, ushering in a period of 'affluence'.

Only if the aggregate distribution of preferences in the electorate as a whole stayed exactly the same across all these epoch-making domestic and international changes is Robertson's analysis defensible. With a completely static ADP, then, the finding linking Labour electoral success with moderation, and Conservative electoral success with extremism, is sound. But if the ADP *shifted position* any single correlation statistic becomes meaningless. A party policy stance which was 'moderate' in relation to one

106

Economic explanations of voting behaviour

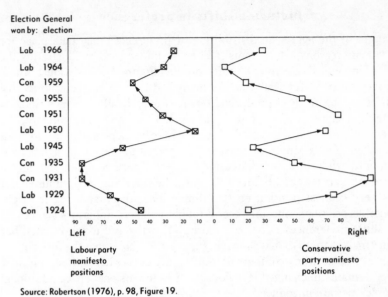

Source: Robertson (1976), p. 98, Figure 19.

Figure 4.8 **Robertson's map of how British parties' policy positions changed, 1924–66**

ADP at a first election might then lie far out on the 'extremes' of a different ADP at a subsequent election.

For example, suppose that voters' views shifted to the left during the Second World War, then although the Conservatives' policy position in Figure 4.8 apparently shifted centrewards in 1945 when they lost by a landslide to Labour, *relative to voters' changed views* their manifesto position may have been more extreme than it was in the 1930s. Similarly, if voters became disillusioned with stringent post-war government controls on the economy 1945–50, then their views may have shifted rapidly to the right, favouring a return to a market economy. In that case the Conservatives' apparently more extreme manifestos of 1950 and 1951 (when they were re-elected) could have been close to the new median voter position. Similarly, a general leftward shift of public opinion might well explain Labour's 'comeback' victory of 1964.

A key implication of this conclusion must be that any kind of empirical testing of public choice models of voting behaviour is unlikely to be feasible unless independent data can be provided showing that the distribution of preferences in the electorate has remained stable throughout the study period. Even in the shortest conceivable election periods – such as Britain's three-week general election campaigns – almost all empirical phenomena will be open to explanation in terms of people changing their minds, and hence causing shifts in the ADP across the electorate as a whole.

107

Picturing shifts in preference

Changes of the aggregate distribution of preferences may take place for three main reasons, whose roots can best be understood by illustrating the alterations in a single voter's utility profile (Figure 4.9). Obviously these changes must be replicated across many individuals before a noticeable impact on the ADP is produced, but it is analytically useful to look at preference changes at the individual level. First, and most directly, the voter may simply change her mind about where her personal optimum point is located. On a single dimension her optimum moves in a left/right direction, while in a two-dimensional system more complex 360-degree movements are feasible. Figure 4.9a shows the voter's initial optimum point as a very centrist position on two dimensions, the first being left/right economic positions, and the second tough/tender moral issues stances. If she shifts preferences to become more right-wing and tough-minded her utility map changes to that shown in Figure 4.9b. Note that the focus of the voter's circular utility contours or indifference curves has shifted, but their shape remains unchanged. Obviously, in n-dimensional space additional complexities are introduced.

Second, in anything except a single-dimension model a voter may change the whole way in which she trades off one issue against another. A shift from (a) to (c) in Figure 4.9 demonstrates such a case, since both the voter's optimum point *and* the shape of her indifference curves change to reflect the new priority assigned to tough/tender issues over economic questions. Even the shape of the graph itself can shift in this case. For example, in times of defence or foreign policy crises public opinion in most liberal democracies seems to assign a high priority to resolving the crisis. In March 1982 very few UK voters were even aware that Britain controlled the Falkland Islands, some 8,000 miles away in the South Atlantic and with a tiny population of around 400 families: their status as a policy priority was hence negligible. Yet after the islands were invaded by the Argentinian armed forces in April public opinion overwhelmingly supported the government's recapture of the islands at enormous financial cost and considerable loss of life. The easiest way to explain this change is to say that people's preferences have radically changed, because recapture/defence of the Falklands suddenly emerged as a new issue of overriding importance.

However, some public choice authors suggest that changes in issue salience do not constitute changes in preferences *per se*. The public reaction to the Falklands invasion could be seen as a response to a situation which had been exogenously transformed. So the public reaction did not constitute a change in what people wanted, merely a revision in the order in which they wanted to achieve fixed goals (such as a consistent value placed on national defence, standing up to aggressors, etc.). This interpretation is quite plausible, but it does not rescue the exogenous preference assumption. A shift in the salience assigned to an existing 'national defence' issue by

Economic explanations of voting behaviour

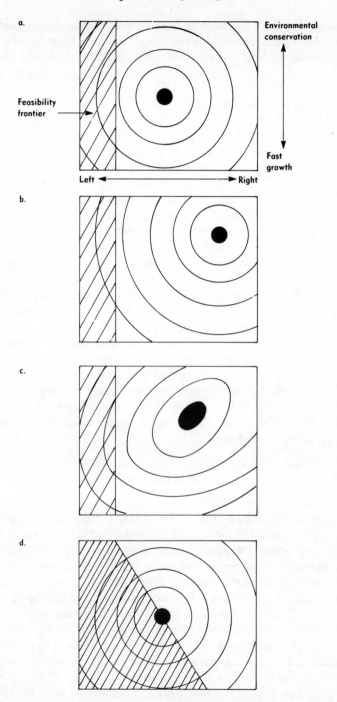

Figure 4.9 **Changes of individual voter preferences in two-dimensional issue space**

contrast with other issues, will constitute a change in the aggregate distribution of preferences in the electorate as a whole, because voters must make simultaneous choices over all issue dimensions at an election. Because issues have to be traded off against each other in casting a vote, any change of issue salience will force a redrawing of the indifference curve map encompassing these dimensions.

Third, people's feasibility perceptions may change in such a way as to debar some parts of their utility profile from being seen as 'realistic' policy options. The shift from (a) to (d) in Figure 4.9 demonstrates a situation where a voter's underlying utility profile remains stable, but a substantial portion of the map is excluded from consideration by a changed feasibility frontier. In this case I assume that because of some external reason (perhaps a world recession) the voter now sees the left-wing economic strategies included in her basic preference map as incapable of being implemented. It might be argued that the situation in (d) is formally compatible with the assumption of exogenously fixed preferences. Yet where the feasibility frontier exerts a decisive influence on people's voting behaviour the difference between situations (d) and (b) or (c) is nominal only. In all three cases the voter's *effective* utility profile has shifted markedly from that in (a). So long as such a change was replicated across other voters – and people's changes of mind did not cancel each other out – then the ADP configuration will vary over time. The importance of context-framing in shaping feasibility perceptions is well illustrated by empirical evidence that people are more concerned about the same welfare change if it is presented as a prospective loss than if it is presented as a welfare gain (Quattrone and Tversky, 1988). Hence a shift in people's reference point alone can serve to alter their policy preferences.

Conclusion

A rational choice account of why people vote at all can be given which avoids the main problems cited by critics. The first key step is to shift away from the objective variables of the existing literature, and to focus completely on subjective variables. The group identity model of why people join groups can be extended to apply in basically similar form to voting decisions. People's calculations of the impact of their vote on the electoral process are barely influenced by changes in the irrelevance of their individual votes to their preferred party's chances of success, but are significantly shaped by changes in their party's perceived viability. Party identities are important in boosting people's perceived stake in electoral outcomes. The private costs and benefits of supporting one party also influence people's choices, and will generally far exceed the costs and benefits of the act of voting itself.

Public choice theories cannot assume exogenously determined voter preferences and yet also undertake effective empirical analyses. No version of the fixed preference assumption is consistent without effectively outlawing changes of mind by the electorate. This pressure explains why:

> The voter's sovereignty and political equality of the simplest theories give way to political inequality and to influence by political and economic elites in theories of greater complexity. Even one of the most cherished axioms of economic theory, the assumption that citizens have fixed policy preferences, must be abandoned in the face of a full treatment of information costs. (Page, 1978, p. 7)

A two-part recognition is needed, firstly 'that preferences are not static but change over time, and secondly [that] . . . they are indeed subject to outside influences in this change' (Bartlett, 1973, p. 43). The argument here has stressed the theoretical and empirical difficulties of picturing political preferences as formed outside political processes themselves. The next chapter shows why any convincing public choice account of electoral competition *must* partly endogenize preferences, by recognizing that rational party leaders will use state power whenever they can to reshape voters' views in favourable directions.

Chapter 5

PARTY COMPETITION – THE PREFERENCE-SHAPING MODEL

with Hugh Ward

The strategies adopted by political parties and candidates trying to win elections are influenced by voters' behaviour, but by no means as completely as the existing public choice literature supposes. Spatial models emphasize convergence upon an equilibrium position close to the median voter in two-party systems, yet empirically sharp public policy alternations are common: 'The pervasiveness of rather large policy swings poses a puzzle for mathematical models of majoritarian processes. We have seen that these models predict either policy convergence or total policy instability, neither of which occurs in actuality' (Romer and Rosenthal, 1984, p. 472). And efforts in formal models to explain more limited cyclical behaviour 'still do not account for one of the most important stylized facts about electoral politics in the United States and elsewhere, namely enduring differences between parties' (Chappell and Keech, 1986, p. 882).

The key requirement is to show how factors internal to the process of party competition can produce or sustain party differentiation. I argue first that public choice theory's focus on preference-accommodating parties and political leaders creates expectations of an anti-incumbency bias in electoral competition, which are empirically implausible. By contrast, an account of how parties and candidates try to change voters' preferences explains the considerable advantages which accrue to incumbents from deploying state power with an eye for partisan advantage. Multiple factors influence how party leaders choose between preference-accommodating and preference-shaping strategies, rooted in the characteristics of the party systems and institutional arrangements of different countries.

ACCOMMODATING VOTERS' PREFERENCES

If voters' preferences are exogenously fixed and cannot be changed by the process of party competition, then the influence of electoral manoeuvres is automatically restricted. Party leaders or political candidates need not waste time or money on fruitless efforts to exercise opinion leadership or to alter citizens' preferences. Consequently, in existing public choice accounts politicians exclusively pursue *preference-accommodating strategies*. If they are to win against viable opponents, rational party leaderships must make their policy stances accord as closely as feasible with the preferences of a majority of voters – or at least with a sizeable block of opinion in a multi-party system.

So political leaders make a difference to election results through two key activities: finding out what most voters want, and then 'presenting a case' which delivers on these preferences (Robertson, 1976, pp. 12–15). With extensive polling research all major parties or candidates presumably know the same things about the basic contours of public opinion. Indeed, in the most formalized public choice models 'candidates are conceived to take a stand on every issue of relevance to any voter in the elections, and issues must identically influence the evaluation of all competing candidates' (Rabinowitz and Macdonald, 1989, p. 99). In practice, however, it is usually difficult to gauge from inherently static survey information how voters will react to the production of new policy ideas or options, or to externally changing foreign policy or economic situations. Practical political dynamics are still understood judgementally for the most part, using 'ordinary knowledge' (Lindblom and Cohen, 1979), although this version of common sense may be informed in sophisticated ways about evidence of the electorate's previous reactions to similar stimuli.

Obviously, politicians can use many equivalent presentational strategies in convincing people that their policy platform accords most closely with voters' views. Wherever a 'grand majority' of voters hold one view, both leaderships in a two-party system endorse these positions. With a narrower majority on one side of an issue, party leaders or candidates adopt more ambiguous stances or make their pledges vague enough to avoid alienating other potential voters. On minority-appeal issues, so long as preference intensities are different, political leaders can still assemble packages of policies which attract intense minorities sufficiently to change their votes, without alerting or antagonizing opposing blocs of opinion to the same degree, thereby realizing a net gain in support. Sophisticated calculation and judgement are also exercised in devising party publicity: differentiating a particular programme sufficiently to provide enough variety throughout an election campaign; waterproofing the party's case against misstatement by multiple party spokespersons and the mass media, or misrepresentation by opposing politicians; and devising ways of putting in a poor light what opponents have themselves said.

Much of the 'information' available to voters about party policy stances is generated adversarially, by rival parties trying to pull holes in each other's positions, and being forced to respond to opposition onslaughts. This active flow of charge and counter-charge adds an extra layer of complexity and dynamic judgement to the presentational and information-generating functions of politicians. Public choice writers argue that the ensemble of activities involved here is completely commensurate with the significance which we normally assign to political leadership. Successful parties are simply those where politicians are more skilful than their opponents in presenting a case, and making multiple and complex judgements about what voters want. If a single equilibrium position exists upon which political parties converge, then political leadership of parties will indeed seem a fairly minimalist activity, with policy positions essentially static. However, if there is no such equilibrium parties' policy positions may move significantly in issue space, especially where party positions cycle through recurrent alternative positions (as in Figure 4.5). The political leadership tasks involved here are considerable, in both candidate-based and party-focused elections.

Political-business cycle models add a very limited role for government to influence the electoral process, but without qualifying the claim that parties or candidates compete solely by means of preference-accommodating strategies. Faced with the need for a given mix of deflationary and reflationary economic stimuli across its term of office, a rational government ensures so far as it can that its policy balance is reflationary at the time of the next election (Frey, 1978, Chapters 10–11; Alt and Chrystal, 1983, Chapters 5–6; Tufte, 1978). Some governments' economic policy decisions may be influenced away from an objectively appropriate balance by their need to secure re-election. But with a vigilant opposition, high levels of mass media coverage, close scrutiny by financial markets and plentiful voter information such partisan enthusiasms are as likely to reduce electoral support as to aid re-election. The most that parties of government can do therefore is to try to accommodate voters' preferences at the time when they make decisions between the parties, and to capitalize upon any short-termism in people's perceptions or attitudes.

The anti-incumbency bias

A fundamental problem arises in simple public choice accounts of two-party competition in conditions of perfect information and with unconstrained political leaderships, able to shift their parties' policy stances freely to optimize their appeal to voters. A rationally-led opposition should simply track all the government's policies which attract majority support, incorporating them into their own programme. However, the party in power is limited in one crucial respect, the need to make policy in some contexts where there is no determinate or transitive preference ordering in the electorate as a whole. For example, consider a very simple example of cyclical majorities where three voters must decide how to allocate 'peace dividend' resources away from defence and towards either cutting taxes, or public health care, or the 'war' on drugs.

	First preference	*Second preference*	*Third preference*
Voter A	Tax cuts	Health care	Drugs war
Voter B	Health care	Drugs war	Tax cuts
Voter C	Drugs war	Tax cuts	Health care

The rankings are such that none of the options receives a clear majority over both the alternatives.

For the party of government, which must commit resources and make a definite choice between outcomes, a no-win situation is created:

[With cyclical majorities] any alternative that the government chooses can be defeated in a paired election by some other alternative. If the government picks [tax cuts], both [voters] B and C prefer [the drugs war]. If the government chooses [the drugs war], both voters A and B would vote for an opposition which picked [health care]. Finally if the government selects [health care], the opposition can choose [tax cuts], which both [voters] A and C prefer to [health care]. As long as the government must commit itself first, the opposition can choose some other alternative, match the government's programme on all other issues so as to narrow the election to this one, and defeat the incumbents, no matter what alternative the incumbents choose!

Since government faces more than two alternative policies in almost every decision, we may assume that it encounters this dilemma at least once during every election period. Any other conclusion requires an extreme degree of consensus among voters on every detail of every issue. . . . Therefore, once elected, a government has no reason to follow the majority principle on any issue. It knows that if a single instance of [a cyclical majority] is encountered, no matter how trivial, it will lose to the opposition. Since this is overwhelmingly likely, the government will act according to some rule other than the majority principle, such as immediate material gain for its members. Thus the hypothesis that government acts so as to maximize votes seems to lead to its own abandonment. (Downs, 1957, pp. 61–2)

In fact with multiple issues to be resolved simultaneously by a large number of voters, theoretical modelling shows that cyclical majorities will occur in over two-thirds of decision situations, so long as all logically possible preference orderings are equally likely to occur (Frey, 1978, pp. 71–3). In practice, many logically possible preference orderings rarely occur, while others occur very frequently – so that cyclical majorities are not as crippling a problem as some formal accounts suggest. None the less: 'The [voting] paradox is not an artefact of 3-person electorates and 3-alternative agendas – many configurations of individual preferences exhibit cyclic social preferences, and these intransitivities can encompass a great many alternatives' (Ordeshook, 1986, p. 58).

Hence, the difficulties confronting the party of government under perfect certainty are likely to be serious over a full term in office. This bias against incumbency is inherent in the pure preference-accommodating model of party competition, so that Downs saw no opportunity to retain complete consistency in its exposition. Instead, by an 'admitted dodge' he decided to 'retain certainty but ignore its effect upon the motivation of party behaviour, i.e., we assume that parties are never discouraged from their desire to be re-elected by their continual defeat after one term in office' (1957, p. 63).

Obviously, when uncertainty amongst voters and party leaders is admitted, it becomes harder for the opposition to match the government on every issue except the cyclical majority problem. Costly and imperfect information also expands the scope for discretionary political leadership, and reduces the accuracy with which either the government or the opposition can accommodate voters' preferences. Both these effects mean that governments are no longer automatically limited to a single term. But formal models strongly suggest that an opposition which closely tracks government policy is still advantaged: the less voters expect any ideological gap between the parties to translate into policy differences, the more an opposition is favoured (Enelow and Hinich, 1982). To make things harder for the opposition party to match the government on issues, it is possible to drop the notion of prospective voting, in which voters evaluate party policies in terms of their promises for the future. Greater levels of uncertainty could be linked to the idea that citizens vote retrospectively – re-electing a government whose term of office has generally benefited their personal welfare, and supporting the opposition when it has not. (This step actually compromises considerably on the public choice idea that voters maximize their net benefits on the basis of their expectations about the future. In its place retrospective voting substitutes the notion of voters as rationally 'satisficing' actors, concerned only to secure a tolerable level of welfare.) If international and socio-economic influences are favourable, then with retrospective voting the government can use the political–business cycle far more powerfully to influence election results. But if external conditions are not benign, or past policy solutions have proved ineffective or simply hard to fine-tune, the government's apparent advantage quickly disappears. Similarly, if voters' preferences about given welfare changes vary depending on whether they are perceived as gains or losses, then incumbent governments are advantaged in good economic times – but challengers are also favoured in bad times (Quattrone and Tversky, 1988).

All these variations in starting assumptions create a less determinate process of competition, and thus help to rescue the pluralist expectation that the party leadership currently in government will adjust public policy so as to maintain their popularity and secure re-election. However, this may not be enough to offset fully the anti-incumbency bias in existing public choice models. The effects of uncertainty are much the same for the government and opposition parties, so that they do not differentially detract from the advantages of a more mobile opposition over a government tied down by the necessity to make commitments. Nor can retrospective voting eliminate the opposition party's greater freedom of manoeuvre and enhanced opportunities to vary its policy stance so as to attract maximum support. To explain why we do not ordinarily view governments as competing on unfavourable terms with their oppositions, we need to analyze more closely what it is that a party gains from winning an election.

PARTIES WITH STATE POWER

Much of the public choice literature treats elections as completely abstract competitions. The participants' objectives are often described as simply coming first: 'The polity is democratic in the sense that the candidate who receives the most votes wins' (Budge and Farlie, 1976, p. 170). But what does winning entail? For the parties involved in seeking mass endorsement the objective is not some gold challenge cup to be handed back next time and competed for once again from an unchanged footing. Nor can we judge a polity to be democratic if the victorious political candidates are simply given a commemorative medal and sent home.

For the public choice literature to count as modelling the political process in liberal democracy, the party (or coalition of parties, or leadership candidate) receiving most votes at an election must take or retain control of the state apparatus and state power. Downs, at least, saw this requirement as an essential feature of his model:

> At each election, the party which receives the most votes (though not necessarily a majority) controls the entire government until the next election. . . . The governing party thus has unlimited freedom of action, within the bounds of the constitution. . . . Economically there are no limits to its power. It can nationalize everything, or hand everything over to private [actors], or strike any balance between these extremes. It can impose any taxes and carry out any spending it desires. . . .
>
> If our model is to be internally consistent, the government in it must be at least theoretically able to carry out the social functions of

117

government. . . . The definition of government used in this study is borrowed from Robert A. Dahl and Charles E. Lindblom [1953, p. 42] who wrote: 'Governments [are] . . . organizations that have a sufficient monopoly of control to enforce an orderly settlement of disputes with other organizations in the area. . . . Whoever controls government usually has the *last word* on a question; whoever controls government can enforce decisions on other organizations in the area'. . . .

In the real world, governments in fact do almost everything which an organization conceivably can. . . . Every government is the locus of ultimate power in its society, i.e. it can coerce all other groups into obeying its decisions, whereas they cannot similarly coerce it. . . . Thus . . . the government is a particular and unique social agent. (Downs, 1957, pp. 11–12, 21–3)

Downs clearly set out to model electoral competition as a mechanism for securing state power, and recognized that as its critical function. But these propositions conflict directly with the strongly held assumption of exogenously fixed preferences discussed in Chapter 4. It is not feasible to hold both parts of Downs' model at the same time. If governmental or state power has the extraordinary significance described by Downs, it will confer on the party of government the ability to shift the aggregate distribution of preferences in the electorate, and indeed to change individual voters' preferences. As the 'locus of ultimate power in its society', capable of having 'the last word' on any issue, the state must be logically capable of accomplishing changes in what people want. If this capability is denied, then it seems clear that voters' preferences are being represented as completely unchangeable by any social agency – in line with the Stigler and Becker (1977) position.

In any public choice account, the party of government is run by rational leaders anxious to maximize their chances of re-election. For them state power has the qualities of a free good which can be used for securing partisan advantage. Wherever their party is not certain of winning enough support to be re-elected, leaders should logically exploit this free good to create at least a minimal majority. In conditions of acute uncertainty party leaders may want to build up a secure margin of victory. In either case it makes sense to use their control of government so far as they can to accomplish changes in aggregate (and hence individual) preferences favourable to their party. For example, Figure 5.1 shows a situation where party A wins an election with the aggregate distribution of preferences given by ADP_1. But during its tenure of office party A pursues policies which accomplish a favourable shift in the voter distribution to ADP_2. Since the state is unique among social agencies in its ability to accomplish such alterations, voters' preferences are no longer fixed exogenously to the

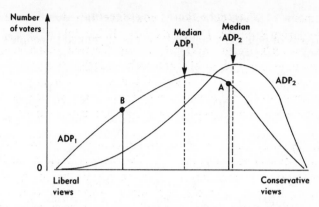

Figure 5.1 Illustrative use of governmental power to reshape the ADP curve

process of party competition. Instead, to the degree that the incumbent party of government adopts *preference-shaping strategies* which change the shape of the ADP curve or surface, people's policy tastes and issue preferences are determined endogenously within the process of party competition itself.

The remainder of this section first sets out in detail the mechanisms which allow governing parties to use state power to alter what people want, demonstrating that the logical possibility of preference-shaping is empirically important. Second, I examine how major parties not in office can to some degree offset or counteract the incumbent government's efforts by using party power in a preference-shaping manner. The last part of the chapter explores the factors which condition how party leaders choose between preference-shaping and preference-accommodating strategies.

How governments can shape preferences

The normal 'constitutional bounds' which limit government behaviour in a liberal democracy include rule-of-law restrictions on non-universalized legislation and against arbitrary or unlicensed executive behaviour. These provisions are justified as ensuring that state power is not used in a 'tyrannical' manner by ministers or officials on behalf of their own interests. In addition, as Downs (1957, p. 12) makes clear: 'The most important of these bounds is that the government – i.e. the governing party – cannot hamper the operations of other political parties in society. It cannot restrict their freedom of speech, or their ability to campaign vigorously, or the freedom of any citizen to speak out against any party.' With these restrictions built into public choice models as part of the definition of liberal democracy, however, there remain four main preference-shaping strategies which the party of government can exploit.

119

Partisan social engineering

Where patterns of political alignments are closely linked to people's social location, the incumbent party can use state power to try to produce favourable changes in the social structure. The government identifies social locations or geographical areas where its support is concentrated and then systematically facilitates their growth, using diverse policy tools. At the same time, growth in social locations preponderantly supporting opposition parties is discouraged. For example, in the 1980s private sector voters in Britain have been differentially pro-Conservative, and people in the public sector more pro-Labour (Dunleavy, 1980a; Dunleavy and Husbands, 1985, Chapter 6). Many Conservative government policies have aimed to reduce public sector employment: by floating public enterprises on the stock exchange (and allocating shares in small packets to the maximum number of voters at less than market prices); selling-off other enterprises to individual private corporations; hiving-off operations from the civil service to private service providers; and introducing mandatory competitive tendering into the National Health Service and local government, which leads to extensive contracting out of services to private firms (Ascher, 1987).

The longer-term history of housing policy in the UK shows the effects of policies saturated by partisan considerations. In the 1930s the Labour leader of the London County Council pledged to 'build the Tories out of London', launching an extensive public housing programme to boost the numbers of pro-Labour tenants. So successfully was this strategy pursued that by the late 1970s in some inner London areas 80 per cent of the housing stock was publicly owned. From the early 1970s onwards the Conservatives retaliated by encouraging councils to sell off houses to their tenants, converting them into home owners – who are preponderantly pro-Conservative. In 1980 the Thatcher government forced all local authorities to sell properties at below the market valuation of properties to any tenant wanting to buy. By the end of the decade tenants could purchase properties with up to 70 per cent of their market value knocked off. When a prestigious Conservative council in Westminster was almost lost to Labour in the 1986 elections, the local party leader responded by freezing all new lettings of council houses and flats in marginal wards. The local Tories inaugurated a programme to sell off 10,000 council properties at full market value, not to existing tenants or poorer people on the borough's waiting list for public housing but to anyone living or working in the area. In practice, this meant affluent gentrifiers able to afford very high central London prices, who could be relied on to vote Conservative. At the next local elections in 1990 the Conservatives duly secured a sharply increased majority against the national swing of votes to Labour. All these partisan practices at national and local level increased the salience of housing tenure on British voting behaviour from the 1960s to the 1980s, by which time it was more correlated with partisan choice than social class, previously the bedrock of British political life (Heath, 1987, p. 10).

Adjusting social relativities

Even if the size of particular social groups is not altered, the government may intervene to alter their relative social and economic positions in order to strengthen its support amongst a target category. If the incumbent party can make its own supporters feel better off by comparison with groups who mainly support opposing parties, it solidifies their support. And to shift the aggregate distribution of preferences in a favourable way the government must make marginal voters in cross-pressured or ambivalent social groups feel relatively advantaged *vis-à-vis* a comparison group.

Again, British housing policy provides extended evidence of this strategy. In the post-war period Labour administrations intervened to keep down rents for all public housing tenants. Their most obviously partisan effort was a rent freeze and special subsidy introduced by a minority Labour government in 1974 to help it win a second election due within six months. By contrast, throughout the post-war period Conservative governments pushed up public housing rents instead to 'economic' levels, cut public subsidies, and reduced new building by local authorities (Community Development Project, 1976). In 1980–2 the Thatcher government raised public housing rents by 80 per cent at the same time as large discounts on home sales were promoted. The *relative* position of home-owners was improved by Tory policies, the main alternative tenure was made less attractive, and so their Conservative allegiances were solidified. Governments do not have to increase the absolute well-being of voters in order to gain increased loyalty, a potent option in times of economic recession or public spending cutbacks.

A peculiarly powerful (but less controllable) form of exploiting relativities is to involve state power in social tensions in a way which advantages the incumbents. For example, the party of government may use the state apparatus and state legitimacy to stigmatize groups associated with the opposition, or employ its discretionary powers in ways calculated to bring an opposing group into conflict with the law, delegitimizing them. Exacerbating social tensions often builds up long-run problems for future governments. But where social polarization on political lines is strong, the gains from exploiting cleavages which mobilize a large majority against a small and stigmatized minority group can also be considerable. In multi-party systems political leaders may even exploit much more evenly balanced and potentially explosive social tensions simply in order to firm up their vote share, as the history of elections in the Lebanon in the 1970s and in Northern Ireland since 1969 both suggest (O'Leary, 1990).

Context management

The party of government may in some situations be able to manipulate the objective situation of the polity as a whole, in a way which confers partisan advantages – epecially through foreign policy decisions. In most liberal democracies citizens will patriotically back their government in short-run crises, especially those which are manageable and non-threatening. In larger crises the government may be able to take exceptional control over voters' lives, dramatically extending the scope for preference-shaping manipulations of voters' feasibility perceptions or information. During the 1982 Falklands War, the Conservative government in Britain at first seemed badly damaged by the Argentinian invasion of the Falkland Islands. But during the military recapture of the territory, the government was able systematically to fillet and colour the news, ostensibly in order not to jeopardize British soldiers' lives. By preventing any hostile scrutiny of the government's policies this news management helped create a 17 per cent surge in the Conservative opinion poll ratings – moving from a post-war record low for any government to touch 50 per cent popular support (Dunleavy and Husbands, 1985, pp. 67–70).

Foreign policy crises can have powerful short-term impacts on many voters' feasibility perceptions (see page 108), blanking out the possibility of negotiated or internationalist solutions to problems, even when they previously supported such policies. For instance, in August 1914, a succession of European socialist movements committed to internationalism none the less supported their governments' wholehearted plunge into the First World War. Internal crises can also be exploited by parties of government, especially in combination with a strategy of accentuating social tensions for partisan advantage. In early 1974 the British Conservative government led by Edward Heath called a snap general election over the strike by the coal miners' union against government-imposed wage limits. In the run-up to voting the government conserved energy by limiting manufacturing industry to working a three-day week and closing down all TV networks at 10.30 p.m. These measures forcefully dramatized the government's perception of the country's situation, and brought home a sense of crisis to voters. However, Conservative strategists were unable to keep the four-week election campaign focused on this single issue, and as other concerns surfaced (such as worsening inflation) the Tories' initially commanding lead was eroded and they eventually lost narrowly to Labour despite these efforts.

Context management strategies using internal or external crises to change the ADP curve work are fairly exceptional and may be risky. By contrast, the conventional political-business cycle involves the government routinely manipulating the country's economy in order to alter the situation of changeable voters. For example, the marginally unemployed will find jobs given appropriate reflation in the election run-up, while those already employed see their take-home pay improve, and find it easier to move jobs or secure promotion. Cumulated across the whole electorate such change can quickly produce radically different public perceptions of the governing party's performance. In the 1980s, governments have used their leverage over financial market interest rates as a key means of electoral context management.

Institutional manipulation

Political leaders in government can often alter the 'rules of the game' which structure party competition. Obviously, in a democracy this intervention cannot take the form of directly limiting the ability of opposition parties to present a case to voters. In some countries the party of government can influence the boundaries of election districts, as with the notorious gerrymandering which sustained unbroken Liberal government in Queensland for many years, or was a feature of Protestant hegemony under the devolved Northern Ireland government at Stormont before 1971. Similarly, southern states in the United States excluded black citizens from voting for decades by discriminatory registration laws (e.g. intelligence tests and charges to register as a voter).

However, similar effects can be effectively accomplished via less direct means. In unitary states, the party in power nationally can often restructure sub-national government structures in ways which confer party advantage. In 1972–4 a Conservative government reorganized the English and Welsh system of local councils in a way which transferred one-sixth of the population outside London from predominantly Labour-controlled or two-party city authorities to overwhelmingly Conservative-controlled county councils (Dunleavy, 1980b, pp. 89–90). As a result of these changes three-fifths of voters lived in 'safe' Conservative areas at the key tier of local government, compared with less than a fifth in safe Labour areas. Reducing or removing alternative centres of political legitimacy (which could serve opposition parties as stepping-stones to national power), can also strongly affect party competition, especially in unitary states where national incumbents may want to prevent opposition parties acquiring institutional bases from which to devise their own preference-shaping strategies. For example, in the mid-1980s the Thatcher government's expenditure cutbacks were strongly challenged by seven Labour-controlled metropolitan county councils. The Conservatives reacted by abolishing these councils in 1985, ostensibly to 'streamline' city government but in fact transferring their expenditure functions to a forest of quasi-governmental agencies or joint committees of lower-tier councils (O'Leary, 1987b).

Major changes of national institutions are rarer because of constitutional constraints (see below, page 138), but again some examples show strong partisan effects. In 1958 General de Gaulle was elected by the French legislature to serve as president for seven years during a major crisis over army dissent from decolonization in Algeria. Half way through his term he called and won a unilateral (and hence unconstitutional) referendum on introducing direct elections for the presidency, instead of indirect election by MPs. This reform changed the whole balance of the Fifth Republic's constitution. Thereafter, the prospect of conflicting parties controlling the presidency and the legislature kept French voters supporting unbroken right-wing control of government for two decades. In 1981, when a socialist Mitterrand finally won control of the presidency he called legislative elections immediately and secured a socialist majority in the parliament. When his government became unpopular and further legislative elections loomed in 1986, Mitterrand changed the voting system used for electing the parliament to proportional representation. This switch preserved the maximum number of socialist seats in their period of unpopularity and also split the right-wing parties, allowing the extremist French National Front into the legislature for the first time. The new parliamentary majority of the right changed the voting system for legislative elections back to the traditional French two-ballot system. But Mitterrand held on in office with a right-wing government for two years, secured re-election as president in 1988, and then again called snap legislative elections which eliminated the right's parliamentary majority and secured another socialist government.

All four preference-shaping strategies – partisan social engineering, adjusting social relativities, context management and institutional manipulation – can have clear partisan advantages for the party of government. However, with all the examples considered above this does not mean that there were *only* preference-shaping reasons for policy shifts. In most cases, considerations of partisan advantage were only partial if none the less important factors influencing government decisions. Nor should the arguments here be taken as implying that partisan uses of state power are always successful in terms of delivering electoral victory for the party which initiated them. My purpose has simply been to establish that a variety of potentially effective preference-shaping strategies exist and seem to have been applied by governing parties in the past.

Preference-shaping uses of state power have some considerable drawbacks. Altering the social structure can only have incremental effects. Hence partisan social engineering is most viable for a party of government already confident of an extended tenure of office, so that incremental changes can cumulate in a noticeable shift in the aggregate distribution of voters' preferences. Privileging supporters and disadvantaging opposing social groups may harm the legitimacy of government or the 'governability' of the country in the longer term – a major problem, too, for strategies which avoidably exaggerate social tensions for partisan advantage. On the other hand, adjusting social relativities can be pursued in the short term and quite flexibly; combined with partisan social engineering, it is likely to produce noticeable effects within the four or five year life span of most democratic governments. Changing the situation of the whole polity can have dramatic short-term effects. But in non-routine situations like external or internal crises this kind of context management will also carry high risks if the government's policies prove ill-advised. However, in more routine forms (such as political-business cycle manipulations) or in manufactured crises where partisan success is over-determined at the outset, as with President Reagan's invasion of Grenada in 1983 or President Bush's invasion of Panama in 1989, short-term gains may be fairly assured, even if long-term impacts on popularity are slight. Finally, the scope for institutional manipulation depends crucially on constitutional factors (see below, page 138). But in at least some major Western countries there is evidence that this strategy can have rapid positive effects for governing parties with relatively manageable and predictable consequences.

Party power and preference-shaping

Major parties with a potential to become the next government (alone or in coalition) can also try to reshape voters' preferences by using their own resources of legitimacy or influence, playing on the probability of their future return to government. Three mechanisms are important.

Capitalizing on social tensions

Main opposition parties (like the government) can maintain or aggravate social tensions in their society for partisan ends. A political leader 'becomes a symbol of some or all the aspects of the state; its capacity for benefiting and hurting, for threatening and reassuring' (Edelman, 1964, p. 73). This potential is at its greatest when one leadership decides to break out of a previous élite consensus which excluded some types of social division from the ambit of party competition. 'Following the crowd' and legitimating unethical or undesirable populist attitudes may reap major partisan gains for established parties. For example, in the 1880s Britain confronted acute problems with Irish nationalism which prompted the Liberal premier Gladstone to propose home rule. Lord Randoph Churchill successfully urged his colleagues in the Conservative leadership to 'play the Orange card' in predominantly Protestant Ulster, whipping up English opposition to home rule for Ireland as a whole (which is overwhelmingly Catholic). This gambit secured the Tories a prolonged period in government while fuelling sectarian bitterness in Ireland. New populist parties may also breach an established élite consensus on a salient issue with dramatic impact, as when the National Front won over one in seven of all French voters by explicitly tapping racist sentiment in the mid-1980s. Even party machines close to government can engage in similar tactics at times, as in the notorious 'Willie

Horton' advertisement used in the then Vice-President Bush's 1980 presidential campaign to associate emotively his Democrat opponent with being soft on black criminals.

Joint institutional manipulation

Established parties in liberal democracies normally acquire a degree of control over the 'rules of the game' which structure their competition. Traditions of bi-partisanship or consultation with all major parties about electoral arrangements allow their leaders to discriminate against new entrants, by colluding to create electoral system thresholds (Taagepera and Shugart, 1989). In West Germany the constitution requires any new party to win 5 per cent of the vote before it gains any seats at all in the Bundestag. In the United States and Britain both major parties benefit from plurality-rule elections which allocate no rewards to third force parties with widely dispersed support. Efforts to preserve oligopolistic rather than open competition also include provisions on campaign financing (for example, allocating government funds for party publicity on the basis of votes gained last time round) or access to publicly controlled broadcasting. All such provisions artificially enhance the viability of established parties, create extra thresholds for new parties to surmount and encourage voters to perceive support for new parties as a 'wasted vote'.

A classic example of joint institutional manipulation is the electoral college system in US presidential races, which gives the Democrats and Republicans extensive protection against 'third force' candidates. The leading candidate in each state wins all its electoral college votes, so that unless they come first in a state, third force candidates can poll millions of votes nationwide without winning a single electoral college vote, as John Anderson did in 1980. This system also insulates the national parties from being much damaged by candidates with only regional support: like George Wallace in 1968 they may win the electoral college votes of their home state and neighbouring areas, but get penalized by the system everywhere else. Finally, the electoral college system institutionalizes major differences in the influence of votes across the United States, to the advantage of the major party organizations. A vote in a large, two-party 'pivotal' state such as California, Ohio or Illinois is around thirteen times more likely to influence the presidential election result than one in a small state such as those of New England (Rabinowitz and Macdonald, 1986).

Party power influences may also discourage a current government from promoting hostile institutional changes for fear of 'tit for tat' behaviour if a viable opposition gains office in future. But when the incumbents are confident that future alternations of power are unlikely this constraint is removed. In Britain, concern that a Labour government might limit political donations by business kept Conservative governments from attacking the political funds of trade unions for four decades. However, after Labour lost the 1983 general election disastrously and was perceived as unlikely to win power in the future, the Conservatives imposed periodic union ballots before political funds could be maintained. Expected by Conservative strategists to trigger widespread union disaffiliations from Labour, crippling its national finances, the law backfired when large majorities of members voted to maintain their funds in all the fifty-nine unions affected.

Agenda setting

Major parties can reshape preferences because of their control over the political agenda. Opposition parties' policy positions are not just adopted to present a vote-maximizing case to the electorate, but also as weapons to blunt government preference-shaping strategies. By vigorously contesting government legislation through all stages of decision-making, pledging its repeal and using sub-national governments or interest groups to frustrate its implementation, a viable opposition party may significantly change how the policy is perceived by voters and whether it endures or is successful. For example, post-war Labour governments in Britain introduced three different systems for taxing unearned land betterment gains in order to create income to finance public holdings of most development land (Cox, 1984). In each case, the Conservative party promised to scrap the legislation and restore a free market in land, advising landowners to withhold their properties from the market until they could be returned to office – thereby helping to negate the policies. By contrast, in Sweden the Social Democrats successfully municipalized all development land, partly because they held unbroken government power for forty years. Using party power obstruc-tively is most effective where decision-makers must use long time-horizons or where bi-partisan consensus is an important determinant of investment.

In a broader way, opposition parties may influence the ADP curve by bidding up voters' expectations of what is feasible, as the new right argue. Over the long term and with party alternations in power such tactics are potentially counter-productive, since each incoming government is as-sessed against the higher expectations which its earlier propaganda in opposition helped to create, and which may quickly prove disabling. Pluralists argue by contrast that voters will discount politicians' promises, thereby negating partisan gains from expectation-boosting. But such optimism may underestimate voters' readiness to believe in the ability of new social or physical technologies to change past policy parameters or their susceptibility to symbolic manipulation. For example, Ronald Reagan used supply-side economics in his winning 1980 campaign to convince American voters that the Republicans could simultaneously cut tax rates, dramatically increase public spending on defence and yet maintain core welfare systems. For opposition parties acting in the short term and needing to win votes, expectation-boosting is often rational despite adverse longer-term consequences or possible counter-plays by the party of government.

PREFERENCE-SHAPING VERSUS PREFERENCE-ACCOMMODATING STRATEGIES

The importance of preference-shaping strategies using state power does not tip the scales of electoral competition decisively towards the party of government for several reasons. In the first place, its effect is partly to offset the anti-incumbent bias in existing public choice accounts noted earlier (page 114). The opposition use party power in preference-shaping ways to counteract the governing party's exploitation of state power. In addition, non-government parties may be able to adjust their policy positions to accommodate to the new shape of the ADP curve or surface. Institutional manipulation by governments is hard for their opponents to combat when out of power, but the impact of other forms of preference-shaping (social engineering, manipulating social relativities and context management) might be offset by preference-accommodating responses. For example, if the Conservatives in Britain successfully engineer large-scale reductions in public sector employment and public housing, why cannot the Labour party simply alter its programme and campaign approach so as to appeal successfully to an electorate with more home owners and private sector employees? The existing public choice literature presents this countervailing reaction as feasible, flexible and simple to accomplish. So why should rational politicians in government embark upon lengthy and hard-to-control preference-shaping strategies when their impact can be so easily offset?

The most general response here concerns the general dynamics of party competition. Parties following only preference-accommodating strategies also face countervailing responses by other parties. In the abstract world of mathematical public choice, perfect information and complete leadership control of parties would seem to imply that almost any initiative by one party leadership could be instantly matched by their opponents. Hence once two competing teams of leaders have reached the supposed equilibrium position as close as possible to median voter views they should effectively renounce all political movement. Since voters' preferences are exogenously fixed in these models, the logic pointing to leadership quiescence is reinforced. Yet even in these accounts, if party A mistakenly adheres to an existing policy stance in a changed situation while its rival B actively pursues new or improved preference-accommodating strategies, then party A will certainly lose.

In real life party systems, however, frictionless adjustments of electoral stances are rarely feasible, generating the potential for an active party leadership to outperform inactive opponents. Indeed, if any leadership is to

128

gain a clear comparative advantage in a public choice model it must rely on lags, discontinuities and imperfect information impeding other parties' reactions. Even if all parties could change their policy positions fairly easily, an incumbent government which renounced preference-shaping strategies would place itself at a comparative disadvantage. If alternations in government occur, then opposition parties will certainly use preference-shaping interventions when they win office. And while still in opposition rival parties can often use party power in a preference-shaping manner.

Hence the general logic of party competition will tend to involve leaderships in reshaping preferences using state power to some degree, just as competitive pressures in economic markets produce multi-faceted efforts by firms to promote and continuously to improve their products. Beyond this background situation there are two main groups of influences which determine whether incumbent parties pursue preference-shaping or preference-accommodating strategies. The structure and operations of the party system determine how easily party leaders can implement preference-accommodating strategies, and hence to what degree preference-shaping approaches are attractive. And the different constitutional and institutional arrangements of liberal democracies determine how feasible it is for party leaders effectively to use state power for partisan advantage.

Party system influences

Political parties' policy stances are characteristically sticky rather than mobile. In many circumstances, significantly reorienting what the party stands for is a difficult and risky operation, which can only be accomplished after considerable time lags. Table 5.1 lists five factors which condition how easy it is for leaders to change party programmes or campaign positions, which I review in turn.

The structure of issues and social conflicts

Parties often base their appeal to voters primarily around zero-sum policies which redistribute but do not enlarge social resources. In this case, if the leadership is to attract marginal voters, policy changes may entail welfare sacrifices for the party's existing voters. If core support groups perceive the change as 'betrayal' and abstain through alienation, any net gain of votes is reduced or negated. In a detailed longitudinal study of seven West European countries, Przeworski and Sprague (1986) argue forcefully that the leaders of social democratic parties were unable to broaden their electoral appeal to include middle-class groups because their existing appeal to manual workers could only be changed by diluting their parties' defence of distinctive class interests. In France and Germany in particular, centrist

Table 5.1   *Party system influences on the choice of preference-accommodating or preference-shaping strategies*

	Preference-accommodating favoured	Preference-shaping favoured
Issues involved in electoral competition	Pareto improvements/ expanding social welfare	Prevalence of zero-sum conflicts
Consistency constraints on parties	Weak	Strong
Role of party ideologies	Weak	Strong
Constraints on party leaders from activists/ legislators/financial backers	Weak	Strong
Comparative organization of parties	Symmetric	Asymmetric

strategies which temporarily swung extra socialist support for one election produced a declining working-class vote at subsequent contests:

It is just impossible to speak of vote maximization ahistorically. The fiction of elections as a series of unconnected events is no longer tenable. If the votes cast in each election are a cumulative consequence of past strategies, then party leaders cannot every few years begin history anew, picking for their parties the strategy that would place it best electorally in a known distribution of public opinion. . . . Parties mold the 'public opinion': they present the public with images of society, evoke collective identities, instil political commitments. . . . Many of today's objective conditions are the errors of yesterday. Therefore, when party leaders choose strategies for the next election they must worry about the conditions they will encounter when they will be making their future strategic decisions. (Przeworski and Sprague, 1986, pp. 125–6)

Even where social conflicts are less polarized, party programmes generally put together a coalition of groups who can agree either a minimum set of common interests and/or a series of priority concerns which do not interfere with each other. Trying to incorporate new groups may radically alter the structure of payoffs and destabilize the previously viable coalition. In such situations, party leaderships will find preference-shaping strategies more attractive. Within the existing structure of zero-sum conflicts social engineering or manipulating social relativities can be used to maintain or expand support.

Consistency

Voters, the mass media and opposition parties scan each party's current pronouncements to check how they match up with its previous programmes and past record in government. Changes of position are seized on by political opponents either as admitting past mistakes, or as indicating the party's lack of commitment to its newfound stance. Picked up by the mass media, such attacks acquire force because voters face a difficult task in assessing whether party leaders mean what they say or will deliver on their promises. The greater the consistency between a party's current position and its past record, the lower the rate at which voters discount its ability and intention to deliver on its formal programme. The stronger such consistency constraints are the more difficult it becomes for party leaders to operate flexible preference-accommodating strategies, and the greater the relative attractions of preference-shaping.

Ideology

In many liberal democracies (such as those in Western Europe) political parties invest heavily in distinctive ideologies which play a large role in insulating and sustaining their long-term appeal to voters and producing policy consistency across multiple issue areas. Ideologies help voters develop strong 'brand loyalties' to a party and create a distinctive public image which cuts citizens' information costs, especially for marginal voters. Downs saw ideologies as parties' key response to uncertainty, representing a major 'sunk cost' which the party can ill afford to write off: 'Ideological immobility is characteristic of every responsible party because it cannot repudiate its past actions unless some radical change of conditions justifies this. Therefore its doctrinaire policies alter slowly to meet the needs of the moment' (Downs, 1957, p. 110). Calling into question or altering an established ideology carries risks of sending confusing signals to voters (especially older voters most resistant to change). Although the strong development of party identities provides its leaders with protection against electoral volatility, it also reduces leaders' freedom of manoeuvre and reinforces normal consistency constraints. Again, this circumscribes possibilities for flexible preference-accommodating behaviour, while preference-shaping strategies offer party leaders the chance to expand support while maintaining party ideology intact.

Since Downs wrote, the importance of substantive ideology to parties' construction of a public image has probably declined. The presentational packaging of parties for the broadcast media has become more sophisticated and effective, while direct political advertising has become more important. Parties can now acquire a mass appeal before they have enunciated specific policies or any very coherent ideology. In Britain a Social Democratic party flourished for several years after its foundation in 1981 primarily on an image of 'moderation', having reputable leaders and denouncing over-

131

polarized Conservative vs Labour conflicts. Subsequently, however, the longer-term importance of party ideology perhaps shows in the SDP's messy split into two rival sections in 1987 over proposals to merge with another centrist party (the Liberals), followed by the demise of the rump party in 1990. Image, leadership reputations and astute political advertising may suffice to sustain or remould a party's short-term efforts at 'presenting a case'. And where elections focus primarily on candidates and not parties, this effect may be all that is needed. But in most parliamentary democracies, where campaigning is party-based, distinctive party ideologies are still crucial for long-term survival.

Organizational constraints on leaders' autonomy

Most existing public choice models rule out internal obstacles to policy shifts by directly assuming that parties are unified teams tightly controlled by leaders, who retain complete autonomy from control by their party activists in deciding what the party stands for. This model fits the US presidential party machines quite well, since they are essentially 'shell' organizations taken over by the winning candidate from the primaries and the party convention. And of course, in the battle to secure the party nomination most candidates (except presidential incumbents) build up their own campaign team from scratch. A higher proportion of national campaign workers are also hired employees rather than volunteers.

However, these assumptions look much less credible as characterizations of the US party system as a whole, where a number of recent studies have emphasized the continuing functional importance of major party organizations (Gibson *et al.*, 1989; Jones, 1981) and the significance of enduring policy differences between party activists. Erickson *et al.* (1989, p. 731-7), conclude that although Democrats and Republicans in state legislatures adopt widely varying strategies across the United States:

> In every state, the Democratic elite is more liberal than the Republican elite. And given [our] scaling assumptions, each Democratic party is more liberal than state opinion, and each Republican party is more conservative than state opinion. In most states, the divergence of the two parties is considerable: typically the divergence between the state's Democratic and Republican positions exceeds the entire range of mean state opinion between the most conservative and the most liberal states. . . . State parties, like national parties, are pushed towards the median voter position by electoral considerations and away from the median voter position by the preferences of their activists. (Erickson *et al.*, 1989, p. 731)

Other research shows that a simple index of legislators' conservative/liberal ideological attachments explains the vast bulk of Congressional voting (Poole and Daniels, 1985). And a number of studies have emphasized the

132

'increasing polarization' of American politics (Poole and Rosenthal, 1984). The strong tendency for incumbent members of Congress to become more 'extreme' in their policy positions than the constituencies they represent is noteworthy, and clearly poses problems for traditional spatial models of electoral competition (Rabinowitz and Macdonald, 1989, pp. 111–14). Because US parties are 'multi-nuclear', binding together diverse 'collective efforts to capture a single [elective] office' (Schlesinger, 1985, p. 1153), it is possible for political leadership to be much more unitary at presidential competitions than in sub-national elections.

The unitary leadership assumption looks distinctly ethno-centric in the context of party competition in most West European systems, where parties are permanent, multi-member organizations. All party leaders in these systems confront substantial constraints on their discretionary ability to shape or reshape party policy from one of three groups: a mass membership of party activists; the party's members of parliament; or consolidated financial backers. Normally in these systems party leaders are directly elected by either their MPs or by the party activists/mass membership. In some socialist parties funded by trade unions (such as the British Labour party), union leaders also play a key role in selecting the party leadership. To have any chance of gaining governmental office, politicians must first win and then retain majority support within their party machine to become leaders. Convergence on the median activist or median MP's position will take place in leadership elections, and an established leadership deviating from this position will always be challenged. Again, the more restrictive these organizational limits on party leaders' autonomy the fewer their options are in terms of accommodating voter preferences, and the greater the attractions of preference-shaping strategies.

Downs acknowledged that uncertainty over party policy always generates internal debates and factionalism, and together with general organizational inertia imposes a special consistency constraint on leaders:

> Rational immobility is strongly reinforced by the institutional immobilities associated with every social organization. Because individual men become identified with certain policies, it is often necessary for a party to shift its leadership before it can shift its platform. This means that intra-party power conflicts influence just how rapidly its policies change. Different groups within the party use varying shades of the dominant party ideology as weapons against each other. (Downs, 1957, pp. 110–11)

But in Downs's account party activists remain committed to achieving electoral victory, so that there is no conflict of ultimate goals between leaders and activists, only debate about means.

This premiss is queried by 'adversary politics' accounts which point out that in a two-party system party activists or legislators come from at most

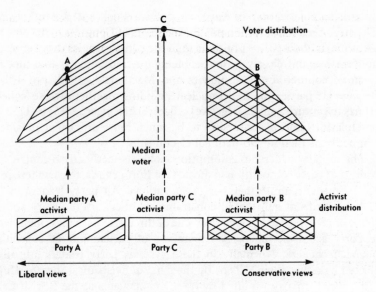

Figure 5.2 **Simplified adversary politics model with three parties**

half of the complete political/ideological spectrum occupied by voters (Dunleavy and Husbands, 1985, pp. 38–46). Hence the processes of internal party democracy prevent both left- and right-wing party leaderships from promoting policies approximating the median voter position. In a two-party system, activist control and internal party democracy implies that neither party leadership can converge on median voter preferences. Both parties offer voters policies which are too 'extreme', an over-polarization which constantly offers a middle majority of voters a 'Hobson's choice' of the lesser of two evils at election time (Finer, 1980). Even in three-party competition this constraint directly conflicts with vote-maximization for non-centre parties (Figure 5.2). Here, rational party leaderships in parties A and B can only compete effectively with party C by shifting position towards the median voter position. But they may be locked into publicly proclaiming their median activists' positions, for fear of losing the party leadership or of prompting damaging dissent inside their organizations. By contrast, the centre party C has no such problems, given the ADP configuration shown.

The adversary politics model also explains why tension between leaders and activists can be sustained despite election defeats for unresponsive parties, by offering an alternative rational choice assumption about activists' motivations:

Assume that party activists are pure ideologues, that is, they join the party initially, and remain members thereafter, because they want to

134

see something close to their personal views being espoused by a major party. Activists may then be almost completely immune to the electoral consequences of advocating particular desired policies. Even if this seems a bit far-fetched we can safely assume that activists are much less vote-conscious than party leaders in the policies which they want to see the party adopt, and much more concerned to see it adhere to a correct political line in terms of their values. (Dunleavy and Husbands, 1985, p. 39)

Where power inside the party machine is assigned to financial supporters or organized interest group backers the constraints on party leaders' ability to make policy changes are less than with direct activist control. Institutional supporters are likely to be more concerned with election success. Similarly, if party MPs select leaders then their own re-election chances will be improved if the party adopts vote-maximizing positions. However, financial backers with strong ideologies of their own (such as the labour movement) may be prepared to fund losing parties for extended periods. And MPs in safe seats may be far less receptive to changing established policy than those in marginal constituencies.

So in two- or three-party systems the adversary politics model provides a strong motivation for any party leadership to pursue preference-shaping strategies to bring the median voters' position closer to the party's fixed policy stance. Politicians can *simultaneously* pursue electoral victory, satisfy activists or MPs, and maintain or improve party unity. The party of government can also be confident that if it successfully pursues preference-shaping strategies, opposition parties will not be able to develop an offsetting preference-accommodating response.

In multi-party systems with no particular peaks in a stable overall distribution of preferences, the constraints on leaders' freedom of manoeuvre may not be so serious in vote-maximization terms. The party activists or MPs occupy only a segment of the complete voter ADP, but in a multi-party configuration the party will anyway draw support only from a similar segment – there may be no pressure at all for convergence on median voter positions. However, if the ADP shifts unfavourably for a party then the internal constraints on leadership mobility could significantly impair their ability to respond quickly or effectively. Again, the party of government can be confident that preference-shaping strategies will afford it real advantages over opposition parties.

Asymmetries in party organization

Where party A is leader-dominated, while its rival B is internally democratic or more controlled by MPs or financial backers, a peculiar dynamic is created fostering maximum use of preference-shaping strategies in two-party systems. If they can gain power, the leaders of party B have a strong incentive to preference-shape because their autonomy to shift the party programme or campaign stance in vote-maximizing ways is so restricted by activist control. Their opponents in party A know that party B is differentially immobile, and therefore cannot respond in a preference-accommodating way to a changed distribution of voter preferences. Party A leaders also know that party B has a strong incentive to preference-shape if it wins power, creating an incentive to get in first. This asymmetrical situation applies well to Britain in the 1970s and 1980s, where Labour elects (and periodically re-elects) its leaders via an electoral college vesting 70 per cent of the votes in the party's constituency membership and affiliated trade unions, while in the Conservative party MPs elect the leader on their own. As the differential in internal democracy has grown, so the Conservative government's use of preference-shaping rather than preference-accommodating strategies has grown more confident and explicit.

Constitutional and institutional influences

The clearer the lines of political accountability connecting the government party to voters, the greater the incentives for incumbents to try to change voters' views in their favour. And the more fractured, confused or weak the linkage between public policy and a single political party or leadership the more probable it is that incumbents will try to accommodate voters' existing preferences. Table 5.2 shows that there are six features of constitutional and institutional arrangements which magnify or reduce the possibilities for preference-shaping.

The centralization of state power

A background influence upon whether party leaderships pursue some kinds of preference-shaping (especially institutional manipulation) is the degree of control over public policy exercised by the incumbent party at national level. Unitary states without independent sub-national governments provide the most scope for national governments to reshape voters' preferences, secure in the knowledge that no alternative centres of state power exist from which opposition parties could organize countervailing efforts. In some liberal democracies, such as the Netherlands and Eire, local government roles have been drastically curtailed, with municipalities run by central government appointees and no regional governments. In Britain local government remains but its powers and institutions can be remoulded at will by the national government.

Greater restrictions on the national government's use of preference-shaping apply in most other unitary states where local government is accorded a measure of constitutional protection, as in Japan; or plays an important part in structuring party politics and political recruitment, as in France; or implements almost all welfare state policies, as in Denmark or

Table 5.2   *Constitutional and institutional influences on the choice of preference-accommodating or preference-shaping strategies*

	Preference-accommodating favoured	Intermediate situation	Preference-shaping favoured
Structure of government	Federal states	Unitary states with strong or entrenched sub-national governments	Centralized unitary states with weak sub-national governments
Constitutional arrangements	Codified constitution/ bill of rights/strong judicial review		Uncodified constitution/no bill of rights or judicial review
Separation of powers	Strong separation/ independent election of legislature and president		Weak separation/one election decides legislature and government
Type of legislature	Congressional system/ no constraint on legislature's powers of budget or law-making/ constituency representation key and weak party role		Parliamentary system/ executive controls budgeting and most law-making/strong party role
Electoral system	Proportional representation system		Plurality rule or non-proportional system

Sweden. Here the national government cannot easily implement non-consensual changes in local government structures or financing, either because special procedures are needed for institutional restructuring, or because the centre is heavily dependent on local authorities for effective public service delivery.

Federal systems, as in the United States, Canada, Australia, Germany or Switzerland, further handicap a national government trying to change voters' views, for here opposition parties normally control state or regional governments and local authorities which they can use in countervailing ways. Efforts by the governing party at the centre to reshape the ADP curve will evoke strong sub-central reactions, perhaps leading to both sides bidding up their use of preference-shaping strategies. Obviously, the balance of power in federal systems is not static. The period of public expenditure growth up to the mid-1970s increased central governments' grant-funding of other agencies and hence policy influence. But in federal systems the capacity to use national power for partisan advantage still remains in a different league from the preference-shaping strategies feasible in unitary states.

Codified constitution

More general constitutional constraints – such as judicial review, a bill of rights and restrictions on the politicized use of power – delimit the scope of preference-shaping by the incumbent party. The United Kingdom has an uncodified constitution, so that a government with a parliamentary majority disposes of unconstrained powers to rearrange state institutions, revoke citizens' rights, and even legislate retrospectively, without any possibility of judicial review. Other liberal democracies have codified constitutions, but in some cases (such as the French Fifth Republic) the constitution is relatively easy to change and contains little effective protection of citizens' rights or judicial review of the constitutionality of government actions. In all these systems, a governing party with a clear majority will not be unduly constrained in using state power for partisan ends. By contrast, where the constitution is very codified, hard to amend, and embodies extensive judicial review and well-specified citizenship rights, as in the United States, using preference-shaping strategies effectively is more difficult.

Separation of powers

The scope for preference-shaping is also enhanced where there is no effective separation of legislative and executive powers. In Westminster systems most governments control a legislative majority. A majority government in Britain can be confident of passing around 95 per cent of its legislation unamended through Parliament. In the Westminster system legislative activity is reduced to showpiece debates between government and opposition which are largely tangential to the policy-making process. By contrast, where a directly elected president heads the executive as in the United States and France, the two branches of government can be controlled by different parties. In the United States, the House of Representatives has been solidly controlled by the Democrats for four decades and the Senate has been predominantly Democratic, while much of the time the president has been a Republican. Where policy measures initiated by one party in the executive can be amended by the opposition in the legislature before being implemented by the executive branch, the scope for either side to reshape preferences effectively is lessened.

Type of legislature

Although systems of legislative oversight and control also vary widely, Breton (1988) suggests that from a public choice perspective the basic divide is between parliamentary systems (especially Westminster systems such as Canada, Britain, Australia and New Zealand) and congressional systems (of which the United States is of course the paradigm, indeed almost the only, case). A parliamentary system greatly strengthens pressures for preference-shaping strategies to be adopted because the balance of institutional roles favours the executive over the legislature. Individual MPs are often barred from proposing public expenditure without government approval, and in practice they make relatively few legislative initiatives against a weight of executive-proposed laws. Budgetary control is centralized in a finance ministry, not run through the legislature, and hence interest group lobbying is also targeted primarily at the executive. Party caucuses in Parliament are strongly developed, influencing the composition of the executive and selection of policy priorities, but also binding individual MPs via tight party discipline into supporting the party leadership line virtually all the time.

By contrast, a congressional system on the US model makes national efforts at preference-shaping very hard to implement, while encouraging preference-accommodating strategies. Congress directly initiates and extensively amends much legislation of all kinds. Budgetary co-ordination takes place primarily in the legislature via a system of committees and budget resolutions. Hence interest group lobbying and pressures from constituents both focus directly on representatives in Congress. Party caucuses and leaders play an important role in determining the legislature's own operations, but cannot directly determine the composition of the government. Party discipline in the parliamentary system sense of a standard voting line is very weak, although party solidarity in roll call voting behaviour may still be significant (Schlesinger, 1985). Multiple pressures here make it difficult for political credit-claiming to be easily developed. Representatives can best secure their individual re-election chances by developing strong records of constituency service.

Of course, the ways that legislatures operate are strongly shaped by party system features as well. Party discipline in the legislature tends to vary directly with the extent of constraints on party leaders – discipline is greatest in mass membership parties with well-developed ideologies and distinct, long-run voter images. In these cases strong party discipline inside the legislature fits with a more general pattern which makes it feasible for a government to exploit state power for partisan advantage. By contrast even with single-party government and an executive based in Parliament, political credit-claiming by the governing party is more difficult with a free-wheeling and relatively independent-minded legislature – as in the Fourth Republic in France, 1945–58. Legislators have a more complex calculus to make in supporting preference-shaping strategies when their voters judge their individual voting record rather than looking primarily at their partisan affiliation. But it is only when generally weak party discipline combines with a developed congressional system, as in the United States, that the development of coherent party-oriented strategies of policy-making fractures and blurs under the weight of log-rolling by sectional lobbies or pork barrel politics on behalf of constituency interests (Mayhew, 1974). Primary elections to determine who becomes the party candidate for legislative seats obviously add a further level of complexity to any party-based efforts at preference-shaping by incumbent legislators.

However, legislators' incentives can still be influenced collectively by voters developing simple response patterns, even in the most fragmented systems. For example, Weatherford (1983, p. 171) explains evidence that US voters penalize incumbent representatives and senators for hard times:

> It is obvious that the impact of economic conditions on midterm congressional elections does not determine macroeconomic policy. Any individual votes in at most one House and one Senate race, many economic policy decisions are taken in response to current circumstances unknown at the time of election, and the role of presidential leadership in this area is pronounced. Given these circumstances, the primary impact of economic voting in congressional elections is less towards effecting policy by changing personnel than towards affecting policy by changing the way that officeholders perceive their incentives. The crux of this process is the requirement that a relatively unambiguous message about potential electoral punishment be transmitted by the midterm vote.

Since the adverse impacts of hard times apparently swamp constituency work effects, even when legislators are primarily oriented to preference-accommodating strategies they may still favour preference-shaping strategies to influence the political-business cycle, and possibly a few other macro-issues as well.

Electoral systems

The diverse ways in which liberal democracies count votes and allocate legislative seats or executive offices has an important influence on the incentives for party leaders to reshape or to accommodate preferences. In some countries, electoral rules assign a high priority to achieving proportionality between votes and seats (Taagepera and Shugart, 1989, Chapter 1), tending to generate multi-party systems and coalition governments where preference-accommodating strategies predominate. Elsewhere, especially in countries with plurality rule elections, the voting system is oriented instead to producing governmental stability by delivering legislative majorities to the largest party. This type of system makes preference-shaping much more feasible and attractive to incumbent governments, which are also significantly longer-lasting.

Majoritarian or coalitional government

Single-party governments on the left or right of the political spectrum can pursue preference-shaping strategies more easily than multi-party coalition governments – where no agreed preference-shaping strategies may benefit all the parties. A single governing party which unambiguously originates policy also makes it simpler for voters to allocate political credit for improvements in their personal situation or the country's welfare. Even where governing coalitions span only a section of the political spectrum, the parties involved may only be able to agree preference shaping strategies which meet their common interests. Political credit-claiming is also more complex for voters. Coalition governments are also likely to include centrist parties in combination with those on the left or right. Centrist parties are probably least interested in distinctive preference-shaping strategies even in multi-party systems. The least favourable conditions for strategies using state power to secure partisan advantage are grand coalition governments.

However, the grand coalitions characteristic of consociational democracy represent an exceptional situation where state power is explicitly committed to an *even-handed* effort at preference-shaping to secure and entrench the position of all parties in the governing coalition. The foundation of consociationalism is the parcelling out of state power to parties representing different 'pillars' of society (Lijphart, 1984). Party leaders co-operate in securing stable government in return for partisan control over their own share of state power, which can be used to reinforce their role as the monopoly channel of representation for their particular social segment (see Rogowski, 1974).

Focus of electoral competition

Constitutional arrangements greatly influence the structure of electoral competition in several ways. Directly elected chief executive positions automatically create more personality-focused elections. Some voting systems strengthen party discipline (especially plurality rule elections), while others create personal competition between multiple candidates for the same party (as with the single transferable vote in Eire). Attempts to remould voters' preferences are more likely in political systems with party-based competition for governmental power than in countries where competition is essentially candidate-based.

Political parties have long histories, but individual candidates and their campaign teams tend to make shorter-term political calculations, and to have a more ephemeral policy impact. Some preference-shaping strategies are incremental and require time to achieve results, and party-based governments are more likely to take the long view than administrations centred on individual politicians. Strongly party-based systems also greatly strengthen the institutional constraints inside parties which impel leaders to adopt preference-shaping strategies. In candidate-based systems by contrast, internal party considerations are generally weak constraints on the winning candidate's freedom of manoeuvre.

Constitutional restrictions on how long governmental leaders can retain office add a further twist. In the party-based Swiss system, the premiership rotates around the Cabinet every year – a provision which strengthens collective party or governmental responsibility to voters, and hence incentives for preference-shaping behaviour. In candidate-based systems a current government leader prevented from restanding has few incentives to use preference-shaping strategies on behalf of a successor candidate. For example, under the Twenty Second Amendment of the US Constitution passed in 1951 no incumbent president can run for a third consecutive term of office.

Summarizing party system and institutional influences

The overall impact of these numerous considerations is complex in any political system, since they pull in differing directions. However, the Westminster-model constitutions and party systems of Britain and other Commonwealth countries clearly embody multiple pressures which make preference-shaping strategies attractive for party leaders, and relatively easy to implement. By contrast, in the United States multiple factors seem to impel political candidates towards accommodating voters' preferences.

Systematic empirical evidence about the extent to which political élites can in practice influence or reshape public opinion is really only available for the United States. The 'dynamics of structural realignment' in American politics seem to involve three stages where new ideological conflicts emerge first in congressional behaviour, are next taken up and dramatized effectively in presidential elections, and then gradually reorganize both the major parties' stances in sub-national elections and how voters themselves view policy issues (Macdonald and Rabinowitz, 1987). And despite the fragmentation of the US political system, analyses of major public opinion shifts suggest that while unpopular presidents have little influence:

> A popular President does indeed stand at a 'bully pulpit'. On an issue
> of great importance to him he can hammer away with repeated
> speeches and statements and can reasonably expect to achieve a 5 or 10
> percentage point change in public opinion over several months.
> (Page, Schapiro and Dempsey, 1987, p. 34)

Opposition party spokespersons also play a significant role in influencing shifts of American public opinion. However, the sum of partisan influences remains fairly restricted in its impact compared with the influence on American voters' attitudes of an élite consensus both expressed through and partially shaped by the mass media. These results, demonstrating significant party preference-shaping capabilities but constrained by other influence, closely fit the analysis here of American politics as an exceptionally difficult context in which to apply preference-shaping strategies.

How parties choose strategies

As a final way of placing the importance of preference-shaping strategies I briefly recap on the wider context in which party leaders operate, where they confront four main strategy choices. First, like interest groups political parties want to send contradictory messages to their supporters (both voters and activists). On the one hand, people's individual participation is important in achieving electoral success. But on the other hand the party is large and viable (so their individual participation is actually objectively irrelevant to any collective benefits they receive). Political parties seem to have a special capacity to convert themselves from endogenous groups to exogenous groups, primarily by using state power (plus party power) to reshape preferences and to secure their support bases. Compared with interest groups, political parties find it easier to create dependency amongst defined sectors of the population, using state power and the oligopolistic nature of most party systems to influence voters. Because parties are few in number and socially inclusive, it is especially difficult to exit from consuming a party's outputs when compared with interest groups.

Second, leaders in democratic parties often confront troublesome choices about maximizing their internal popularity with activists or their external appeal to voters. For left- or right-wing parties in two- or three-party systems the internal pressures to maintain a distinctive party programme and external pressures to converge on a median voter position are likely to be contradictory. By contrast, for centrist parties in two- or three-party systems, and for all parties in stable multi-party systems internal and external pressures are more compatible.

Third, even if party leaders operate exclusively with preference-accommodating strategies as public choice models suggest, they none the less confront some interesting dilemmas in adopting static or dynamic positions (Page, 1978). When party leaders offer voters a clear 'choice' they are anticipating or leading public opinion, initiating a new political project, or responding to changing conditions in a dynamic way. When leaders simply 'echo' current opinion configurations (or each other), they are taking a shorter-term and more risk-averse view, but one unlikely to offer any breakthrough dividends. An analogy might be drawn here between 'choice'-oriented leaders and Schumpeter's picture of entrepreneurs as originating and implementing product innovations or differentiations. By contrast 'echo'-oriented party leaders resemble the entrepreneurs of neo-classical theory, whose primary emphasis is upon cost-cutting in producing standard goods. Fourth, party leaders must choose some mix of preference-accommodating and preference-shaping strategies to follow, responding to the complex factors discussed above.

These strategy decisions are closely interconnected. How strongly internal and external pressures constrain party leaders or pressure them in conflicting directions affects their motivations to consider shifting the ADP curve. Preference-shaping strategies are also a useful way of managing size-manipulation problems, especially by shifting towards an exogenous group configuration and strengthening voters' dependency upon a particular party. Altering people's preferences also ties in very effectively with 'choice'-oriented efforts to anticipate voters' long-run positions.

Conclusion

Existing public choice accounts of party competition claim to offer a positive (that is, an empirical, non-normative) account of the central dynamic of representative government. But by focusing exclusively upon preference-accommodating strategies as the mechanisms of competition this literature risks being contaminated by ideological thinking – offering a positive (that is, an over-optimistic) image of electoral competition. This danger has been compounded by too rapid a process of generalization from a very stylized view of the US political system to other liberal democracies with quite different party system characteristics and institutional arrangements. As the public choice literature has become more formalized in ways which disguise its founding assumptions, the importance of the exogenous preferences axiom in sustaining a picture of voters' one-way influence over parties has dropped from view. And the object of party competition has been refined into a strange dedication by party leaders to winning for its own sake, with little attention paid to how party leaders might use governmental power for their own advantage.

By contrast, the preference-shaping model offers an account of party competition in which the shape of public opinion (that is, the ADP curve or surface) is determined endogenously within the competitive process. It also provides propositions about the influences acting upon rational party leaders in choosing between preference-shaping and preference-accommodating strategies. Logically, the involvement of state power in party competition requires that the exogenous preference assumption must be jettisoned. Empirically, there is considerable evidence to suggest that feasible preference-shaping strategies exist and are adopted by party leaders in appropriate contexts. Still a significant area of investigation remains largely unexplored, as David Robertson (1976, p. 191) noted:

> Many . . . aspects of the interaction between the party and the voter
> are cloaked in appalling ignorance. . . . We know very little about the
> extent to which political parties are able, or even forced, to change
> public opinion itself, to create a market for their goods.

144

PART II

—

BUREAUCRACY

—

Chapter 6

EXISTING PUBLIC CHOICE
MODELS OF BUREAUCRACY

During the 1970s, conventional public administration approaches began to look tired and undynamic. By contrast, political economy offered a logical/deductive model of how government agencies behave, with clear directions for policy analysis and simple normative recommendations for reform (Ostrom, 1971, 1974). Public choice accounts became widely accepted because they fit closely with everyday or common-sense views of bureaucracy. Officials and civil servants are basically portrayed as wanting to maximize their budgets, within external political constraints. Many people experience bureaucracies as expansionist organizations, constantly seeking to increase their size, staffs, financing, or scope of operations.

The economic literature on bureaucracy is sometimes traced back to von Mises (1944) or to Gordon Tullock's lengthy essay on his time in the US State Department, *The Politics of Bureaucracy* (1965). However, von Mises' account is not a recognizable public choice work, while in Tullock's contribution 'in fact, there is little "economics"' (Niskanen, 1987, p. 136). Hence the two key public choice works which form the focus of this chapter are later contributions, Anthony Downs's *Inside Bureaucracy* (1967), and William Niskanen's *Bureaucracy and Representative Government* (1971; see also Niskanen, 1973, 1975, 1978). Downs gives a basically pluralist picture of the complex micro-level workings of government agencies, discussed in the first section. By contrast, Niskanen offers a new right account of the aggregate behaviour of bureaus, discussed in the second part of the chapter. In the third section, I show how both models share common failings inherent in existing public choice approaches. In the next chapter, the 'bureau-shaping' model is introduced as a solution to these problems.

147

THE PLURALIST MODEL

Downs's model can be considered under four headings: what bureaucrats want, how government agencies work as organizations, the external environment in which agencies operate, and the overall strategies which rational officials pursue.

Bureaucrats' motivations

Bureaucrats are officials working permanently for large (public or private sector) organizations in circumstances where their own contribution to organizational effectiveness cannot be directly evaluated (Downs, 1967, pp. 24–5. This source is referred to by page number only for the rest of this section.) Bureaucrats play the same supply-side role as entrepreneurs/managers in the theory of the firm, and to 'drive' his account, Downs makes role-specific assumptions about their preferences (just as the theory of the firm debate focuses on alternative assumptions about what firms maximize). Significantly, models treating bureaucrats as the counterparts of consumers in demand theory have failed to develop substantive propositions about their policy-making behaviour (Breton and Wintrobe, 1982). At the same time, just as pluralist accounts of voting and group-joining stress the variety of reasons behind people's actions, so Downs's account of bureaucracy places motivational diversity at its core. His central difficulty was how to combine this emphasis with the need for some simple substantive assumptions about what bureaucrats want. His solution combined a general model of how rational officials behave with a typology of different bureaucratic personalities.

General model of self-interested behaviour

In their public as well as private roles bureaucrats are rational utility-maximizers, optimizing benefits net of costs. 'Every official acts at least partly in his own self-interest, and some officials are motivated solely by their own self-interest' (p. 83). And 'every official is significantly motivated by his own self-interest, even when acting in a purely official capacity' (p. 262). Their 'general motives' include five self-interested motives and four potentially altruistic goals:

Self-interest motives
Power – inside the bureau or outside it.
Money income.
Prestige.
Convenience – minimizing personal effort.
Security – defined as a 'low probability of future losses of power, money income, prestige or convenience'.

148

Broader motivations

Personal loyalty – to the immediate work-group, bureau as a whole, the wider government, or the nation.

Identification with a specific programme of action, or 'mission-commitment'.

Pride in proficient performance of work.

Desire to serve 'the public interest' – that is, what the official believes the bureau should be doing to carry out its social function.

Instrumental motivations in bureaucrats' behaviour show up in four key biases running through all aspects of agency operations (pp. 77–8). First, officials always distort information communicated upwards to superiors or politicians so as to present their own or their section's activity in the most favourable light. Second, officials respond to decisions by their superiors or politicians in a discretionary way, implementing decisions consistent with their self-interest more speedily, and de-emphasizing those which are inconsistent. Third, in choosing between broadly equivalent policy choices officials always favour outcomes advantageous to their interests. Finally, officials' 'search' behaviour for new policy solutions is heavily influenced by self-interest.

To analyze how parts of agencies or whole bureaus behave, these micro-level propositions are simply scaled up. Every section of an organization is in partial ecological competition for more funding, staffing, policy 'territory' or other resources (pp. 53–4). A similar picture applies to whole agencies: 'Every large organization is in partial conflict with every other social agent it deals with' (p. 216); 'Bureaus tend to invest excessive resources in territorial struggles [to defend their existing functions or acquire new ones], that is more than they would if officials had no biases' (p. 216). Similarly, bureaus tend to be inertial, 'to continue doing today what they did yesterday' (p. 195), as a result of sizeable 'sunk costs' consisting of past investments in plant and staffing, standard operating procedures, and modes of relating to clients, politicians and the rest of society.

Like other organizations, bureaus have inherent tendencies to expand, but fewer than normal constraints on their ability to do so (p. 17). Agency growth helps retain and upgrade personnel; enables leaders to acquire more power, income and prestige; reduces internal conflicts; facilitates economies of scale; helps insulate top officials from change and strengthens the agencies' ability to survive. Large agencies can also better stabilize their environment than can small ones. And 'if [the top official] does not have to pay the costs of adding more personnel he will be motivated to increase the size of the organization indefinitely, since each new member adds somewhat to his total direct-action capabilities. This is usually the case in bureaus' (p. 141).

Democracy, Bureaucracy and Public Choice

Motivational diversity

The ways in which people construct or interpret self-interested behaviour will be variable and not standard. Different weightings of the nine motivations listed above combine to yield five bureaucratic personality types of officials, two focusing on narrowly egoistic motivations, and the others mixing self-interest and broader altruistic considerations:

Climbers want to maximize their own power, income and prestige. Senior climbers may over-commit to the organization and push through radical changes which foster their individual aggrandizement.
Conservers are equally egoistic, but want a quiet life and a stable future. They maximize convenience and security, and may want to marginally upgrade their existing levels of power, income and prestige. But conservers resist almost all radical organizational changes, including major agency growth or functional expansion.
Zealots are a mixed type, strongly committed to the specific programmes in which they are involved, which become for them 'sacred policies' (p. 109). Like climbers, zealots gladly embrace radical changes which expand the bureau's responsibilities or resources to pursue these sacred policies, but they are not interested in acquiring broader functions or roles unless they advance the programmes with which they are identified (p. 110).
Advocates have a more general, idealistic orientation to maximizing the power of their agency to pursue its mission or better serve its client groups. They identify their personal welfare with the organization or loyalty to its clients. Advocates may encourage limited competition inside their bureaus and take an even-handed view of its internal affairs. But to the outside world they are enthusiastically partisan in search of wider roles and more resources. 'The most aggressive and persistent "bureaucratic imperialism" usually comes from advocates rather than climbers' (p. 109).
Statesmen take a broad view of the general welfare, which they seek power in order to implement. Thus they approximate the model of altruistic civil servants set out in older public administration textbooks.

The schema of personality types generates a range of 'laws' and lesser propositions about how bureaucracies behave under different internal and environmental conditions. Bureaus have a regular life-cycle. New agencies are born by splitting off from an existing organization; or because of the entrepreneurial activities of a group of zealots; or to routinize the charisma of a political leader and institutionalize her influence in government. New agencies attract disproportionate numbers of climbers (who see them as a ladder for fast-track promotion), and zealots (who become mission-committed to the agencies' new programmes). As agencies age so the number of climbers decreases to normal. Agencies in old age become decreasingly expansionist, overwhelmingly oriented to maintaining their established roles. The longer an agency has been in existence without rapid growth or

150

personnel turnover, the more it becomes dominated by conservers and the more resistant it becomes to any form of change – the *'law of increasing conservatism'*.

At the individual level all bureaucrats tend to become conservers over time, the *'law of increasing conserverism'*. Fast-track upwardly mobile officials cease to be climbers as they exhaust the promotion options open to them, and become conservers in response. Middle-rank officials who fail to be promoted adopt conserver attitudes as a means of accommodating to their situation. Middle-rank officials with mixed self-interested and altruistic motivations slip into conserverism as they recognize that their attitudes cannot noticeably shape agency policy. The only type of officials immune to this law are strong zealots (whose commitment to specific programmes survives either promotion or confinement to the ranks), plus advocates or statesmen sufficiently senior to have a recognizable individual influence upon agency policies (pp. 101–11).

Overall, the typology of officials, the model of bureaus' life-cycles, and the two 'laws' which derive from it constitute the most distinctively pluralist elements in Downs's account. They contrast with and heavily dilute the general axioms of self-interested behaviour.

Bureaus as organizations

Most economic analyses of bureaucracies posit a fundamental dichotomy between two ways of co-ordinating social activities in industrialized societies – markets and command structures (see below, page 162). Downs labels this contrast the *'law of hierarchy'*: 'Co-ordination of large-scale activities without markets requires a hierarchical authority structure. This law results directly from the limited capacity of each individual, plus the existence of ineradicable sources of conflict among individuals' (p. 52). In particular, the general self-interest axiom implies that actors will not co-operate unless compelled to do so by a clear command structure. Yet this ultra-Weberian picture of government agencies keeps on being qualified by a more pluralistic stress upon people's capacities and self-interested inclinations to resist the demands of their superiors. The typology of bureaucratic personalities also blurs expectations of hierarchical control being fully effective. Four main implications follow.

First, any individual has a necessarily limited span of control in supervising the behaviour of others, so controlling a large organization requires an extended, multi-level hierarchy. But at each stage in the upward flow of communications officials filter the information they pass upwards in order to defend their self-interest, suggesting some key limits on the effectiveness of top-down systems. In particular: 'No one [person] can fully control the behaviour of a large organization', the so-called *'law of imperfect control'* (p. 143).

151

Second, as an agency gets larger so the resources devoted to immediate task-implementation decline, because internal management tasks consume more time and effort, and control/supervision problems increase. Hence unless large organizations can reap substantial economies of scale they are less efficient than smaller bodies. Information losses and evasion of control inside agencies both increase the greater the distance separating top officials from implementing tiers. Of course, senior officials develop methods of 'counterbiasing' the information they receive from subordinates and control techniques for bypassing intermediate organizational tiers and finding out about policy implementation. But all these efforts consume resources. This seepage can only be partially offset by boosting the bureau's overall budget or staffing, or by giving senior officials extra backup or more sophisticated management information and control systems. Hence the *'law of diminishing control'* states that: 'The larger an organization becomes the weaker is the control over its actions exercised by those at the top' (p. 143).

Third, the four general biases produced by self-interested behaviour (namely, information losses, selective implementation of superior's orders, marginal diversions of resources to private goals and instrumental patterns of search behaviour) all imply that middle- and low-ranking people can partly offset attempts to tighten up hierarchical management. Hence Downs's *'law of counter-control'* holds that: 'the greater the effort made by a top-level official to control the behaviour of subordinate officials, the greater the efforts made by these subordinates to evade or counteract such control' (p. 147). Countervailing mobilization does not imply that greater top-down control is impossible, but only that it is rarely costless.

Fourth, in rank-structured bodies, conflicts between individual officials or whole sections which cannot be amicably resolved, get pushed higher up the chain of command for arbitration by a single authoritative actor (pp. 147–8). Where too many issues are bid up in this way, top managers become overloaded and strategic guidance suffers. Where too few issues are bid up, discretionary behaviour by lower-ranked officials can produce a large 'implementation deficit' of policies not carried through because of resistance. Because control diminishes with size, these considerations mean that: 'the larger any organization becomes, the poorer is the co-ordination among its actions' - *'the law of decreasing co-ordination'* (p. 143).

Some alternative mechanisms might concert action by all the members of an agency, such as a strong ideology justifying and guiding its operations, or the inculcation of a common organizational culture. Yet Downs views these mechanisms simply as devices for defending collective interests or facilitating smoother management, and not as qualifying the importance of hierarchy. Bureaus develop ideologies to help rationalize their activities, present them in a positive light, and insulate the agency from external scrutiny or criticism. Some bureaus (such as the armed forces) also require their members to take extreme risks on occasion, and hence need special motivational back-up devices to cover such contingencies. Similarly all organizations develop particular cultures which enhance their officials' identification with its activities, especially at senior levels. But none of these channels or devices can substitute for authoritative guidance. Using ideology to guide detailed policy-making risks becoming ossified, unable to respond to new problems or circumstances. And over-strengthening agency culture exacerbates organizational rigidity, which will be strong in any case. So hierarchical guidance is vital if the organization is to pursue key goals effectively.

Agencies' external environment

For one organization to monitor another or to co-ordinate activity by multiple agencies also requires hierarchical inter-organizational relations to overcome resistance from staff in the subordinate bureaus. The law of counter-control combined with the stress on hierarchy produces the '*law of control duplication*': 'any attempt to control one large organization tends to generate another' (p. 148). Of course, controlling organizations need not become as large as implementing agencies. But the law does mean that contrasts between 'line' and 'staff' organizations often become blurred, as supposedly supervisory agencies absorb increasingly substantial resources. A spiral of top-down control efforts, followed by subordinate agency evasion, followed by increased attempts to secure control, is likely.

In addition, strong pressures push monitoring bureaus to extend their control over subordinate agencies. Climbers or zealots in top-tier agencies want their organizations to grow and to extend their influence. Even if top agencies are run by risk-averse conservers, they may seek more controls over lower-tier bodies as an insurance policy against mistakes. Hence the logic of one agency placed in hierarchical supervision over another creates a '*law of ever-expanding control*' whereby: 'The quantity and detail of reporting required by monitoring bureaus tends to rise steadily over time, regardless of the amount or nature of the activity being monitored' (p. 150).

In addition, Downs provides a terminology for describing environmental influences acting upon agencies. The 'sovereign' is any person or body placed in a position of legal authority over the bureau, such as a minister in parliamentary systems. Some bureaus may have multiple sovereigns, as with US federal agencies where the department head appointed by the president and the relevant committees of Congress occupy this role. 'Rival' agencies are alternative implementation channels. Agencies can also be significantly affected by their suppliers, by clients (the people or firms who benefit from their activities) and by those whose behaviour they regulate. A 'territorial' drive in all organizations leads them to define core functions central to the organization's mission, and more peripheral or penumbral activities which surround this core and are used to insulate it from erosion or attack. But all these propositions are primarily typological rather than substantive.

Rational officials' strategy

Although officials vary widely in their behaviour, exclusively public-interested officials are extremely rare. Agency behaviour is determined most commonly by the actions of multiple officials defending their self-interest, and by a dialectic of supervision and evasion endemic to hierarchical organizations. Bureaucracies need to be constantly supervised by representative bodies if they are to work at all well in fulfilling social rather than sectional individual or organizational goals of their own. Agency behaviour also varies over a regular life-cycle. At any one time some agencies are expanding and others stagnating. New agencies will set up in competition with established bureaus. And complex hierarchical battles between monitoring bureaus and their subordinate agencies are constantly in progress.

THE NEW RIGHT MODEL

Bureaucrats' motivations

Niskanen shares two distinguishing features of new right public choice theory, a concentration on a narrow and economistic conception of what people want, and a strong view of individuals as inherent maximizers. 'An assumption about the objectives of individuals is a necessary element in any theory of social behaviour. . . . Purposive behaviour by individuals is the essence of social behaviour' (Niskanen, 1973, p. 20). His account of what bureaucrats want is a direct analogy of the standard neo-classical assumption that the managers and owners of private firms maximize profits – because their remuneration is often performance-related (a rationality motivation), and because high profit levels safeguard the existing management against possible hostile takeover bids which would otherwise jeopardize their positions (a survival motivation).

Bureaucracies are 'non-profit organizations . . . financed, at least in part, from a periodic appropriation or grant' (Niskanen, 1973, p. 8). So with no profit index, what do bureaucrats maximize? The basic public choice answer (apart from Downs) has been that officials maximize the size of the agency (Tullock, 1976, pp. 26–35). Some writers have suggested that size is assessed primarily in terms of personnel (Noll and Fiorina, 1979). Niskanen argues that the agency's budget, its 'periodic appropriation or grant', is the central focus for top officials. Bigger budgets increase their well-being in multiple ways:

> Among the several variables that may enter the bureaucrat's motives are: salary, perquisites of the office, public reputation, power, patronage, output of the bureau . . . all [of them] are a positive function of the total budget of the bureau during the bureaucrat's tenure. . . . A bureaucrat's utility need not be strongly dependent on every one of the variables which increase with the budget, but it must be positively and continuously associated with its size. (Niskanen, 1973, pp. 22–3)

Unpacking these 'rationality' claims in more detail, larger budgets help bureaucrats push up salaries and fringe benefits (such as pensions), since increased responsibilities merit higher remuneration. They improve officials' promotion prospects, since budget scale increases normally trigger regrading directly or via increases in staffing and bureaucratization. Officials can more easily divert resources into creating perks (such as larger or more prestigious offices, more beautiful secretaries, additional functionaries or more policy analysts under their direct control). Bureaucrats in larger agencies have enhanced public reputations for influence, and higher status among their peer group. Senior civil servants commonly regard the comparative budget increases across departments as indicating winners and losers in the ecological competition for resources (Aberbach, Putnam and Rockman, 1981), a kind of 'virility index' (appropriate terminology in this case since top officials in most Western countries are still men). Bureaucrats in larger budget agencies also control more patronage and have a greater capacity to influence events and overcome resistance. They can also create organizational slack and resources more easily to meet unusual risks or crises when they occur.

In addition, maximizing budgets is critical for an agency's survival in two ways. The organization's budget is allocated to it by a 'sponsor', a 'single, dominant collective organization' such as a government, minister, chief executive, or a committee of the legislature. Sponsors expect to be presented with proposals for enlarged funding; during the scrutiny process attention will focus overwhelmingly on the marginal increases being sought. If no increase is asked for, the sponsor will be thrown into confusion, and its procedures become inoperative (see below). Completely static budget demands will tend to be decoded as signifying the bureau's stagnation or loss of role.

Second, senior bureaucrats seek budgetary expansion as a lubricant which facilitates making changes in agency operations. In large or growing agencies, difficult or incompetent officials can be moved sideways to sinecure appointments; the costs of reorganization can be more easily absorbed; and wage militancy or staff resistance to changes can be more easily bought off. Maximizing budgets enlarges demand for staff skills, and keeps wages and promotion prospects buoyant. Client groups also value top officials who boost budgets, co-operating more easily with the agency and generating public enthusiasm for its operations – especially where key clients are well-organized interest groups.

Bureaus as organizations

Niskanen's account says little explicitly about the internal organization of government agencies. It adopts the general economics view of bureaus as command organizations run in a completely top-down manner and contrasting starkly with the operations of markets as decentralized discovery systems. In addition, he follows the theory of the firm tradition of treating corporations and government agencies (however large) as run by a unified management team, in order to focus on their aggregate behaviour *vis-à-vis* other actors.

The external environment

Each bureau usually has a single sponsor, which provides a budget in return for a whole block of outputs. In dealing with them, bureaus have four main advantages. First, sponsorship is normally fragmented between committees of a legislature or political department heads. In any policy area the people exercising the sponsor role have a higher demand than citizens in general for the relevant bureau's outputs. For example, in legislatures the agriculture, defence or energy committees are generally dominated by representatives from constituencies with strong interests in farm subsidies, defence industry contracts, or oil depletion allowances respectively. Similarly, if ministers or political department heads exercise the sponsor role, they often come from a favourable background and have strong incentives to make sure policy implementation in their area is successful. The performance of a political department head will be judged principally by a specialist audience, dominated by vested interests with a stake in expanding agency budgets. Interest group support and political popularity will all increase with higher budgets, whereas budget cuts will attract only opprobrium, declarations of no confidence in the politician responsible, and reduced interest group co-operation.

The fragmentation of the sponsor role also means that each committee or political department head competes with others for public expenditures and other resources. As much as agencies themselves, the political standing of committees, department heads or ministers is judged by their success in committing public resources to their policy areas. Hence, agencies seeking higher budget appropriations from sponsors are pushing at an open door.

Second, the bureau is advantaged because only its personnel know in detail what the costs and benefits of different levels of output are. Each agency offers its sponsor a whole block of outputs in return for a total budget, thereby minimizing the information revealed. In addition, many liberal democracies such as the United Kingdom have powerful traditions of government secrecy which deny huge amounts of non-sensitive information to legislators, the mass media and public opinion. In other countries such as France the legislature has explicit rules whereby ongoing government spending programmes are reapproved without scrutiny, and automatically indexed for inflation. Such practices formalize the existence of an unanalyzed 'base budget' for which bureaus need not provide any detailed justification. Even in the United States where congressional budget scrutiny remains formally vigorous and comprehensive, and where freedom-of-information legislation curtails government secrecy, the sheer scale and complexity of information included in the *Budget Appendix* ensures that sponsor bodies focus attention overwhelmingly on year-on-year changes, new programmes and marginal spending increments.

Third, the agency normally has monopoly control over a given policy area – it does not have to compete with other agencies or firms in terms of its functional responsibilities. Conventional public administration stresses that duplication of functions between agencies is wasteful and should be eliminated; that bureaucratic organizations should be consolidated into a 'rational' pattern covering large, functionally defined programme areas; and that line agencies should combine the roles of developing, funding and implementing policy. In extreme cases, alternative modes of providing services may be prohibited, and citizens compelled to consume the bureau's services whether they want to or not. For example, mandatory schooling requirements in most countries compel parents to enter their children in the local public school system for a decade, unless they can afford private education or can teach a demanding curriculum themselves. All these practices make sponsors acutely dependent upon a single bureau for outputs. Sponsors must by and large fund the whole budget package submitted by the agency: they cannot easily pick and choose within the package, or consider competing bids from alternative providers.

Fourth, in a much stronger version of the previous point Niskanen even apparently envisaged that bureaucracies would enter into negotiations with sponsors on an overt 'take-it-or-leave-it' basis. Here the agency would demand that the sponsor fund the whole budget, or risk having to do without any agency outputs at all if it could not agree the agency's funding requirement (Eavey, 1987). If this bargaining stance were feasible, then the agency's position would be immensely strengthened. However, this version of the monopoly power thesis seems implausible for several reasons. Top bureau officials pursuing such a *force majeure* strategy would risk being replaced, while agency employees' livelihoods would also be jeopardized if the threat of non-supply were ever implemented. Sponsors' fallback positions would only rarely be to receive no services at all. Instead, they could easily fund the agency in line with last year's budget, confident that any service reductions experienced would be decremental only (Romer and Rosenthal, 1978). Even if the sponsor were highly dependent upon an agency for a specific service, rival bureaus or the private sector will normally offer a partially competing alternative. Lastly, congressional committees in the United States are certainly tough-minded enough to resist any attempt at agenda-setting as crude as Niskanen implies, and always have been so (Fenno, 1966).

The one instance where agency employees might adopt strategies resembling the all-or-nothing position is in withdrawing their labour during industrial disputes, which can often push up agency budgets noticeably. However, there are multiple reasons why this effect is of little help to Niskanen. It conflicts directly with his insistence on modelling only top bureaucrats' behaviour. And the crudeness, inflexibility and all-out character of the strike weapon is widely recognized as a key limitation on trade union influence, both in public choice work (Crouch, 1982) and outside.

Turning to the sponsor bodies' powers, Niskanen does acknowledge three different kinds of limits which legislatures or ministers can impose on agencies. First, agencies which promise certain outputs in return for a budget must deliver services consistent with their programmes. Of course, bureaus can extensively manipulate sponsors' perceptions of their performance. But long-term or conspicuous gaps between promised and achieved outputs make the sponsor discount the bureau's future pledges. A second general constraint is that sponsors can generally stop bureaus from reducing the *total* social welfare. Bureau activities which produce only net costs for society will trigger strong complaints from interest groups and voters, who pressure the sponsor to cut back the scale of the agency's operations. Hence legislators and ministers can at least ensure that agency operations are *neutral* in welfare terms.

The third constraint which sponsors can maintain is that each individual unit of output must have some value to society – although, of course, the costs of providing these outputs may well exceed their social benefit. For example, if a police agency recruits and deploys so many personnel that additional units begin to cause avoidable riots in sensitive city areas, then the extra units of police begin to erode the social welfare. The sponsor will conclude that marginal police outputs are counter-productive and refuse their funding increments. But the sponsor could do little about personnel who fill out their schedules with trivial duties, so long as they make some positive contribution to the social welfare in part of their time, and so long as the police force as a whole costs no more than it delivers in benefits.

158

Rational officials' strategies

The interaction between budget-maximizing bureaucrats with monopoly power and fragmented sponsors characteristically produces a radical oversupply of agency outputs (Figure 6.1). The horizontal axis of the graph measures the level of the bureau's output, and the vertical axis the marginal costs and marginal social benefits of each unit of output. For the sake of convenience I have drawn the marginal cost (MC) curve and the marginal benefit (MB) curve as straight lines, but the analysis remains the same with other patterns. The MC curve rises with increased outputs, perhaps because of increased factor prices with rising demand (but it makes no difference to the analysis if the MC curve is perfectly flat). The MB curve falls as output increases, reflecting the general presumption in economic analysis of diminishing marginal utilities. Early units of output are intensely valuable to society, much more so than their costs, but as the MB curve falls this differential is progressively eliminated and at point E the marginal costs and marginal value of output are equal. If the agency produced at this point, which is also the welfare optimum and the point at which a profit-maximizing firm would stop, then a net benefit to society would result equivalent to the area GEH. The bureau's total budget at point E is given by the area HEQ0, whereas the gross benefits accruing to society would be GEQ0, creating the consumers' surplus area shown.

However, rational officials take advantage of the sponsor's weak position to push output up beyond point E. Indeed, they only stop expanding output when constrained to do so by the sponsor, which in Figure 6.1 occurs at

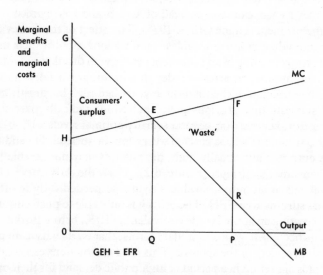

Figure 6.1 **Niskanen's model of why bureaucracies oversupply outputs**

159

point F. Here the bureau has created an area of 'waste' (given by the area EFR) which exactly offsets the consumer surplus created by early units of output (area GEH). 'Waste' is used in the technical sense of avoidable costs, outputs whose value to society is less than the marginal costs of producing them. This does not imply that the bureau is slack, inefficient or necessarily has organizational 'fat' built into it. Waste arises simply because the bureau is delivering far more outputs than society at large or the sponsor body require, even if the bureau is being relatively efficient (= cost-effective) in doing so. At point F the total benefits from the bureau's activity are given by GRP0 and its total costs by HFP0. When these two areas are exactly equal (as here) the bureau neither increases nor decreases the social welfare. Pushing up outputs beyond point F begins to actively reduce the social welfare and can be resisted by even the most pusillanimous or poorly informed sponsor, so that point F represents the equilibrium output for budget-maximizing bureaucrats. Thus Niskanen predicts that with weak sponsor control agencies deliver up to twice as much output as a profit-maximizing firm, and twice the level which would be optimal in social welfare terms.

This model can sometimes appear very abstract, and as I note below (page 210) it has not been widely applied in empirical work. Hence it is useful to look at an empirical example of the over-supply behaviour Niskanen hypothesizes. In 1984 the Metropolitan Police in London arrested around 25,000 people, charged them with being 'drunk and disorderly', held them in jail for a brief period and processed them through the local courts for minor offences. The following year the police's sponsor body, a central department in Whitehall, decided to 'decriminalize' drunkenness, urging police forces to use 'cautions' instead of arrests and court proceedings to combat the problem (Home Office, 1985). The effect of this policy change was that individual police constables could no longer boost their monthly arrest records by pulling in and charging people with drunkenness offences. By 1987 the number of arrests under this heading had fallen to around 7,000, only a fraction of the total three years before. This drastic cutback strongly suggests that previous police behaviour radically over-supplied arrests for drunkenness, far beyond socially optimal levels.

In some situations where costs are very low or societal demand for the bureau's output is abnormally high, bureaucrats may not be able fully to exploit consumer's surplus (Figure 6.2). Here the MB curve cuts the horizontal axis at an output level less than that needed fully to offset the consumers surplus area GEH. The bureau is only able to push output up to point K, creating an area of waste equivalent to EJK, before further output increments become negative in welfare terms, that is, they have no positive value at all to society or the sponsor. This kind of situations can arise where new bureaus are set up in a period of high public demand for their outputs; or where agency outputs are valued as peculiarly salient (as Goodin (1982b,

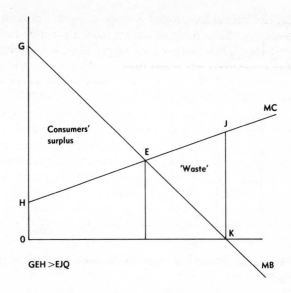

Figure 6.2 'High demand' conditions preventing full oversupply

Chapter 11) suggests is especially true of 'national defence' arguments); or where an agency's historic costs have been radically reduced through technological change (such as computerization) and the sponsor has not yet absorbed the implications of the innovation. When oversupply behaviour is thus unusually constrained, budget-maximizing bureaucrats have strong incentives to create spending increments by becoming less efficient.

A final implication of the Niskanen model is worth noting, since it is so apparently counter-intuitive (McGuire, 1981). Suppose that a bureau's costs fall radically over time: how should it behave? Niskanen's answer is that the bureau will significantly expand its outputs (Figure 6.3). For a profit-maximizing firm the cost reduction would directly trigger some increased output, from E to E_1 in Figure 6.3. But for the bureau the cost reduction moves its equilibrium point from F to F_1 where an enlarged area of waste offsets the increased consumers' surplus, allowing the bureau's output to rise radically. The price elasticity of demand for bureaus will thus be up to twice that for competitive industries.

Niskanen's overall conclusions strongly affirm new right attitudes: 'All bureaus are too large. For given demand and cost conditions both the budget and the output of the bureau may be up to twice that of a competitive industry facing the same conditions' (Niskanen, 1973, p. 33). There is none of the variability in motivations or bureaus' strategies found in Downs's account. Essentially, all bureaucrats everywhere seek to maximize their budgets by radically oversupplying outputs.

161

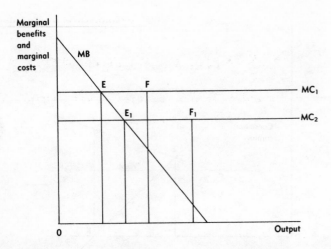

Figure 6.3 **The impact of cost reductions on the equilibrium levels of firms' and agencies' outputs**

PROBLEMS IN ANALYZING BUREAUCRACIES

Despite their apparently different approaches, Downs's and Niskanen's work shares four basic failings:
1. They assimilate all agencies into a restrictive line bureaucracy paradigm.
2. They adopt overly broad definitions of the components of bureaucrats' utility functions.
3. They offer essentially homogeneous accounts of all bureaucratic behaviour, and thus they cannot legitimately explain variations in agencies' goals and strategies.
4. They analyze systems of bureaus as simply scaled-up analogues of single bureaus.

The line bureaucracy paradigm

All economic analyses of bureaucracies view them as uniformly hierarchical organizations for two reasons. First, early authors in the field posited a fundamental contrast between organizations run in a centralized command mode and markets, which are decentralized discovery systems: 'In the absence of profit goals, bureaus must be centrally managed by the pervasive regulation and monitoring of the activity of subordinates' (von Mises, 1944). For many polemicists, such as Hayek (1960), it became axiomatic that government agencies in the West are closely similar in their operation to the bureaucracies of communist states, especially in their reliance on hierarchic

162

planning and control systems. Second, methodological assumptions carried over from the neo-classical theory of the firm invariably included an undifferentiated management team, behaving as a unitary rational decision-maker, and able to control their organizations in top-down manner.

Downs's and Niskanen's experience of government strengthened this orientation for a third reason – both authors focused mainly on defence organizations. Downs wrote *Inside Bureaucracy* on a US Air Force grant to the Rand Corporation. Defence-related examples (chiefly the air force) figure four times more frequently than any other source of empirical references. Niskanen worked as an economist in the Pentagon from 1967–70, and wrote *Bureaucracy and Representative Government* because of his belief 'that I had something important to say if I could abstract from my own experience as a defence analyst' (Niskanen, 1987, p. 140). The book was written on a sabbatical at the Institute for Defense Analysis in Washington. Both Downs and Niskanen seem to have taken their experience of defence agencies as a microcosm of government as a whole. Yet in practice the armed forces of any country are usually the limiting case of centrally run, authoritarian, hierarchy-obsessed and inclusive agencies, with developed internal identifications, and a single multi-tiered chain of command linking top policy-makers and the rank and file. Chapter 7 demonstrates that such organizations are far from typical of modern state agencies.

Downs

Downs's account pictures government agencies' internal organization as a classic Weberian line bureaucracy, despite his discussions of subordinates' resistance to control efforts. He makes a series of logical jumps to move from the proposition that voting cannot resolve conflicts within large organizations to the blanket 'law of hierarchy': 'Co-ordination of large-scale activities without markets requires a hierarchical authority structure.' By bifurcating all non-market mechanisms of co-ordination into voting or hierarchy, Downs excludes other options such as:

- voluntary co-operation between self-interested actors (Axelrod, 1984);
- other interactive modes of conflict resolution, such as 'partisan mutual adjustment' (Lindblom and Braybrooke, 1963);
- other non-market but also non-hierarchical systems, such as the 'kinship' systems of personnel relations developed by large Japanese corporations, which place a premium on fostering employee identification with the firm (Ouchi, 1980).

Even if we could establish that these methods of co-ordination do not play central roles within large line bureaucracies in Britain or America, they certainly operate in inter-organizational relations between agencies. And the 'law of hierarchy' cannot apply only to intra-organizational relations

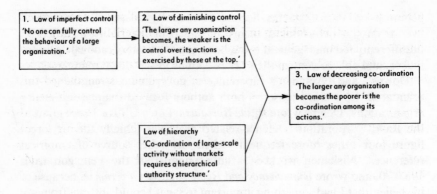

Figure 6.4 **How Downs derives the 'law of decreasing co-ordination'**

within large line bureaucracies, for then it becomes tautological, claiming only that 'hierarchical organizations must be run hierarchically'.

Downs's later discussion of 'the basic nature of control problems in bureaus', starts from the truism that no one individual can fully control an organization of any size (box 1 in Figure 6.4) and then notes that as an organization gets larger so the control exercised by any one leader or fixed leadership group must decline. A logical gap opens, however, with the next proposition that larger organizations are inherently less well co-ordinated than smaller ones (box 3 in Figure 6.4) – which only makes sense if an expectation of decreasing control is combined with the 'law' of hierarchy. If large organizations are less hierarchical than small ones, they may also be more co-ordinated. For example, influential views of large corporations argue that they are inherently less hierarchical than small entrepreneurial firms because they use complex committee structures run by an extensive 'technostructure' which undertakes large-scale planning in fields such as technology development or market manipulation (Galbraith, 1969, 1974). Alternatively, the shift to M-form (multi-firm) structures may extensively decentralize control of operational matters in giant corporations compared with unitary structures (Williamson, 1975). Thus if we query the law of hierarchy, Downs's law of decreasing co-ordination fails as well.

Niskanen

Niskanen's focus on the aggregate behaviour of bureaus is buttressed by a far-reaching assumption about who controls agencies, which is smuggled in by a terminological device. A 'bureaucrat' is defined as 'the senior official of any bureau with a separate identifiable budget' (Niskanen, 1971, p. 22). All other officials in an agency or department are defined as 'employees', and are relevant only to the bureau's role in factor markets. In effect, Niskanen claims that all bureaus are monocratically run by a single top official – which means that internal agency politics cannot affect overall policy and there are no collective action problems inside bureaus. Characteristically, however, Niskanen does not stick consistently to his terminology. While he uses 'bureaucrat' 'for the most part' in the specialized sense above, he also admits that: 'The term "bureaucrat" will sometimes be used in the more general sense to define any full-time employee of a bureau: in this sense it is nearly synonymous with "civil servant"' (Niskanen, 1973, p. 11). This equivocation means that Niskanen often generalizes from conclusions reached about top officials' behaviour when in sole charge of their organizations to more realistic situations where policy influence is dispersed amongst many officials inside government agencies.

Bureaucrats' utility functions

For the notion of rationally self-interested officials to have any empirical cutting power, their utility functions must be defined in terms of clearly self-regarding, hard-edged motives. If officials' utilities include other-regarding elements from the outset, then a superficially more comprehensive but in practice completely vacuous account of bureaucratic behaviour will result.

Downs

Downs's list of bureaucrats' utility functions is excessively loose. Five elements (money income, power, prestige, security and convenience) are clearly instrumental concerns likely to be positively associated with the pursuit of budget increments. But four other elements clearly incorporate other-regarding elements which are simply illegitimate within a public choice perspective. 'Personal loyalty to the work group, bureau or nation' is described in a form which makes it essentially a non-rational motivation in public choice terms. 'Desire to serve the public interest' seems exactly on a par with regarding 'civic duty' as a component of rational voters' utilities. It is hard to see how it would be feasible to discover action which is even formally non-rational (i.e. not directed to the satisfaction of bureaucrats' personal preferences) if such factors can be mixed with instrumental motives in individuals' preferences. Downs's last two components – pride in the proficient performance of work, and commitment to specific programmes – seem objectionable for another reason. These are behavioural traits which a public choice model of bureaucracy should be aiming to predict as likely or unlikely to occur, rather than directly incorporating them into the model assumptions.

Niskanen

Niskanen gives the following list of utility components: <u>salary, perks, public reputation, power, patronage, ease of making changes, ease of</u>

managing the bureau and output of the bureau. Only one element here seems unrelated to individual self-interest, namely 'output of the bureau'. This might mean either that officials consume part of their own outputs (which would be consistent with a public choice approach, but unlikely to be generally true or to influence them much). Alternatively (top) bureaucrats might intrinsically value their agencies' activities (which would conflict with an instrumental model).

More important questions centre on whether larger budget agencies are any easier to manage or to make changes in than small agencies. As the size of a hierarchically organized bureau increases, the single (top) bureaucrat could well find life more rather than less difficult – as Downs argued. Where officials experience restrictive pay and perks ceilings (as in most liberal democracies), the convenience components of their utilities should increasingly influence how they regard budget increments. So do (top) bureaucrats have some equilibrium level of budget beyond which the costs of single-handedly controlling a large and growing agency more than offset the small gains of prestige or power available?

However, Niskanen is apparently determined to retain a view of (top) bureaucrats as open-ended budget maximizers:

> The problem of making changes and the personal burdens of managing a bureau are often higher at higher budget levels, but both are reduced by *increases* in the budget. This effect creates a treadmill phenomenon, inducing bureaucrats to strive for increased budgets until they can turn over the management burdens of a stable higher budget to a new bureaucrat. Hence an interesting cyclical pattern emerges: bureaucrats interested in making changes resign when budgets are stabilized; their replacements will be satisfied with the other rewards of high budgets, or strive for further increases, or, possibly, cut the budget in order to provide a basis for further increases. (Niskanen, 1973, p. 22)

The problems here are obvious. The idea of a cycle of increases, cutbacks and more increases qualifies the budget-maximizing model in a completely *ad hoc* manner. No rationale is provided to explain why a given (top) bureaucrat should follow one strategy rather than another. If rationally self-interested officials could regularly improve their welfare by cutting budgets, what can remain of the oversupply thesis to which Niskanen accords such emphasis? In addition, the cycle or 'treadmill' account is ethnocentric, relying heavily on the US model of politically appointed bureau-chiefs coming in from outside for short periods. But in most other liberal democracies, permanent officials work their way up to top positions mainly within a single bureau. This lifetime career path means that they certainly cannot move on easily to new positions, except by retiring from the civil service altogether.

Some recent exponents of budget-maximizing models distingush between a 'static' argument that bureaucrats are better-off in large-budget than in smaller organizations, and a 'dynamic' version that 'bureaucrats are better off in rapidly growing agencies, or agencies receiving large-budget increments, than in slow-growing agencies' (Blais and Dion, 1988, p. 7):

It remains plausible . . . that everything else being equal,
bureaucrats are better off in larger bureaus, where senior positions are
likely to be more powerful and to command higher salaries. Whatever
the case, Niskanen's dynamic proposition – that bureaucrats gain
from increased budgets – is on firmer ground.

No such option can rescue Niskanen's aside on budget cycles from inconsistency, nor be reconciled with his basic analysis. If bureaucrats want rapidly growing appropriations, then small budget agencies will be attractive since any given increment in funds mathematically produces higher growth. Yet over time, rapidly growing agencies will themselves quickly become large agencies, and their growth rates will tend to slacken. If the dynamic variant of budget-maximizing is true, then the oversupply thesis could not be sustained as a general proposition. Instead, it would become a *temporary* feature of smaller, new or rapidly expanding bureaus. In fact, however, the oversupply thesis is the key to the new right model. The radical implications of Niskanen's account derive precisely from the claim that larger budgets are always better than smaller ones for bureaucrats.

Variations in bureau behaviour

Downs

On the face of it, explaining why agencies behave in different ways should pose severe explanatory difficulties for simple public choice models. Yet Downs defines bureaucrats' utility functions in such a fuzzy way, and uses his typology of bureaucratic personality types (climbers, conservers, zealots, advocates and statesmen) so extensively that he seems to have no difficulty explaining variegation amongst bureaus.

It is unclear whether Downs thinks that all five types are allowable variants of utility-maximizing bureaucrats, since their utility function anyway mixes self-regarding and other-regarding motivations. If so, the vagueness of Downs's self-interest axioms is obvious. Alternatively, Downs sometimes presents the personalities as indicating a continuum of motivations from self-interested rational bureaucrats at the climber/conserver end, through the mixed zealot/advocate types, to pure altruism at the statesman end. If so, he is clearly not putting forward an economic model of bureaucracy at all, but simply some sort of mixed public choice/sociological account.

Downs's typology is clearly inconsistent with the basic neo-classical approach which stresses that only role-specific variations in preferences can legitimately be assumed. Within any given role, economic theory does not make substantive assumptions about inter-personal variations in preferences, for they are likely to be so diverse as to be incapable of being adequately modelled. Yet Downs cheerfully imputes different substantive preference sets to actors within the same role, apparently on the a priori basis that his typology captures basic mind-sets in the population at large, so that some officials will correspond to each ideal type:

> The use of the five particular types is admittedly arbitrary. We could
> have used any number of types, or defined these five somewhat
> differently. The five types used here represent our own best
> judgement of the 'optimal classification' of bureaucrats. . . . [And]
> the particular form of simplification and arbitrariness developed [in
> our theory] enables us to make forecasts about the behaviour of
> officials and bureaus that will hopefully prove more accurate than
> forecasts made with alternative forms. . . . Furthermore much of the
> analysis is wholly independent of how the five specific 'ideal types' of
> officials are defined. (Downs, 1967, p. 4)

But if it is legitimate to make direct assumptions about substantive preferences between personality types, then a huge number of initial axioms can be connected by different chains of deductive reasoning to the same empirical predictions. There really is no reason why we should accept the existence of the 5 types of bureaucrat, rather than 50, 500 or 2. Equally there need be no empirical phenomena immune from economic 'explanation' if it is allowable to fine-tune our assumptions about personality types to accommodate it. Within Downs's proclaimed methodology it is simply impermissible to explain variations in individual or bureau behaviour in terms of reasoning about the mix of assumed personality types within roles, or about how given individuals change over time from one personality type to another. Nor is the typology of officials incidental as Downs claims, but rather an integral part of the analysis, the source of its characteristically pluralist stress on motivational diversity. Two of the most empirical-sounding of the fifteen 'laws' – the laws of increasing conservatism and of increasing conserverism – are wholly dependent on the typology. And much else which seems descriptively compelling stems from speculations about personality types.

Venturing into amateur social psychology in this way has been a constant temptation for other economists writing on bureaucracy from Tullock's early (1965) efforts onwards. The adverse implications for intellectual standards are well illustrated by the recent claim that public agencies are disproportionately staffed by patriots, the risk averse, 'shirkers' concerned to maximize leisure time, 'those who have extreme views about the consequences of alternative policies', and people with 'an unusually large, perhaps inflated sense of their own importance' (Auster and Silver, 1979, p. 81). Here, a supposedly deductive analysis of differential recruitment to the public and private sectors crosses over into assertive stigmatizing of people in particular occupations based on nothing more than commonplace prejudices.

Niskanen

Niskanen focuses on the aggregate behaviour of bureaus and says little about variations across different organizations. Factor market conditions can alter the mix of capital and labour which bureaus adopt in producing outputs – as when government agencies can acquire some factors at less than market costs. And significant differences in behaviour are created by 'normal' and 'high' levels of demand for an agency's output. But all these variations reflect environmental conditions: Niskanen's use of 'bureaucrat' prevents internal politics in agencies from generating variations in bureau behaviour. And his account of the bureau's budget function is a direct assumption:

$$B = aQ - bQ^2 \quad \text{where} \quad 0 < Q < a/2b$$

where B is the maximum budget a sponsor will grant a bureau in a specific year, and Q is the sponsor's expectation of the level of output which the bureau will supply during the same time period. This relation is consistent with Niskanen's remarks about individually rational bureaucrats, but so are many possible functions. This specific budget function is not *derived* from the analysis of individual officials' behaviour – any more than the aggregate distribution of preferences in public choice theories of voting can be derived from assumptions about individual voters' utility profiles. Where such an important element in predicting overall bureau behaviour is directly assumed in the same way about all agencies, the model must claim that essentially all (top) bureaucrats want the same things (budget-maximization), and given the same initial conditions will act in the same way.

In later work attempting some empirical demonstration of his model, Niskanen (1975) modifies the oversupply thesis slightly in a different direction, while retaining open-ended budget-maximization. He envisages that agencies could differ in their ability to divert budgets away from public policy outputs and towards producing direct benefits and perquisites for themselves. Where perks production is well-developed and influences bureaucrats' policy judgements, tendencies to oversupply may be somewhat constrained. Agencies might also be oriented towards supplying benefits to particular political constituencies, for example by producing in uneconomic locales to maximize the regional impact of programmes, or using out-of-date production technologies in order to mop up surplus labour. In either case oversupply behaviour could be reduced and inefficiency increased. But again these modifications have an *ad hoc* feel about them, and mesh badly with Niskanen's original, highly determined model. No criteria are suggested for determining agencies' ability to produce perks independently of their observed pressure for higher budgets.

Later work on the formal modelling of bureaucracy has concluded that because Niskanen's account deals only with bureau/legislature relations, and says little about what agencies do with budgets once they are obtained, the uses to which maximized budgets would be put remain strictly indeterminate:

> Although the model indicates the presence of socially excessive budgets, without a model of production one cannot conclude that *output* is excessive. . . . We cannot say how excess budget is used, whether it is allocated to nonproductive slack (the 'plush carpeting' syndrome), to produce more output ('After we maximize our budget, all we care about is production'), or to invest in activities that do not increase *current* output but which may increase future output (policy analysis). (Bendor *et al.*, 1985, pp. 1047–8)

Systems of bureaus

Organizational boundaries make a difference to communication and influence flows. Inter-organizational relations are qualitatively different from the relationships between ranks, sections or groups of actors within one relatively unified institution. These propositions will seem obvious to political scientists – but apparently not to existing public choice accounts of bureaucracy. Using simply specified parameter conditions (such as perfect competition, oligopoly or monopoly), economists can move easily from the analysis of how one enterprise behaves to conclusions about the behaviour of the industry as a whole. Carrying over this tradition of 'heroic aggregation', public choice writers seem wedded to the claim that once they have understood how 'the bureau' works they have also *ipso facto* understood how the state apparatus works. Aggregate behaviour across bureaus is described only as an afterthought or aside, as in the following account of how poor agency performance stimulates state growth:

> The solution to any instance of [bureaucratic] failure is perverse. It is usually to create another bureau to oversee those who have lapsed into sin. Bureaux are piled on bureaux and the bureaucracy grows on. From the resulting mountain it is soon impossible to unearth the molehill that started it all. (Perlman, 1976, p. 76)

There is no hint here that relations between bureaus are vastly more varied

170

than those between firms, with complex permutations of authority relations and radically different kinds of interaction and interdependence.

Downs

Downs stands out from the rest of the economic literature because of his explicit coverage of inter-bureau relations. But any insights here are largely vitiated by the destructive impact of the 'law of hierarchy' in forging direct analogies between superior/subordinate relations within a hierarchical organization and control problems in inter-organizational contexts (Figure 6.5). Here the 'law of counter-control' (box 1) is simply generalized to apply to situations where one bureau is charged with monitoring or controlling the activities of other agencies, to give the 'law of control duplication' (box 2). A specific discussion of inter-organizational relations leads to the view that budget-maximizing and a struggle for information by the control bureau will generate 'ever-expanding control' (box 3). In practice, however, boxes 2 and 3 cannot be derived from box 1 except within an assumption that somehow a separate control bureau will be in analogous position to the higher-ranked official in superior/subordinate relation within an organization.

In practice, a monitoring bureau needs far less information (either in quantitative or in qualitative terms) than a superior within a line bureaucracy. The whole point of moving away from intra- to inter-organizational relations (by devices such as hiving-off or contracting-out) is to reorganize communication channels and cut back the level of necessary information-loss recorded in hierarchic line bureaucracies. Williamson's work on private corporations stresses that the external sourcing of supply entails greater managerial certainty, whereas in-house staffs are retained precisely in areas where it is more difficult to specify in advance what services will be

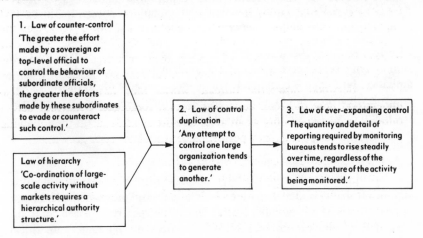

Figure 6.5 **How Downs derives the 'law of ever-expanding control'**

171

needed (Williamson, 1975). Within government, monitoring bureaus want to achieve a 'hands off' form of regulating their subordinate agencies, without getting involved in the minutiae of bottom-tier agencies' management. This helps explain why formula-based rules for allocating grants or expenditure targets to local governments have increasingly been adopted (Rhodes, 1988; Dunleavy and Rhodes, 1988). Control duplication and ever expanding control only make sense if we see inter-organizational relations through the distorting lens of the line bureaucracy paradigm.

Niskanen

Niskanen's account pays little attention to systems of bureaus, despite occasional asides recognizing that most agencies conventionally discussed as unitary actors are in practice congeries of bureaus and sub-bureaus. This omission is serious, however. When Niskanen argues that (top) bureaucrats budget maximize, what exactly does he mean? Do officials maximize the entire budget flowing through their hands, perhaps *en route* to other public agencies? Or do they maximize only that part of it which is retained within their own bureau or organization? The first position seems commensurate with the new right emphasis on bureaucratic oversupply fuelling the growth of the state. But only a positive answer to the second question seems consistent with an egoistic account of rational bureaucrats' motivations.

Niskanen's discussion of agency outputs again makes clear that bureaucrats maximize that budget which relates only to their own agency's activities, since Q in his budget equation in practice stands for (immediate and quantifiable) activities rather than for final outputs:

> The output of most bureaus (even sometimes the concept of output) cannot be precisely determined . . . [so that] For those readers who have trouble with the concept of the output of the bureau, [my] theory may be better understood in terms of the relation between the budget or cost and the activity level of a bureau. (Niskanen, 1971, p. 27)

Clearly then, the official running a top-tier agency in a system of bureaus should only be concerned about the budget for her own department's activities. Niskanen is completely silent about her attitude to the funds she controls which flow out to subordinate governments – so strong is the grip of the line bureaucracy paradigm upon his model.

Conclusion

This critique suggests some useful, if necessarily interim, conclusions. It is significant that two such disparate pieces of public choice work, standing at opposite ends of the methodological and value spectrum, share common basic defects (albeit in different forms). Downs's and Niskanen's uncritical ①adoption of a line bureaucracy paradigm; their use of fuzzy and soft-edged

172

accounts of bureaucrats' utility functions; their inability to come up with methodologically legitimate supply-side variations in bureaucratic behaviour; and their use of crude generalizations to move from explanations of a single bureau's behaviour to that of systems of bureaus – each of these is a fundamental trait of public choice models of bureaucracy, rather than a casual or easily correctable mistake. In the works of lesser authors these defects become more rather than less visible. For example, the *reductio ad absurdum* point in neglecting systems of bureaus is reached by the American economists Auster and Silver (1979) who treat the whole state apparatus of liberal democracies as a single firm – thus achieving a level of explanatory crudity which not even conventional Marxists any longer aspire to reach. Similarly, Mitchell (1983, p. 89) sums up his survey of 'the peculiar economics of government' by deriving 'a principle that is everywhere ignored by governments: "*Nobody spends somebody else's money as carefully as he spends his own*"' – a conclusion that is simply anti-organizational rather than distinctively relevant to the complex institutional structures of the public sector. But these defects do not mean that the public choice literature on bureaucracy should be abandoned or ignored. In the next chapter, I show that reconstructing a public choice model from a radically different standpoint can generate useful insights into administrative behaviour.

Chapter 7

THE BUREAU-SHAPING MODEL

Rational bureaucrats have few incentives to pursue budget-maximizing strategies, as this chapter seeks to show by building on the core public choice assumptions. I assume that bureaucrats maximize self-regarding and hard-edged utilities in making official decisions. A bureau's overall policy is set by some combination of individual decisions made by its officials, and by interactions with a sponsor body. Within broad limits, officials' influence on bureau policy is always extensively rank-structured, with those near the top being most influential. Sponsors depend extensively on bureaus for information about their costs, benefits and outputs, although they also receive some general information from citizens.

There are four reasons why rational bureaucrats should not budget-maximize. First, collective action problems exist within bureaucracies and have an important influence upon overall bureau behaviour. Second, the extent to which bureaucrats' utilities are associated with budget increases varies greatly across different components of overall budgets, and across distinct types of agencies. Third, even if some rational officials still budget-maximize, they will do so only up to an internal optimum level. Fourth, senior officials are much more likely to pursue work-related rather than pecuniary utilities – in which case, collective strategies of reshaping their bureaus into different agency types can best advance senior officials' interests. Whether senior bureaucrats pursue bureau-shaping or budget-maximizing strategies varies systematically with agency type.

COLLECTIVE ACTION PROBLEMS
INSIDE BUREAUCRACIES

Bureaus are rank-structured environments. But it is very rare for any sizeable government agency to be completely dominated by one individual or even a small leadership group with cohesive interests: 'The monolithic bureau is a myth' (Downs, 1967, p. 133). To realize collective benefits for

174

bureau members will require concerted action by a number of officials which may be quite large, especially in hostile or turbulent environmental conditions. Most US federal departments are congeries of between five and ten major bureaus, administrations or offices, running programmes which operate in quite distinct ways and policy fields. Each bureau or administration has an extensive sub-structure of senior officials, and there is a smallish departmental core of central administrators built around the Office of the Secretary and the Inspector General, who pull overall policy together. In this system, and given the large size of most US federal departments, a large number of officials are involved in constructing bureau or departmental budgets. Even in the much smaller and highly integrated departments characteristic of British central government there may be up to eighty policy-level staff. In neither country can budget-maximization be a private good pursued by a single hegemonic official. But if budget-maximizing requires a collective effort, how do officials choose between individual or collective strategies for boosting their welfare, and between increasing sectional or overall bureau budgets? And do bureaucrats encounter collective action problems in maximizing budgets?

Budget-maximizing as a collective strategy

Any given bureaucrat has a range of both individual and collective strategies open for boosting her welfare. She can most directly and strongly improve her personal position using an individual strategy – for here a successful effort generates a pay-off which does not need to be shared with others. By contrast, with any collective strategy there is a more indirect and complex link between a successful outcome and a welfare boost for the individual. When multiple officials shape a bureau's policy, then budget-maximization is a collective rather than an individual way of increasing bureaucrats' welfare:

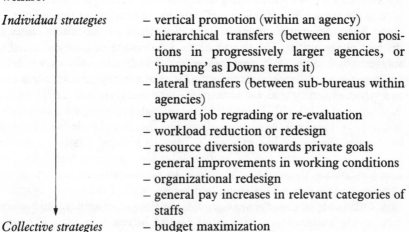

Individual strategies	– vertical promotion (within an agency)
	– hierarchical transfers (between senior positions in progressively larger agencies, or 'jumping' as Downs terms it)
	– lateral transfers (between sub-bureaus within agencies)
	– upward job regrading or re-evaluation
	– workload reduction or redesign
	– resource diversion towards private goals
	– general improvements in working conditions
	– organizational redesign
	– general pay increases in relevant categories of staffs
Collective strategies	– budget maximization

175

An overall budget increase for the agency has particularly indeterminate implications for any official, however senior. Consequently, rational bureaucrats put their efforts primarily into individual utility-maximizing strategies. They only pursue collective goods strategies if other options are foreclosed or are already fully exploited.

Studies in occupational sociology show that blue-collar workers are more attracted to collective forms of pay bargaining than white-collar staffs, because people in manual grades have little prospect of significantly improving their situation by individual strategies of promotion, career advancement, or renegotiating individual contracts with employers (Crouch, 1982, pp. 67–74). Similarly, we might expect that within a government agency the opportunities for individual welfare maximization will be fewest in the bottom ranks of bureaucrats: here collective strategies for improving officials' welfare may be resorted to more readily. But senior officials have much greater scope for exploiting individual strategies, so they are less likely to resort to collective strategies.

A closely related issue arises over the assumption in the existing public choice literature that budget-maximization focuses solely on boosting an agency's entire expenditure, its global budget. With multiple officials influencing policy, surely rational officials will primarily seek budget increments for their section or division inside the agency? Sectional budget increases could offer individual benefits to the one or two policy-level staff in each division. So surely a more realistic focus on budget increments tagged to specific sections can rescue Niskanen's assumption of a single hegemonic official?

But in practice dropping a whole-bureau focus on the global budget is difficult, and cannot rescue budget-maximizing models from their difficulties. Trying to model bureaucratic behaviour *vis-à-vis* sectional budgets requires very complex models which are even more difficult to operationalize than those focusing on global budgets. I noted above that US federal departments are congeries of bureaus, but this is not the end of the story. Even within bureaus or administrations there are sub-offices running distinct programmes. The degree of sectionalization of bureaus and the ways in which senior staffs aggregate sectional budget bids also vary widely across agencies. A developed apparatus for measuring both these properties in a standardized fashion would be needed if a disaggregated model was to be developed. It is highly improbable that officials in general would see their interests as advanced by all (tagged) budget increases inside their bureau or department, as budget-maximizing models assume. Instead, rational bureaucrats will only favour sectional budget increases with positive implications for them. They are likely to be indifferent towards, or to oppose, budget increments going to other sections of their own organization. Officials in stagnant or slow-growing sections of an agency could easily face severe welfare losses because of budget increases in more dynamic sections. Not only would they experience 'relative deprivation', but the balance of influence and prestige within the agency would shift towards the growth areas at their expense.

Consequently, an account of how officials behave with sectional rather than global budget increases would need to be constructed in terms of the emergence of minimum winning coalitions for certain types of budgetary expansion rather than others. Because such an approach would be very complex and require great methodological sophistication before it could be applied empirically, the analysis here follows the existing public choice literature's focus on global budgets. None the less I recognize explicitly that this is a drastic simplifying assumption, which should ideally be superseded at a later stage by a more complex account.

Collective action and maximizing budgets

Because bureaucracies are significantly rank-structured organizations, the existing public choice literature assumes that collective action problems have no bearing upon agency policies. Yet once we recognize multiple policy-level officials, then a rational official must meet the following condition before deciding to pursue the shared goals of global budget-maximization:

$$(B_j * P_j) - C_j > A_j$$

In words, B_j the official's net utility derived from a marginal budget increment (i.e. the individual benefits she receives after allowing for any costs associated with budgetary growths); discounted by P_j, the probability that the individual official's advocacy will be decisive in securing the budget increase; minus C_j, the costs of personally advocating the budget increment; must be greater than A_j, the rate of return on individual efforts to improve her welfare, or available on alternative collective strategies.

In the theory-of-the-firm debate a number of authors pointed out early on that even if a collective goal such as profit-maximization could be plausibly ascribed to a large firm, managers' behaviour could rationally diverge from it (Loasby, 1968):

> Any individual manager is one amongst many and as such he might rightly assume that his activities will only make a small contribution to the achievement of the collective goal. It would be rational for him to assume that the others are contributing to the goal, thereby allowing him to serve his own goals and to become a 'free-rider' in the group. (Jackson, 1982, p. 55)

Only one or two public choice authors recognize collective action problems inside bureaus, and most assume that officials' work conditions are calculated to produce co-operative behaviour:

Hierarchy and organization are especially effective at concentrating the interactions between specific individuals. A bureaucracy is structured so that people specialize, and so that people working on related tasks are grouped together. This organizational practice increases the frequency of interactions, making it easier for workers to develop stable cooperative relationships. Moreover, when an issue requires coordination between different branches of the organization, the hierarchical structure allows the issue to be referred to policy makers at higher levels who frequently deal with each other on just such issues. By binding people together in a long-term, multilevel game, organizations increase the number and importance of future interactions, and thereby promote the experience of cooperation among groups too large to interact individually. (Axelrod, 1984, pp. 130–1)

In the terms used in Chapter 3, a bureaucracy is a strongly defined exogenous group, with a clear group identity of which all bureau members are aware. By retaining a whole-bureau focus on global rather than sectional budgets, difficulties arising from potentially conflicting identities are excluded. So in respect of budgets at least, bureaucrats automatically perceive their collective interest, although they may not rank it highly compared with individual strategies for maximizing their welfare.

However, the rank-structured nature of bureaucracy also changes the basic collective action problem in an interesting and important way which is likely to more than offset these influences fostering co-operation. Each of the terms in the equation above – undiscounted benefits, probability of influence, advocacy costs and returns on alternative strategies – will vary systematically across 'top'-, 'middle'- and 'bottom'-ranked officials, as shown in Figure 7.1.

The utility pay-offs from generalized budgetary increments are likely to vary, roughly inversely with rank. People who are already senior officials gain least, since their position is already well established. The same features of public service systems which foster co-operative behaviour (such as civil service tenure systems) also heavily insulate existing permanent staff from being affected by budget fluctuations. Really large benefits from budget increments will be concentrated on marginal staff – those with no job security, people acting as consultants, spin-off staffs or those on part-time contracts. Certainly these groups have most to lose from budget reductions, and they are a significant (if largely unstudied) component. In the United States, where federal government employment has been subject to strict manpower limits set by Congress, minimum estimates suggest that an extra 5 to 25 per cent of staff are 'contracted in', that is, employed by federal agencies directly without ever showing up in official personnel returns (Bennett and Johnson, 1980, pp. 38–41). The wide range of variation here

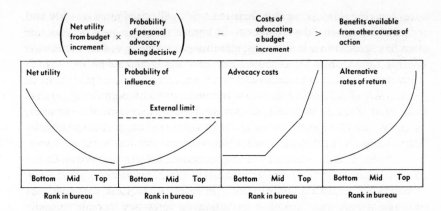

Figure 7.1 **The distribution of net utilities, influence probabilities, advocacy costs and alternative rates of return within a hypothetical bureau**

also reflects a hazy boundary with the much larger phenomenon of agencies' contracting out tasks to firms.

The probability that an individual's advocacy of a budget increment is decisive obviously increases dramatically with rank. Top-down, hierarchic forms of organization clearly imply that part-time, hived-off and bottom-rank officials have negligible individual impact upon their agency's policy, while the influence of middle ranks is not much more. Within policy-making ranks, however, the probability of influence rises sharply with seniority, reaching a threshold of maximum influence which is environmentally determined. In a super-favourable environment the combined probability of top officials in securing increases may approximate 1. But contrary to Niskanen's account, such a situation is very exceptional (Goodin, 1982a). In a hostile or turbulent environment, the agency's overall probability of success declines rapidly, and even the most influential official can have only a fraction of that chance to be decisive in getting a budget increment approved by the sponsor.

With the distribution of influence shown here, environmental conditions have a major impact upon how top bureaucrats discount their utility pay-offs from budget increments. Formal models of the interactions between bureaucracies and legislatures demonstrate exactly this relationship, suggesting that increases in the legislature's oversight activities can dramatically curb the ability of budget-maximizing bureaucrats to secure increments (Bendor and Moe, 1985, p. 772). But external changes hardly affect the attitudes of lower staffs, whose probable influence is small, even in a favourable environment. Top bureaucrats are also likely to be much better informed about shifting environmental conditions than

179

lower-ranking officials, so that their reactions will adapt more quickly and accurately to external developments. By contrast, bottom-rank bureaucrats often have anachronistic attitudes, remaining conservative in environments suitable for organizational growth, or carrying over established growth orientations into an era of cutbacks.

The costs of advocating a budget increment are also significantly rank-structured. Because bottom-rank personnel have little chance to influence bureau policy, their pursuit of collective gains from budget increments may be confined to supporting a labour-movement case for more spending. Beyond the middle ranks of the organization, greater opportunities for actively promoting budgetary expansion (over and above normal or technical incremental adjustments for inflation, etc.) mean that advocacy costs rise steeply with rank. For top officials a budgetary increase typically involves preparing special papers, attending difficult meetings, cultivating external allies and contacts, responding to sponsor criticisms or investigations and justifying the bureau's case in public. Empirical studies of budget-making show that most budget scrutiny, negotiations and controversy concentrates on marginal changes to a largely unanalyzed 'base budget' (Jackson, 1982, Chapter 5). So the advocacy costs of seeking increases on the base budget are substantial in senior ranks.

Alternative rates of return on individual welfare-boosting efforts will be much higher for senior officials (with multiple opportunities to better their positions) than for rank-and-file workers (for whom other options are foreclosed or ineffective). I also argue below that alternative collective strategies focusing on work-related utilities are more important to senior officials (see the final section of this chapter). On both counts, top bureaucrats require higher individual benefits before it is worthwhile to commit effort to budget-maximizing, while lower-ranked officials have fewer viable alternatives.

With utilities, influence probabilities, advocacy costs and alternatives patterned as in Figure 7.1, then bureaucrats will experience severe collective action problems in maximizing budgets, even though annual budgeting is a frequently reiterated game. Even if budget-maximization could benefit bureau members as a whole, officials will none the less free-ride on advocating increases, for different reasons. Bottom-rank bureaucrats gain most from budget increases, but they also know that they can make virtually no difference to the outcome individually. Hence even though their advocacy costs are small, and they have fewer welfare-boosting options to pursue, low-ranking officials with secure jobs are unlikely to find it worth their while to press for increased spending. By contrast, officials at the top of the bureau can significantly affect outcomes, but stand to gain least from budgetary expansion, confront high advocacy costs in exercising their influence and have more opportunity to boost their welfare in alternative ways. They are particularly unlikely to incur high advocacy costs in a hostile or turbulent environment where the agency's overall chance of success is low or unpredictable.

Of course, much will depend on the cardinal values assigned to the variables in the equation above. By itself this analysis cannot demonstrate that bureaucrats *necessarily* confront collective action problems in maximizing budgets. But fleshing out the equation with some intuitively realistic values and examples suggests that collective action problems will be the norm rather than the exception.

KEY CONCEPTS FOR ANALYZING BUDGETS AND AGENCIES

To claim that bureaucrats maximize budgets is unilluminating until we can know precisely *which* elements of agency expenditure rational officials seek to boost. Although this chapter deals with whole-agency budgetary changes rather than sectional budgets, important distinctions are still feasible within this focus. And differentiating types of (whole agency) budgets highlights the existence of very different kinds of agency, many of which do not conform with the line bureaucracy paradigm in existing public choice accounts.

Types of budget

An agency's *core budget* (CB) consists of those expenditures which are spent directly on its own operations (rather than going outside the agency in transfers, contracts or grants to other public sector bodies). The CB includes items such as salaries and personnel costs, equipment and material costs consumed directly in the agency's basic functions (such as office equipment or computers), and accommodation expenditures (such as rent for premises and recurrent capital spending on buildings). The concept is very similar to the definition of 'running costs' used in the UK central government (Thain and Wright, 1989), except that the CB also includes some capital spending on the agency's own operations.

The *bureau budget* (BB) includes all the core budget items above, plus any monies which the agency pays out to the private sector, for example by awarding contracts to private firms, or by making transfer payments to individuals or firms, or by directly paying interest on capital debts. In Western countries, most spending on construction and major equipment purchasing is included in the bureau budget, since these tasks are carried out under contract by private firms. The BB covers all expenditures which are directly controlled by the bureau's own decisions. So long as the funding stays inside the public sector (e.g. up to the point where contracts are let or transfers disbursed), policy implementation rests solely with the bureau's own staff. No separate or subordinate public sector organizations are involved in handling any part of the BB.

An agency's *program budget* (PB) includes its bureau budget, plus any monies which the agency passes on to other public sector bodies for them to spend. Thus the PB encompasses any expenditure for which the agency must account to the sponsor (and the courts), and over which it exercises some direct supervision – even if large parts of this total are passed on to other public sector agencies for final implementation. Inter-organizational transfers of this last kind can only be included in the agency's program budget total if it exercises some degree of hierarchical control over the ways in which the funding is spent.

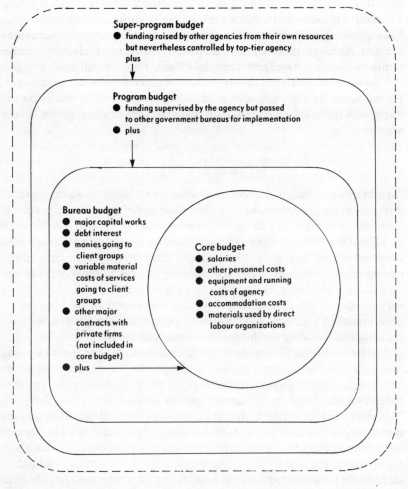

Figure 7.2 **Components of core, bureau, program and super-program budgets**

Finally, the *super-program budget* (SPB) consists of the agency's program budget plus any spending by other bureaus from their own resources, over which the agency none the less either exercises some policy responsibilities, or which it can limit or expand in planning terms, or for which it can wholly or partially claim political credit (and hence also incur political blame). This concept may well have no application in countries with a federal constitution, but is useful in analyzing centralized unitary states such as the United Kingdom.

These types of budget interrelate like Chinese boxes (Figure 7.2). The core budget is at the centre, enclosed by the larger bureau budget, which is in turn enclosed by the larger program budget. Each level has a different theoretical significance. The core budget is the agency's own activity spending; the bureau budget is the public spending over which it retains complete authority and control (before it reaches private sector firms or individuals); the program budget is the agency's total throughput of funding from the sponsor, including money channelled elsewhere in the public sector. For many agencies, the PB is the end of the story.

However, the super-program budget concept is necessary because in some countries top-tier agencies which make inter-governmental transfers to regional or local governments thereby acquire the ability to control large chunks of these lower-tier agencies' spending. Sometimes the existence of grant funding is used to justify legislation giving top-tier agencies extensive policy control or supervisory powers, which are especially strong in European countries like the United Kingdom, the Netherlands and Eire. Alternatively, with linked or matching grants, each unit of central government entitlement has to be paired with some locally sourced funding. These and other devices (such as formula-based grants) often mean that cuts or increases in top-tier agencies grants have multiplier effects on lower-tier governments' finances and behaviour.

Types of agency

The relative sizes of core, bureau and program budget levels fluctuate systematically across agencies, creating an important basis for distinguishing theoretically based agency types. In deciding what is to count as an 'agency', it is normally necessary to decompose officially unified organizations into components consisting of the different agency types set out below, which are themselves functionally defined.

Delivery agencies are the classic line bureaucracies of Weberian theory and economic analyses. They directly produce outputs or deliver services to citizens or enterprises, using their own personnel to carry out most policy implementation. Employees no doubt often work in complex networks of sub-bureaus. But there is a clear line of authority or responsibility from top bureau officials to those at the grass roots. Delivery agency functions are usually labour-intensive. Consequently they tend to have large budgets in relation to their functions. And their core budgets absorb a high proportion of their bureau and program budgets, mostly on staffing costs. Delivery agencies tend not to have significant relationships with subordinate public sector bodies, so that there is no super-program budget increment over and above the program budget. Picturing the stylized interrelationships between types of budgets as in Figure 7.3, both the core budget and the bureau budget rise steadily with program budget increases, with the CB absorbing the great preponderance of the PB. A good example of a delivery agency in the US federal government is the health services wing of the Department of Veterans' Affairs, which employs 200,000 staff, and spends 91 per cent of its $10 billion budget (in 1988) on its own operations. A smaller-scale example is the National Parks Service (in the Department of the Interior) which employs 16,500 staff, and spends 83 per cent of its $1 billion budget on running costs.

Regulatory agencies have the same CB/BB and BB/PB curves as delivery agencies, but much smaller budgets. Regulatory agencies' key tasks are to limit or control the behaviour of individuals, enterprises or other bodies, using licensing systems, reporting controls, performance standards or some similar system. All these devices externalize many of the costs onto the people being regulated, so regulatory agencies appear relatively cheap to run in tax-funding or public expenditure terms. Because regulatory agencies are primarily paper-moving and inspecting organizations, their core budgets absorb a high proportion of their bureau and program budgets. However, if subsidies are used as secondary elements to back up regulations, the bureau budget may differ somewhat from the CB. Because they externalize compliance costs, regulatory agencies employ far fewer staff than delivery agencies, and their program budgets are much smaller. Again, there is no super-program budget increment. A good US example is the Food Safety and Inspection Service (in the the Department of Agriculture) which employs just over 9,000 staff, and spends 87 per cent of its $390 million budget (in 1988) on administrative costs.

Transfer agencies handle payments of some form of subsidy or entitlement by government to private individuals or firms. They are above all money-moving organizations. Since subsidy payments are easily systematized within centrally administered administrations, all national governments are likely to have at least one transfer agency with a large staff. None the less the administration costs of transfer payments are small in relation to the subsidies paid out, so that the core budget should absorb a very low proportion of the bureau budget. Transfer agencies do not usually pass on much money to other public sector bodies, unless a decentralized implementing tier is required for a particular benefit. (If such intermediating bodies are used very extensively to carry out direct service implementation, then the top-tier bureau will be reclassified in my schema as a control agency

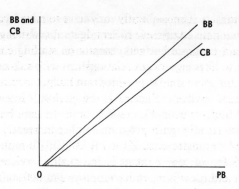

Figure 7.3 **How budgets change in delivery and regulatory agencies**

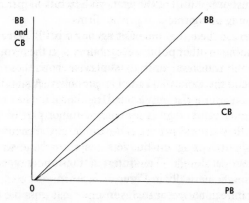

Figure 7.4 **How budgets change in transfer and contract agencies**

– see below.) So the bureau budget usually absorbs almost all of a transfer agency's program budget. The interrelationship of the core, bureau and program budgets to be expected on theoretical grounds is shown in Figure 7.4. Here, unlike delivery or regulatory agencies, the core budget does not keep on expanding with the program budget. Once a basic administrative apparatus is in place, sizeable BB and PB increases may have no impact on running costs. For example, an agency paying out public pensions could simply inscribe larger values on the cheques it mails to the elderly, without its core budget changing at all. The benefits wing of the US Department of Veterans' Affairs is a good example, employing nearly 19,000 staff, with administrative costs of $840 million, which none the less amount to only 4 per cent of its program budget of nearly $20 billion (in 1988).

Contracts agencies are concerned with developing service specifications or capital projects for tendering, and then letting contracts to private sector firms (or to commercially-run public sector organizations, such as public corporations). Contracts agencies' staff work on research and development into projects, drawing up equipment or service specifications, liaising with companies, contract management and compliance, etc. The actual implementation of the projects or services, the ordering of plant and materials, the employment of most of the staff needed and the production of physical outputs are all carried out by contractors. Consequently, contracts agencies' core budgets typically absorb only a modest share of their bureau budget (following the pattern of Figure 7.4), although considerably more than would be the case for transfer agencies. A typical CB/PB ratio is 20–30 per cent. Bureau budgets, of course, absorb almost all of contracts agencies' program budgets, and there is again no super-program budget increment. The US space agency NASA is a good example. Its 22,000 staff carry out research and development and prepare contracts for space projects, at a cost of $2.2 billion, just over a fifth of the agency's $10 billion program budget, the remainder going in contracts to private firms.

Control agencies are the last of the basic agency types. Their primary task is to channel funding to other public sector bureaus in the form of grants or inter-governmental transfers, and to supervise how these other state organizations spend the money and implement policy. Again, the administrative costs involved comprise only a small fraction of the sums transferred, but this time the bureau budget is also only a minor part of the program budget. Because they often supervise sub-national governments or bureaus, control agencies' super-program budgets can show large-scale increases over program budget levels. The interrelationship of control agency budgets is shown schematically in Figure 7.5. As in the previous diagram, once a basic organizational apparatus is in place it is possible for large PB increases to take place without affecting the core budget. But since grants to other public sector bodies are also excluded from the bureau budget, the BB line, too, remains flat. Finally, a super-program budget line growing faster than the 45 degree angle is sketched in, indicating that in some countries the provision of central funding confers leverage over subordinate agencies' spending from all sources. A good American example of a control agency (but with no super-program budget) is the Federal Highways Administration (in the Department of Transport), which employs just 3,400 staff, at a cost of $194 million, but pays out grants and subsidies for national highways totalling $13 billion, chiefly to the state governments. The FHA's core budget absorbs just 1.5 per cent of its program budget.

In addition to these basic types, some additional categories need to be included to achieve comprehensive coverage. *Taxing agencies* raise government finances. They closely resemble regulatory agencies in externalizing administrative costs onto individuals, enterprises or other bureaus, and in being labour-intensive, paper-moving organizations. Their administration costs tend to be small in relation to the yield of taxes gathered. However,

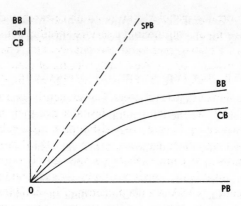

Figure 7.5 **How budgets change in control agencies**

taxing agencies are much larger in staffing and core budget terms for a number of reasons. In Western Europe, governments have used fewer and more general taxes, such as simplified income taxes or value-added tax, concentrating personnel into one or two major taxing organizations (Rose and Karran, 1988; Rose, 1981, pp. 94–127). In all liberal democracies subsidy systems have been extensively integrated into the tax collection apparatus, with tax expenditures seen as a politically acceptable substitute for public spending in areas such as home ownership, occupational pensions, company cars or private health insurance. So taxing agencies have gained a stake in many different policy areas. In the US federal government the Internal Revenue Service employs 113,000 staff and has a program budget of $9.5 billion (in 1988), of which some $5 billion is in the core budget (virtually all the rest is repayment of over-collected taxes).

Trading agencies were defined for the UK central government analysis as full governmental bodies (that is, excluding public corporations with their own intermediating board from the scope of the central state). In other contexts a broader definition might be more appropriate. These agencies operate directly in economic markets in a fully or quasi-commercial mode, and when they deliver service to other public sector bodies they do so on a full recharging basis. Trading agencies normally do a single job, without other policy responsibilities. Good US examples are the various Power Marketing Administrations (in the Department of Energy) which distribute electricity generated from government-built hydro-electric schemes to utilities and other customers in the south-west United States.

Servicing agencies are very similar in function, providing services or facilities to other government bodies, sometimes on a recharged basis but with no private sector customers, or else on a non-priced basis where their outputs are seen as collective benefits for a set of agencies or a whole tier of government. The General Services Agency which manages land acquisitions and property for the US federal government is an example.

Agency types: empirical evidence

This theoretical analysis has been empirically operationalized in a detailed study – still ongoing – of the US federal budget, in which 205 analytically separate government agencies have been identified (including the examples of each agency type mentioned above). However, since these data are still undergoing analysis at the time of writing, the rest of this section draws instead on a completed study of the British central state (Dunleavy, 1989a and 1989b). Preliminary analysis of the US data suggests that they closely follow the patterns in the UK data.

To what extent are the theoretical expectations about agency types set out above borne out in practice by the British data? Table 7.1 shows that seventy-six analytically separate central state agencies were identified, more than a third of which were either pure delivery agencies or mixed types predominantly carrying out delivery functions. This group accounted for 63 per cent of the overall central state core budget (which was £19,000 million in 1987–8) and 64 per cent of staffing (1.02 million in 1987–8). The second most numerous single type were control agencies, a fifth of the total agencies but accounting for only one-twentieth of total staffing or core budgets. Transfer agencies and contract agencies both predominantly direct funding to the

Table 7.1 *Agency types in the UK central state, 1987–8*

Type of bureau	Number of agencies	Total core budgets (£m)	Total staffing
Delivery agencies	22	10,810	591,400
Delivery/transfer	5	1,050	54,410
Delivery/control	1	210	9,910
Delivery/DT group	28	*12,070*	*655,720*
Transfer agencies	8	2,200	126,530
Contracts agencies	4	1,000	45,990
Transfer/contracts group	12	*3,200*	*172,520*
Regulatory agencies	7	540	26,560
Trading agencies	7	735	25,810
Servicing agencies	5	185	6,770
Taxing agencies	2	1,290	84,050
Miscellaneous group	21	*2,750*	*143,190*
Control agencies	15	990	45,420
Total central state	76	*19,000*	*1,016,830*

Source: Dunleavy, 1989a and 1989b.

Table 7.2 *Average budget levels by agency type, UK central state, 1987–8*

Type of budget (£ million)	Control	Type of agency		Miscellaneous
		Transfer/ contract	Delivery/ DT	
(a) Exploratory statistics: medians (midspreads)				
Core budget	49	39	104	50
	(98)	(118)	(405)	(117)
Bureau budget	317	1,110	211	52
	(306)	(1,133)	(856)	(147)
Program budget	2,363	1,277	211	52
	(3,059)	(6,325)	(884)	(147)
Super-program budget	3,990	1,277	211	52
	(7,101)	(6,325)	(884)	(147)
(b) Confirmatory statistics: means (standard deviations)				
Core budget	66	267	431	131
	(56)	(581)	(759)	(227)
Bureau budget	264	4,948	910	153
	(182)	(11,959)	(1,528)	(274)
Program budget	3,142	6,229	947	153
	(3,900)	(13,416)	(1,541)	(274)
Super-program budget	5,316	6,229	960	153
	(5,681)	(13,538)	(1,539)	(274)

Source: Dunleavy, 1989b, p. 407. These figures correct two small errata in the originally published table.

private sector: this group accounted for just over a sixth of all agencies and a similar proportion of staffing and core budgets. The remaining agency types (regulatory, trading, servicing and taxing agencies) are grouped into a miscellaneous category accounting for over a quarter of all agencies, but only around a seventh of total staffing and core budgets.

Because of double-counting problems it is not possible to aggregate figures for bureau, program or super-program budgets. However, it is feasible to look at the average size of these budgets across the different agency types. Because some of the types have only a few agencies in them I present the data for four larger groups used in Table 7.1, namely control agencies; delivery plus DT agencies; transfer and contract agencies; and the miscellaneous group. A final problem is that summary statistics for agency types in the UK central state can be a bit misleading because a few very large bureaus distort means and standard deviations: to counteract this problem Table 7.2 includes an additional sub-table using more robust exploratory statistics, the median and midspread.

Table 7.2 shows clearly that the patterns which apply to core budgets are not the same as those which apply to more inclusive levels of budget. The budgets for miscellaneous agencies show the least change of any agency type when moving from the core budget to the bureau budget level, and do not shift at all at the program and super-program levels. On average, miscellaneous agencies are consistently the smallest of all the types. Delivery agencies by contrast are much the largest agencies at the core budget level, reflecting the fact that their staffing levels are on average twice as large as any other type of agency. Delivery agency budgets also double at the bureau budget level, but thereafter they scarcely increase at the program and super-program levels. Transfer/contract agencies have fairly small core budgets on average. But as their payments or contracts to the private sector are included at the bureau budget level, transfer/contract agencies become the largest of any type. Because some agencies in this group have secondary functions of paying grants to other public bodies their program budget average is somewhat higher, but the super-program budget is unchanged. Finally, control agencies have the smallest mean core budgets, and their bureau budgets show a marked increase. But control agencies' key function of grant-giving to other public sector organizations means that their program budget levels record a massive increase. In fact, at this level the median control agency is bigger than any other type (although the presence of one very large social security agency in the transfer/contracts group keeps their mean program budget level above control agencies). Control agencies in Britain also show a sizeable increase at the level of super-program budgets. In terms of program and super-program budgets, control agencies are considerably more bunched, and hence much more uniformly large-scale, than any other type of central state organization.

To see how effectively the UK central state data confirm the theoretical analysis of agency types, Table 7.3 shows average percentage ratios for the control budget/program budget (PB), the bureau budget/PB and the super-program budget/PB. The core budget/PB ratios are smallest among control agencies, which also have far and away the lowest bureau budget/PB ratios, and the only super-program budget/PB ratios significantly over 100 per cent. Thus these agencies exactly match the theoretical types described above. The transfer/contracts group has the next lowest CB/PB ratios but their bureau budgets account for virtually the whole program budget: again, the fit with the model description is exact. The miscellaneous group also fits closely with the theoretical pattern, since their CB, BB and PB figures are more or less identical.

The one group of agencies to deviate empirically from the theoretical description turned out to be the delivery/DT group where a number of core budget/program budget ratios were somewhat lower than predicted – in the 50–60 per cent range instead of (say) 80–90 per cent. Three factors account for this small discrepancy (Dunleavy, 1989b, pp. 392–3) – the inclusion of

Table 7.3   *Average percentage ratios for core, bureau and super-program budgets divided by program budgets, across agency types*

% of program budget	Control	Type of agency		Miscellaneous
		Transfer/ contracts	Delivery/ DT	
Medians				
Core budget	2.1	5.2	60	98
Bureau budget	10.8	100	100	100
Super-program budget	126	100	100	100
Means				
Core budget	3.0	6.8	62	87
Bureau budget	11.1	91	95	100
Super-program budget	160	100	101	100

Source: as Table 7.2.

some mixed delivery/transfer agencies, where existing official statistics did not allow a clearer analytic separation of agency functions; technical problems in attributing major equipment costs in the armed forces between core and bureau budgets; and some similar problems with the greater than expected numbers of smaller delivery agencies uncovered. However, delivery agencies remain quite distinct from the control or transfer/contracts agency groups in their configuration, and in all other respects fit the model closely. Overall, the analytic features predicted for different agency types show up extremely well in Tables 7.2 and 7.3.

THE CONDITIONS FOR BUDGET-MAXIMIZING

Whether officials want to maximize their budgets can vary in three main ways: depending on their rank and the type of budget; on the type of agency involved; and on variations over time. The last part of the section sums up the arguments about variations by showing how bureaucrats' optimal program budget levels are determined.

Variations with type of budget

The personal utilities of bureau members are unlikely to be equally involved in the expansion of different elements of the overall budget. Table 7.4 shows a rough-and-ready list of the reasons why public choice writers have seen budget-maximization as improving bureaucrats' welfare. The

191

Table 7.4   *Welfare gains for bureaucrats from budget-maximization*

Type of welfare gain	Associated budget	Salience for ranks		
		Bottom	Middle	Top
Improving job security	CB	++	+	0
Expanding career prospects	CB	+	++	0
Increased demand for skills and labour	CB	+	++	0
Triggering upward regrading	CB	0	++	+
Reducing conflict in bureau management	CB	0	+	++
Boosting bureau prestige	BB	0	+	++
Improved relations with clients or contractors	BB	0	+	++
'Slack' creation to cope in crises	BB/PB	0	+	++
Increased patronage powers	PB	0	0	++

Key: ++ = high salience;   + = medium salience;
    0 = low salience;   CB = core budget;
    BB = bureau budget; PB = program budget.

first section of this chapter strongly suggested that the salience of different utility considerations will vary considerably for top, middle and low-rank bureaucrats.

The most basic individual utility gains from budget increases, and those which are most important for bottom- and middle-ranking officials, are all associated with the core budget. By contrast, the more diffuse utility gains from budgetary expansion, and those which are most important for top-ranking officials, are primarily linked to the bureau budget. In this group of pay-offs only facilitating non-conflictual management of the bureau can be regarded as associated primarily with the core budget. And only an agency's patronage power is positively and directly associated with the expansion of the program budget. An enlarged program budget allows top managers to build up slack resources, which can be deployed to cope with sudden crises or calls for action. But since most of the program budget may have to be passed on to other agencies, top officials gain maximum flexibility from retaining any slack in the bureau budget under their own direct control.

Turning to the costs of advocating budgetary expansion (note that these are not the drawbacks of budgetary growth itself, but of advocating it), an important asymmetry becomes apparent. While the benefits of budgetary expansion are associated mainly with the core budget or the bureau budget, the costs of advocacy (in terms of time spent, effort and resources required, increased scrutiny by the sponsor and the public, and level of external criticism received) are all likely to be closely associated with the program budget. It is on program budget performance that sponsor bodies and citizens in general base their judgements about the overall funding levels

192

appropriate in particular policy areas. Within a given level of environmental hostility, a rise in that part of an agency's program budget flowing outside the agency tends to squeeze its chances of achieving core budget increases. Similarly, both core and bureau budget increases will be more difficult if funds flow to expanding subordinate public sector bureaus.

Variations with type of agency

To the extent that rational bureaucrats are primarily concerned to maximize their core budget and perhaps their bureau budget, this incentive will be strongest in organizations where there is a close relationship between core, bureau and program budgets. Delivery agencies are the largest budget organizations which fit this pattern, and here the welfare of both senior and lower-ranking officials seems to be the most closely tied to program budget increases. The same pattern of CB/BB/PB ratios holds for regulatory agencies; but they are much smaller bodies and officials may make utility gains by externalizing costs as well as pushing up budgets. Taxing agencies are large and spend most of their money on their own operations. Budget-maximizing pressures may also be present here, especially where revenue yields are high *vis-à-vis* administrative costs – although environmental hostility (and hence scrutiny by critics in the legislature) is also high in most Western countries. Trading and service agencies also have core, bureau and program budgets which are similar. However, market opportunities and competitive pressures (from other suppliers, or from other goods) normally inhibit trading agencies' expansion, together with requirements to break even or make a given financial return. Servicing agencies are fairly small and their growth is constrained because demand for their services depends on other agencies.

In some kinds of contracts and transfer agencies, self-interested senior officials may also have a strong incentive to maximize their bureau budgets. These agencies' core budgets account for only a fraction of the program budget, so that lower-level staffs have little reason to seek PB expansion. However, senior managers may be able to derive large welfare gains from pushing up the bureau budget (here almost identical with the PB), so long as certain conditions are met. These include:

- the scale of single decisions about contracts or transfers must be large;
- final decisions about the allocation of funding must be one-off and discretionary in character, and made at top levels – rather than routinized, rule-bound, or formula-based, and made at grass roots level;
- the recipients of contracts or transfers must be a relatively few, large organizations – such as big corporations or meso-corporatist interest groupings or lobbies;
- these recipients must be able to organize a flowback of benefits in return for officials' exercising patronage on their behalf.

193

For example, officials in procurement agencies like the Pentagon or NASA have strong reasons to maximize their bureau budgets, since defence and other contracts often confer considerable patronage potential. There are many opportunities for corporations involved in tendering to organize substantial reciprocal benefits for official contacts who are helpful: benefits such as side deals which help win promotion, or yield lucrative opportunities for what the French call *pantouflage*; career moves into the corporate sector for the still vigorous managers; or post-retirement directorships for older individuals. Where transfer agencies are dealing with very well-organized corporate 'clients', such as the powerful farmers' organizations and food-manufacturing interests in most liberal democracies, the same sort of incentives apply for top officials. In these circumstances, it could be rational for bureaucrats to push up bureau budgets, even though the extra monies involved mainly flow outside the agency in question.

However, for all control agencies, and for the remaining contracts and transfer agencies dealing with multiple, fragmented 'clients' (for example, small firms in a highly competitive industry, or recipients of state welfare benefits), no such incentives apply. These agencies' core budgets are only a small fraction of the program budget, and no significant flowback of benefits will follow for senior officials if the bureau or program budgets are inflated. For example, the Department of Education in the US federal government and the Department of Education and Science in Britain both spend less than 2 per cent of the total budget they control on their own activities. Hence it is highly unlikely in public choice terms that self-interested officials would constantly seek program budget increases. No rational actor in policy-level ranks would seem to have much reason to push for increases in funding (still less Niskanen's oversupply levels of funding), when the monies concerned are almost all passed on to low-status or disorganized private sector recipients, or are channelled to other public sector agencies. To take another example, why should policy-level staff at a welfare agency want to push up payments to the unemployed or to old-age pensioners? Rational managers in top-tier agencies have even less reason to care about whether the super-program budget spent by lower-tier agencies in their policy area increases or declines. To worry about such totals, central officials would have to make a fetish out of a particular budgetary aggregate, or be mission-committed, or be afflicted by some form of altruism – all motivations which need to be excluded from any useful public choice model. Indeed, for officials in these types of agency, program or bureau budget increases may be a liability. Since costs attach to the program budget, but benefits to the core or bureau budgets, overall funding boosts can substantially raise environmental hostility while carrying no significant utility gains for top managers. Control agencies in particular may become even more dependent upon subordinate agencies' performance if program budgets grow.

Variations over time

So far I have assumed that the relationship between core, bureau and program budgets is fairly constant, after an initial phase of bureau-consolidating growth. But for any substantial agency there may be a limit beyond which it cannot expand without becoming too unwieldy or unmanageable. Common constraints include:

- the funnelling of management into political-administrative bottlenecks, especially representative institutions with finite capabilities and size;
- the spreading of top management and political attention over too wide an area, and too thinly;
- the accumulation of inertia in very large departments.

For example, in British central government problems of limited ministerial time, finite spans of control and giganticism have repeatedly led to the splitting of departments and the failure of experiments such as 'super-ministries' in the post-war period (Pollitt, 1983; Kellner and Crowther-Hunt, 1980, pp. 174–238).

A large agency coming up against such constraints and pushing for further growth can trigger a period in which it loses some of its existing functions to other (rival) agencies. At the central government level, such rivals could be other departments which acquire slices of territory, or they could be quasi-government agencies set up to hive-off less salient functions. Either threat could produce a zig-zag growth curve for the core and bureau budgets graphed against the program budget (Figure 7.6). With this sort of curve, rational budget-maximizing officials in senior positions should not advocate program budget increases when the bureau's growth has brought it within the danger area – shaded in Figure 7.6. To do so could produce a

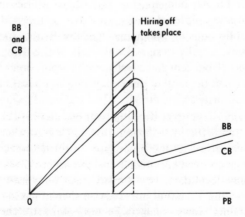

Figure 7.6 **Zig-zag bureau budget curves**

195

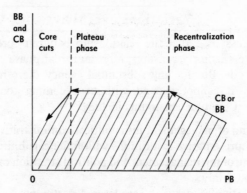

Figure 7.7 **How recentralization cutbacks can expand core or bureau budgets**

quantum reduction in the core and bureau budgets to which their utilities are most linked. Zig-zag core and bureau budget curves are most likely to occur in delivery agencies, plus those contracts, transfer and taxing agencies with large staffs.

The relationship between core, bureau and program budgets also raises some interesting issues when contracts or control agencies enter a period of *declining budgets*. Dwindling program budgets can be associated with a period of rising core and bureau budgets as the control agency re-centralizes powers or functions from subordinate agencies, or as the contract agency brings back in-house functions it has previously sent to outside professionals (Figure 7.7). After a while, the re-centralization phase might be followed by cutbacks striking home within the central department itself. But there may well be extensive periods when officials in contract or control agencies welcome cutbacks in the program budget as a means of increasing or stabilizing their bureau budgets, to which their utilities are linked. For example, Dunleavy (1981a) demonstrates that in the mid-1960s, at the height of a public housing boom managed by British local authorities, council architects actually designed only half of the dwellings involved, private architects 30 per cent and construction corporation architects 20 per cent. By 1973, when the level of public housing starts was half its previous size, the local authority architects' share had increased to 75 per cent. What this meant for one large city, Birmingham, was that in the mid-1960s its architects designed virtually no housing at all – their role was limited solely to contract drafting and supervision, plus minor landscape architecture. Ten years later the council architects had regained full design control of most of their housing output. This kind of effect will exist wherever public agency staffing does not expand fully to accommodate workloads in 'boom' periods, so that the character of agencies' work tasks stretches to absorb the variation – even in delivery agencies which use consultants or contractors.

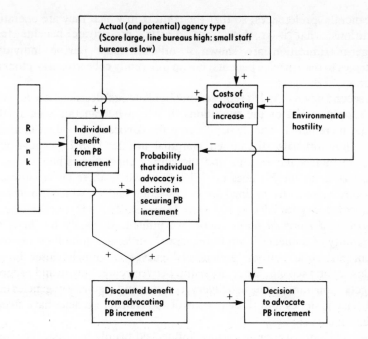

Note: All variables except rank are subjectively perceived.

Figure 7.8 **Influences on whether bureaucrats budget-maximize**

Staff utilities at all levels in the agency may rise quite sharply in periods of limited budgetary reductions when workloads are reinternalized.

Bureaucrats' optimal budget levels

Thus there are multiple reasons why self-interested officials vary greatly in the extent to which they push up expenditures, so that Niskanen's picture of bureaucrats as open-ended budget-maximizers is highly unlikely to be accurate. Summing up the previous discussion, there are two ways of picturing how senior officials make budget decisions. The first is a diagram of the influences upon an individual bureaucrat analogous to those already given for potential interest group members and for voters (Figure 7.8). An obvious difference from earlier diagrams is the importance of rank inside bureaucracies. Rank conditions the undiscounted benefits that officials receive from program budget increments, their individual influence assessments and their costs of advocating budgetary growth. In addition the type of agency determines what stake senior officials have in program budget increases, and to a lesser degree the advocacy costs which they confront. Both these influences have the effect of endogenizing senior bureaucrats' preferences, so that the context in which they are operating conditions what it is they want. Lastly, no private benefits from budget-maximization are shown – officials must pursue individual strategies to reap private benefits, not an inherently collective effort to push up program budgets.

A second key method of representing bureaucrats' decisions is a demand-and-supply model of the conditions in which bureaucrats seek further budget increments. The demand curve for advocacy of budget increases shows how officials' discounted marginal utilities (DMU) change with program budget increments; and the supply curve shows how advocacy costs change as the PB goes up. The point where these curves intersect indicates bureaucrats' optimal level of program budget, which is internally determined (Figure 7.9).

Discounted marginal utility curves are influenced mainly by: first, the probability of influence – top bureaucrats' curves are quite far away from the origin while bottom bureaucrats' curves are much closer in and shallower; and second, the relationship between core, bureau and program budgets – top bureaucrats in delivery, contract and regulatory agencies have fairly elastic slopes, but those in control and transfer agencies have steeply declining curves.

Marginal advocacy cost curves are influenced mainly by: first, the size of the existing PB, set against the sorts of functions which the agency is carrying out, since with constant functions successive budgetary increments become progressively more costly to obtain; second, external hostility to an agency getting a PB increment – at the point where an agency is unlikely to get a further increase however hard it pushes, the cost curve becomes vertical (for top bureaucrats especially); third, changes in external hostility – if it increases or decreases then the cost curve shifts up to the right or down to the left respectively; fourth, alternative rates of return – since marginal advocacy costs are net costs, they take account of other welfare-boosting options, which are extensive for top bureaucrats; and fifth, rank – cost curves are higher and rise more steeply the further up the rank hierarchy officials are located.

In these graphs bureaucrats advocate expansion in the agency's activities if its current program budget is to the left of their equilibrium PB position. But if the bureau's current position is to the right of the equilibrium, officials do nothing, switching attention instead to other individual or collective strategies for improving their welfare. Note that the alternative to budget maximization is inaction, not advocacy of budgetary reductions.

Because of the varying shapes of the discounted marginal utility and marginal cost curves, changes in the external environment have different impacts upon bureaucratic behaviour. For senior bureaucrats in delivery, contract or regulatory agencies a shift of cost curves to the left triggers large decreases in the equilibrium level of PB, since increased external hostility

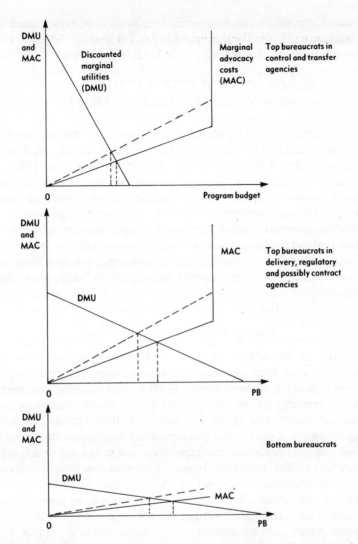

Figure 7.9 **The choice problem for bureaucrats in deciding whether to advocate budgetary increases**

produces sharp adjustments of the cost curve back along a utility curve that slopes fairly gently. But in control or transfer agencies at the same rank a large-scale adjustment in the marginal advocacy cost curve may not affect bureaucratic behaviour much because their DMU curve is already so inelastic. For bottom bureaucrats the same external shifts which manifest themselves as marked changes in the top bureaucrats' cost curves will produce only small increases in the shallow slope of cost curves. But since their discounted utility curves typically are also shallow, even a small shift may produce a sharp fall in their equilibrium PB level.

BUREAUCRATS' MOTIVATIONS AND BUREAU-SHAPING STRATEGIES

The bureaucratic empire-builder is not an off-beat theoretical construct, but also an important everyday image of government officials, especially in the United States (Lineberry, 1989, Chapter 15; Kaufman, 1981). To define an alternative model of what bureaucrats want therefore entails uncovering a more plausible set of official objectives, one which can explain observed behaviour with more precision or over a wider range of situations than the budget-maximization hypothesis. This section develops such an account, the bureau-shaping model. I explore bureaucrats' motivations; the collective strategies which facilitate bureau-shaping; and how differently situated officials choose between bureau-shaping or budget-maximizing strategies.

Motives for bureau-shaping

Welfare-maximizing officials in policy-making ranks are primarily concerned to improve their welfare by providing themselves with congenial work and a valued work environment for three main reasons. First, there is a general presumption in the existing public choice literature, most organization theory and in the first section of this chapter, that senior managers put less stress than lower-ranking bureau members on the pecuniary or near-pecuniary components of their utility function (such as income, job security, or perks). Instead, higher-ranked bureaucrats place more emphasis upon non-pecuniary utilities: such as status, prestige, patronage and influence, and most especially the interest and importance of their work tasks (Halperin, 1974; Kingdon, 1984).

Second, public service employment systems are designed to place severe limits on officials' ability to increase their pecuniary utilities by either individual or collective action, whether budget-maximization strategies or the discretionary ability to divert resources to personal welfare-boosting. Salaries are constrained within restrictive and standardized upper salary ceilings. In Sweden, West Germany and the United Kingdom the ratio between top civil service salaries and the wages of bottom-rank government employees consistently declined from 1950 to 1980, when the three countries' figures were 6.0, 4.3 and 5.5 respectively (Peters, 1989b, pp. 41–4). Hence there is no public sector counterpart to the very large and individualized 'prizes' paid out as salaries to key executives in private corporations. Similarly, blanket limits on staff numbers, centralized audit systems, and lifetime career paths to senior positions, are all common features of public service employment systems which tend to reduce officials' ability to pursue their individual interests in pecuniary terms. In addition, public sector perks are strictly controlled, with very few company cars or fringe benefits, strict rules against officials having additional employment or business activities, standardized provision of accommodation and equipment, and scarce support of secretarial staff rationed out by across-the-board formulae. In most public administration systems personnel, accommodation, finance and information technology are centrally administered to minimize the creation of slack by individual managers. Only recently have such patterns begun to be eroded by 'cost centre' budgeting imported from the private sector.

Compared with their counterparts in private companies, senior government officials are likely to find that budget-maximization is a remarkably frustrating activity in terms of direct near-pecuniary utility pay-offs. The distinctive traits of public service systems are designed to displace senior officials' energies and efforts into work and policy-related aspects of their careers rather than into feathering personal nests. Senior officials' pay and conditions are normally maintained at levels sufficient to preserve their pre-existing position in the occupational class structure. But they are also calculated to sift out from promotion people anxious to maximize pecuniary utilities. Thus a realistic individual-level model of why people enter career paths leading to senior positions in public agencies, or of why people temporarily transfer into such positions from the private sector in the United States, is likely to emphasize non-pecuniary utilities related to the intrinsic characteristics of the work involved.

Third, work-related utilities seem to be a major continuing influence on the ways in which officials behave within the public sector. Without positing an other-regarding or ideological commitment by officials to their bureau or its mission, a good deal of evidence suggests that self-interested officials have strong preferences about the kind of work they want to do, and the kind of agency they want to work in. Table 7.5 gives a list of the most common pro and anti values cited in the administrative sociology literature, and which can plausibly be ascribed to self-regarding bureaucrats pursuing their own welfare.

Clearly, there is always a pecuniary parameter in bureaucrats' concerns – a level of income and of near-money benefits which they will seek to achieve as a condition of the pursuit of other utilities. But this is likely to be a constraint which is surmounted relatively easily and thereafter is not very influential positively or negatively in structuring individual behaviour, especially when officials are making policy decisions. Officials are certainly not likely to be trying to maximize pecuniary elements of their utilities. There will be sharp differences in the perceived welfare of officials who share comparable salaries but are located in different agencies and

Table 7.5   *Positive and negative values ascribable to bureaucrats*

Positively valued	Negatively valued
Staff functions	*Line functions*
• individually innovative work	• routine work
• longer-time horizons	• short-time horizons
• broad scope of concerns	• narrow scope of concerns
• developmental rhythm	• repetitive rhythm
• high level of managerial discretion	• low level of managerial discretion
• low level of public visibility	• high level of grass roots/public visibility
Collegial atmosphere	*Corporate atmosphere*
• small-sized work unit	• large-sized work units
• restricted hierarchy and predominance of élite personnel	• extended hierarchy and predominance of non-élite personnel
• co-operative work patterns	• work patterns characterized by coercion and resistance
• congenial personal relations	• conflictual personal relations
Central location	*Peripheral location*
• proximate to the political power centres	• remote from political contacts
• metropolitan (capital city location)	• provincial location
• conferring high-status social contacts	• remote from high-status contacts

positions. Rational officials want to work in small, élite, collegial bureaus close to political power centres. They do not want to head up heavily staffed, large budget but routine, conflictual and low-status agencies.

Collective strategies for bureau-shaping

If officials have the values posited in Table 7.5, they can most effectively pursue these objectives at an individual level, searching for career or promotion paths which lead them to an appropriate rank in a suitable sort of agency – just as I argued in the first section that officials pursuing pecuniary utilities can best do so using individual means, rather than relying on collective budget increments.

None the less, once individual opportunities are exhausted or show diminishing returns, or in addition to them, are there collective strategies (akin to budget-maximization) by which bureaucrats can foster their work-related utilities? And can these strategies be continuously developed – as with budget-maximization because of the annual budgetary cycle? I argue that rational bureaucrats oriented primarily to work-related utilities pursue a *bureau-shaping* strategy designed to bring their bureau into a progressively closer approximation to 'staff' (rather than 'line') functions, a collegial atmosphere and a central location. Essentially, these pro-values imply that national-level delivery agencies in particular become transformed over time into control, transfer or contracts agencies. Policy-level officials maximize this objective within a continuous bureau budget constraint, but one which varies systematically with the character and size of the agency. At each stage of the process, senior officials seek to achieve a satisfactory level of budget, but this level in turn is set by their previous success in restructuring the bureau's tasks and organization. As a reshaped bureau takes on more of the small, central, élite character – becomes more of a control, transfer or contracts agency – then the budget constraint is eased. Senior officials' utilities become progressively unlinked from dependence on a high absolute level of program or bureau budget.

There are five key means of pursuing bureau-shaping strategies.

1. *Major internal reorganizations.* Changes in structure can regularly increase the degree to which an agency conforms with the élite policy-making ideal. Expansion is concentrated at the policy-making level, while existing routine functions are shunted into well-defined enclaves which need to be involved as little as possible with senior management. Often geographical separation is a key means of achieving this result, especially where it saves costs or fits with regional policy objectives. Other current functions inconsistent with the bureau's ideal image may be 'hived-in' to separately designated departmental agencies or accountable management units.

2. *Transformation of internal work practices.* Policy-level officials want to increase the interest of their work tasks, lengthen the time horizons used in decision-making and extend their discretionary ability to control policy. A shift towards more sophisticated management and policy analysis systems insulates the agency from criticism by rival bureaus, external partners or the sponsor body. It also tends to change the balance of bureau personnel towards more high-level, skilled or professional staffs, improving existing bureau members' status and work content, as well as their career advancement prospects.

If personnel ceilings are being enforced then the automation or computerization of clerical tasks can free manpower quotas to be redeployed at policy-making levels (for instance, by hiring in more policy analysts). In many public service systems restrictive personnel limits are placed on whole groups of agencies by political fiat. Congress has long imposed rigid manpower ceilings on the US federal government departments. In Britain the incoming Conservative government froze civil service manpower in 1979, and then programmed manpower targets reduced by 15 per cent over five years (Fry, 1986, p. 102; Dunsire and Hood, 1989, pp. 17–19). Where such constraints apply, a pre-condition for regrading changes may be the contracting out, reduction, computerization or automation of routine work tasks so that the staffing allocations involved can be redeployed in ways which confer more fruitful pay-offs for senior officials. Bureau policy staffs also tend to promote more accountable management for routine enclave areas or lower-level staffs, but emphasize collegial decision-making, 'team production' methods and hence diffused responsibility amongst policy-rank officials.

3. *Redefinition of relationships with external 'partners'.* Where agencies deal extensively with external organizations – such as subordinate public agencies, contractors, regulatees or client interest group – these relationships can be readjusted so as to cut down on routine workloads while maximizing the agency's policy control. Policy-level officials promote hands-off, autopilot controls for run-of-the-mill matters but increased discretionary involvement in policy-relevant issues – often implying a shift towards a more corporatist style of relationship (Cawson, 1982 and 1985). The bureau also tries to minimize its dependence upon external organizations, as the inter-organizational literature argues (Hanf and Scharpf, 1978). A high-density managerial or control workload can be a liability for a bureau if external or subordinate organizations refuse to co-operate. Replacing such arrangements with a more robust and insulating control apparatus is usually a priority. Bureaus also seek to extend the scope of their patronage of external bodies, but only where this can be achieved in line with their preferred image.

4. *Competition with other bureaus.* Bureaus always defend the *scope* of responsibilities involved in their existing program budget, although they may be only weakly committed to defending given program budget levels. Agencies are by no means simple-minded imperialists. They compete with rival bureaus at the same tier of government for program tasks and policy areas which fit in with their ideal bureau form (especially those tasks with a high proportion of policy-level staff, which command useful resources and confer prestige or influence, and which tend to increase the average level of managerial discretion within the bureau). But bureaus may want to export troublesome and costly low-grade tasks to rivals, especially where doing so carries no major implications for a reduced program budget.

5. *Load-shedding, hiving-off and contracting out.* By far the most radical possibilities for top-tier agencies to reshape their functions arise from their ability to export responsibility for functions inconsistent with senior officials' agency-type ideal. Especially in unitary states, central government departments may simply be able to legislate the transfer of functions to sub-central governments, as the UK Department of Health and Social Security did in 1985, transferring a complex and troublesome system of implementing housing benefits administration to local governments. Alternatively, routine or non-core bureau functions can be hived-off to closely supervised quasi-government agencies (QGAs) (see page 225 below). Both load-shedding to subordinate governments and hiving-off to QGAs preserve bureaus' program budget levels, but reduce core and

bureau budgets. Finally, ancillary functions especially can be contracted out to private firms or made subject to competitive tendering, producing radical reductions in the personnel absorbed on routine functions. Core budgets fall, but the contracted services remain within the agency's bureau budget (see page 239).

Individual officials in policy ranks can contribute to bureau-shaping strategies just as easily and frequently as they can push up budgets. Like budget-maximization, the pursuit of a bureau-shaping strategy requires collective action, especially by top- (and perhaps also, middle-) ranking officials. But bureau-shaping has a much more important and visible connection with these officials' welfare than does generalized budgetary expansion *per se*. Maximizing a bureau's conformity to an ideal, high-status organizational pattern, within a budget constraint contingent on the existing bureau configuration, provides a powerful explanation of a wide range of observed administrative behaviour. Bureau-shaping activity appears to be every bit as commonplace and as frequently pointed out by scholars of administrative behaviour as are tendencies to budget-maximization.

Choosing between bureau-shaping and budget-maximization

The graphs of discounted marginal utilities and advocacy costs developed above can be used to diagram the rival ways in which budget-maximizing and bureau-shaping strategies expand bureaucrats' welfare. Niskanen's model suggests that oversupplying bureaucrats are always trying to push outwards against a restrictive external constraint imposed by the legislature or other sponsor body (Figure 7.10a). Hence the DMU curve often intersects the MAC curve in its vertical section at point A, because of the requirement that the bureau be at least neutral in its impact on social welfare. However, officials realize that if the vertical section of the MAC curve could be pushed further outwards, a new equilibrium at point B would be feasible.

Figure 7.10a implies that no long-term budgetary expansion can take place, unless officials are in a position to change the shape of the MAC curve. In fact, new right accounts stress that bureaucrats invest in reorganization because it shifts the DMU curve upwards, as in Figure 7.10b where DMU_2 and DMU_3 are the curves after successive reorganizations. Even if the MAC curve stays at MAC_1, reorganization can improve officials' welfare, as in the shift from J to R. However, reorganizations also normally enable officials to expand the legislature's tolerance of budget increases, so shifting the vertical section of the MAC curve outwards as shown to MAC_2 and later MAC_3. Agencies will promise that reorganization or work automation will increase efficiency, improve service quality,

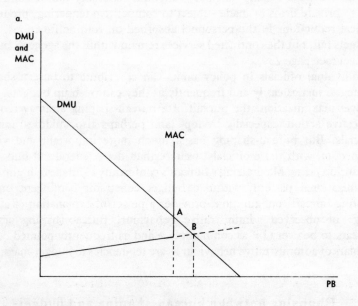

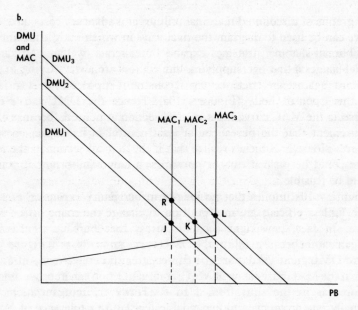

Figure 7.10 **The new right's view of the impacts of reorganization in a line bureau**

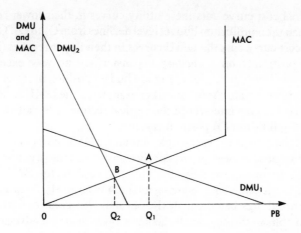

Figure 7.11 **The bureau-shaping model's view of the impacts of reorganization in a line bureau**

modernize service standards, or allow them to undertake new tasks with resources freed up by reorganization. Thus the equilibrium program budget levels will continuously expand over time, from J to K and L. On this account, the level of PB which bureaucrats seek can only stabilize when further expansion of the DMU and MAC curves is ruled out by a taxpayers' revolt, constitutional amendment, or accession to power of a new right government (Mitchell, 1983).

By contrast, the bureau-shaping model argues that normally equilibrium program budget levels lie on the sloping section of the MAC curve, because senior officials respond to changes in environmental favourability or hostility in much more sensitive and diffident ways than budget-maximizing accounts assume, and these responses affect the shape and placing of the whole MAC curve, not just its vertical section. In many circumstances, the existing PB level could already be larger than senior officials' optimum, and the agency quiescent. Over the longer term, the bureau-shaping model argues that major internal reorganizations are very unlikely to simply inflate the DMU curve along its existing shape. Far more commonly, the DMU curve changes shape, swinging in a clockwise direction so as to maximize the benefits which senior bureaucrats derive from lower levels of the program budget, while reducing their dependence on high levels of PB in order to maintain their welfare (Figure 7.11). Numerous strategies discussed above allow top bureaucrats directly to improve their own welfare: for example, by shedding troublesome direct managerial responsibilities and gaining increased staff and time resources for intellectually more attractive tasks such as planning and guidance. All these kinds of change will produce shifts like that from DMU_1, to DMU_2 shown here. So long as

207

the marginal cost curve cuts these utility curves in their lower reaches as shown, then the equilibrium budget level declines from Q_1 to Q_2. Only if the marginal cost curve cuts the DMU curves in their upper reaches (i.e. if the external constraints on budgetary expansion are anyway exceptionally restrictive) will the equilibrium program budget position move outwards if the DMU curves rotate. As in the earlier example, if the DMU and marginal advocacy cost curves intersect in the vertical section of the advocacy costs curve the equilibrium PB position is static.

A particularly interesting example of rotating DMU curves occurs where a delivery agency has been progressively transformed into a control agency, transfer agency or contracts agency. This change shifts the DMU radically clockwise, at the same time changing its shape from an elastic to an inelastic curve. Other things being equal, the optimum program budget level for top bureaucrats in the new small agency is lower than that advocated while they still had direct line responsibilities. It should be clear that a prerequisite for an internal reorganization of this kind is that the area under the DMU curve but above the advocacy costs curve should be greater with a control/transfer/contract agency configuration than under delivery agency arrangements – as in the curves diagrammed here.

Conclusion

Public choice models of bureaucracy which predict open-ended budget-maximization are badly flawed internally. Bureaucrats typically do not embark on collective action modes of improving their welfare unless they have exhausted individual welfare-boosting strategies. If they do choose to try to increase budgets, rational officials usually confront familiar collective action problems. In particular, although lower-ranking bureaucrats have most to gain from budgetary expansion, they will know that the attainment of increments is almost completely insensitive to their individual advocacy, so that even though their advocacy costs are small, campaigning for budgetary expansion is unlikely to advance their individual utility. Higher-ranking officials are aware that the attainment of budgetary growth will be much more sensitive to their personal contribution, but typically they have much less to gain from increments and confront substantial advocacy costs in seeking to push through increases in the agency's base budget.

Budget-maximization is anyway an ambiguous concept, since utility pay-offs are primarily associated with growth in the agency's core or bureau budgets, while advocacy costs are associated with the program budget. In addition, there are major differences between agency types in the extent to which officials associate their welfare with the growth of the program budget. In delivery agencies (the classic line bureaucracies dwelt on in public choice models) the connection is close and positive. But in control agencies it is remote and variable. Top bureaucrats' decisions about budget-maximizing can be modelled in terms of discounted marginal utilities and marginal advocacy costs, whose interaction identifies an optimal budget position which is an equilibrium point.

The characteristics of public service employment systems make it likely that the welfare of higher-ranking bureaucrats is closely bound up with the intrinsic characteristics of their work, rather than near-pecuniary utilities. Rational bureaucrats therefore concentrate on developing bureau-shaping strategies designed to bring their agency into line with an ideal configuration conferring high status and agreeable work tasks, within a budgetary constraint contingent on the existing and potential shape of the agency's activities. Changes in the ways in which agencies are organized may shift this equilibrium point outwards over time – if the change involves simply reorganizing the way in which an agency carries out a fixed role. Alternatively, organizational changes can cause the equilibrium PB point to become smaller – if the change involves reshaping an established delivery agency by hiving-off line functions so that it becomes a central control, transfer or contracts agency.

Chapter 8

COMPARING BUDGET-MAXIMIZING
AND BUREAU-SHAPING MODELS

The oversupply model of bureaucracies has been fully specified in Niskanen's work for nearly two decades, and existed in the less rigorous form long before that. In 1776 Adam Smith described a type of self-interested, empire-building official whose aim is 'to support with rigorous severity [his] own interest against that of the country which [he] governs' (quoted in Dunsire and Hood, 1989, pp. 98, 110). Over time, the appeal of the budget-maximizing view seems to have grown apace, so that economists, conservative politicians and media commentators now cite it routinely, as an uncontentious part of the conventional wisdom. Yet this view has rarely been subjected to critical attention or systematic empirical testing. Even when relevant evidence has been collected, the budget-maximizing model has almost never been tested comparatively, to see how it performs *vis-à-vis* rival approaches in analyzing empirical phenomena. This chapter aims to sketch in an agenda for such a critical comparison by looking at how budget-maximizing and bureau-shaping views stand up against existing empirical evidence; and by exploring how these views interpret two important contemporary trends – privatization and deinstitutionalization.

STATE GROWTH AND ORGANIZATION

Evaluating models of bureaucrats' motivations and behaviour is a complex undertaking, and the development of knowledge has been uneven. Economists' empirical testing procedures in this area (as elsewhere) have tended to focus on deriving predictions and seeing if they are falsified in rather aggregate-level data: yet in many cases outcomes compatible with budget-maximizing accounts are also consistent with a range of other utility-maximizing views, such as Downs' pluralist view (Orzechowski, 1977). By contrast, political science and public administration studies

210

mainly examine how hypotheses stand up to much more micro-level tests. Five aspects merit closer attention: the legislature's role in the Niskanen model; micro-level tests of the budget-maximizing and bureau-shaping models; the role of bureaucrats in government growth; the balance of growth across tiers of government; and interpreting major reorganizations in central government departments.

The role of the legislature

The demand-side of Niskanen's account was largely ignored in Chapter 7 (which deals solely with bureaucrats' motivations and behaviour), but has attracted some important critical attention. Early critics argued that Niskanen's account seemed ethno-centric, generalizing too much from rather exceptional American institutional arrangements. In a wide-ranging review covering fourteen European liberal democracies, Peters (1989b) analyzed the strength of the executive and legislature, and the mix of programmes between those directly administered by the centre and those funded by moving money to other organizations. 'In general these conditions are almost all less favourable for the [budget-maximizing] bureau chief in Europe than they are in the United States' (p. 30). With the reorganization of congressional procedures in the mid-1970s (such as the inauguration of full-house budgetary debates and the work of the congressional Budget Office) other critics argued that Niskanen's analysis of a weak and fragmented sponsor body was also rooted in the late 1960s and early 1970s, a period of exceptional congressional weakness *vis-à-vis* the executive (Goodin, 1982a).

Formal analyses have stressed that Niskanen's picture of bureaus as able to make all-or-nothing budget offers to the legislature, completely dominating the agenda-setting process, is extremely artificial.

> In effect, [Niskanen's] position on the 'bureaucracy problem' assumes a specific legislative structure: oversight by very-high-demand committees, total bureaucratic flexibility in framing decisional alternatives, and final choice by a representative middle-demand group. Under these conditions it does indeed follow that bureaucracy generates big government. But when committee demand is less extreme, bureaucrats are constrained by legislative rules of thumb, or the middle-demand group is to some degree unrepresentative, very different substantive conclusions may be entailed. (Miller and Moe, 1983, p. 320)

> The power of bureaucrats to get what they want has been exaggerated. Although [in formal models] bureaus can sometimes move to a paradise of exploding budgets and slack, they cannot do so when checked by even a primitive form of legislative oversight, nor

when their adjustment is slowed by inertia, nor when their constituents are aware of the burden of taxes. In the most general case they wind up at the pluralist equilibrium. (Bendor and Moe, 1985, p. 772)

In experimental studies very few decision-makers playing the role of bureaucrats maximize without limit, while nominally competing bureaus often rationally collude to make agreed bids to the sponsor. Simulations also demonstrate that when the sponsor can find out some information about alternative budget packets and partially penalize oversupply behaviour, the sponsor–bureau relation becomes more even-handed. Bureaus are forced to reveal their marginal costs, oversupply behaviour is quickly cut back, and in some cases optimally-sized budgets maximizing the social welfare result. The more risk averse officials are and the more resources legislators devote to oversight, the more pronounced these improvements become. In addition, of course, legislators can change the structure of the budgetary process, conceal their demands for services, and use their control of administrative procedures as means of enhancing their influence over bureaus' budgeting behaviour (McCubbins *et al.*, 1987; Weingast, 1984; (Bendor *et al.*, 1985).

In formal models, control problems for the legislature actually tend to be less severe when they are dealing with budget-maximizing bureaucracies than with those which are 'mission-committed' (Bendor *et al.*, 1987). Niskanen's model has thus emerged as an extreme special case, for which there is little or no supporting evidence. Actual bureaucracy/legislature relations are likely to run a wide gamut of patterns between configurations closely fitting the pluralist picture of legislative control and a limited degree of budget-boosting or oversupply. A priori there is no way of establishing which patterns are more likely to occur, and quite small shifts of the balance of relations have significant effects on equilibrium budget outcomes (Bendor, 1988, pp. 354–62)

For the bureau-shaping model the development of more sophisticated formal accounts of variable sponsor–bureau relationships poses no problems. Greater scrutiny by the legislature (or by political department heads in parliamentary systems) enters into the model simply by cutting the likelihood that any bureau can be decisive in securing budget increments and by raising its officials' marginal advocacy costs. In turn, these shifts alter the position of the DMU and MAC curves, so that bureaucrats' optimal program budget levels adjust downwards. Whereas the budget-maximizing model pictures such a change as highly conflictual, in the bureau-shaping account the process is likely to be accomplished with much less friction between officials and politicians – especially in agency types where senior officials' welfare is least dependent on high program budget levels.

Formal studies of bureaucracy–legislature relations have relatively few implications for the bureau-shaping account because: 'Most models in the Niskanen tradition represent exchange, not production. . . . The bureau promises to deliver a certain quantity of output in exchange for a budget: how revenues are transformed into programs is not explicitly represented' (Bendor *et al.*, 1985, pp. 1047–8). Even when variations in bureaucrats' maximands are considered, they are directly assumed, and presented as quite independent of the means that the agency uses to translate revenues into outputs (Bendor *et al.*, 1987). By contrast, the bureau-shaping model offers an endogenized explanation of why bureaucrats in the main types of agencies behave in varying ways – precisely because bureaus use very different policy technologies, and many do not directly produce outputs themselves in the way that the line bureaucracy paradigm assumes.

Micro-level tests

Propositions deriving from the budget-maximizing and bureau-shaping models can be examined using a variety of data. An early direct extrapolation was noted by McGuire (1981) who pointed out that if Niskanen's account was accurate then the demand for bureaus' services should always appear to be elastic, so that reductions in costs trigger greater-than-proportionate increases in budgets (see p. 161). In practice, however, US state and government agencies react to cost reductions with only modest increases in outputs.

Looking at the staffing, grade structure and remuneration of public officials should also shed light on the budget-maximizing model. Hood *et al.* (1984) argue that if officials benefit from agency expansion and expenditure growth then we should expect to see their salary levels prospering *vis-à-vis* the private sector; salary payments growing faster than total budgets; and senior officials' salaries outstripping those of junior staffs. In no case in the United Kingdom could these propositions be supported in the 1971–82 period. Personnel numbers did grow somewhat more rapidly than overall program budgets in a few departments, as did the number of senior staff in comparison with lower-grade employees – but neither of these was a strong or general pattern. In later extensions of this work covering the 1975–84 period these cases of faster expansion also attracted more cutbacks (Dunsire and Hood, 1989).

Analyzing a decade of cutback management these authors derived and tested detailed empirical predictions about how bureaucrats will react according to a conventional Weberian administrative sociology model and the new right's budget-maximizing account. They conclude:

'Popular' expectations about the effect of bureaucratic cutbacks based on a stereotype of *homo bureauensis* as self-regarding and self-serving

(and in particular, wielding the axe on anyone but him or herself in time
of trouble) do rather less well as predictors than do the rather less
popular and more prosaic 'Weberian' expectations. Whereas only two
out of the seven [new right] expectations can be said to gain any kind
of support from this inquiry, only two out of seven 'Weberian'
expectations are clearly inconsistent with what we found here, and
one of these is only partially so. (Dunsire and Hood, 1989, pp.
109–10)

In particular, bureaus did not try to resist cutbacks by offering only
reductions in planned expenditure (the 'fairy gold' gambit); did not cut
salaries' share of expenditure last, nor cut money-moving in preference to
salaries-heavy programmes; nor were top echelons of officials protected
from staffing cuts, or cuts concentrated on temporary and part-time staff.

A similar study of the US federal government from 1971 to 1984
established that civil service pay increased less than half as fast as total
personal incomes, and did not even keep pace with inflation:

Salaries . . . declined significantly as a proportion of total federal
expenditure. Rather than being labour intensive, federal spending has
become 'transfer intensive'. There have been large increases in
spending programs (for example, Social Security) that require
relatively few employees per dollar spent. . . . To judge from its
performance [the federal civil service] is not an institution which
wants to maximize its own income and finds it relatively easy to do so.
(Peters, 1989a, p. 134)

Civil service personnel have not expanded as a share of the US labour force
but contracted; pay levels have been sluggish; health and pension benefits
have grown fast but chiefly for exogenous reasons (such as increased
inflation); pay rises across grades have not benefited top ranks; and
personnel changes favoured middle-ranking officials more than bottom or
top-ranked people – a finding also applicable to the UK civil service
(Dunsire and Hood, 1989, p. 104). Peters looked in detail at high- and low-
spending federal bureaus, finding that the correlations between expenditure and staff increases were low among both growing agencies ($r = 0.08$)
and declining bureaus ($r = 0.19$). He concludes:

We cannot test the underlying assumption of the budget-maximizing
motivations of the bureaucrats, but I have been able to test some of the
predictions about the success of the public bureaucracy in feathering
its own nest at the expense of the public and the bureaucrats'
preference for employment when there is any 'surplus' in the
appropriations granted to them. The data . . . for the United States
offer almost no support for the predictive validity of these models.
. . . The[se] results . . . are especially damning, given that the

models were developed with the decentralized and entrepreneurial nature of American government in mind. (Peters, 1989a, pp. 141–2)

The bureau-shaping model has not yet been explicitly tested in a similar way to budget-maximizing models, but seems to have little difficulty in explaining existing results. Dunsire and Hood (1989, p. 111) note that its 'expectations about bureaucratic behaviour come much more closely into line with [the] "Weberian" expectations' about cutback management that they found were supported. At the same time, the bureau-shaping account can explain the two aspects of UK cutback management also consistent with the budget-maximizing model, namely the tendency for central spending to be cut last, and for budgets to be cut before staff. Although their data operate only with officially defined groupings of departments rather than theoretically specified agencies, Dunsire and Hood's analysis of the distribution of cutbacks can be cross-checked in terms of bureau types (Table 8.1). None of the seven delivery agencies in their figures suffered a real terms PB cutback, although two DT agencies (delivery bureaus with subsidiary transfer functions) did so. Transfer and control agencies had a more mixed record, while the miscellaneous agencies (especially those with trading roles) predominantly incurred PB cutbacks.

Referring back to the more detailed UK central state data analyzed in Chapter 7 shows a high degree of association between agency types and policy areas (Table 8.2). Delivery/DT agencies predominate numerically and in core budget and staffing terms, and within this group defence-related agencies are most important, followed by law-and-order agencies. Social insurance is similarly important in the transfer/contracts group, while just under half the agencies and core budgets in the miscellaneous group are concerned with carrying out common organization functions for central government. Over half the control agencies are concerned with collective consumption activities, that is, welfare state public services. This pattern of

Table 8.1 *Distribution of program budget cutbacks across bureau-types in twenty-nine UK central departments, 1975–84*

Bureau type	Level of spending cut 1975–84	
	No real cutback	*Real cutback*
Delivery/DT agencies	7	2
Control agencies	5	3
Transfer/contract agencies	2	3
Miscellaneous agencies	2	5
Total	*16*	*13*

Source: computed from Dunsire and Hood (1989), p. 125.

215

Democracy, Bureaucracy and Public Choice

Table 8.2 The distribution of British central state agencies and core budgets across agency types and policy fields

Type of agency

(a) Number of agencies

Control		Transfer/contracts		Delivery plus D/T		Miscellaneous	
Collective consumption	7	Social security	2	Law and order	13	Central govt org	10
Law and order	2	Land, built env	2	Defence/overseas	6	Empl/trade/energy	5
Mixed con/production	2	Central govt org	2	Empl/trade/energy	3	Land, built env	3
Empl/trade/energy	2	Empl/trade/energy	2	Agriculture	2	Law and order	2
Central govt org	2	Defence	1	Collective consumption	2	Agriculture	1
		Law and order	1	Land, built env	1		
		Collective consump	1	Central govt org	1		
		Agriculture	1				
Total	**15**	**Total**	**12**	**Total**	**28**	**Total**	**21**

(b) Percentage of all central state core budgets

Control		Transfer/contracts		Delivery plus D/T		Miscellaneous	
Collective consump	2	Social security	11	Defence/overseas	44	Central govt org	8
Law and order	1	Defence	4	Law and order	12	Empl/trade/energy	3
Mixed con/production	1	Land, built env	1	Empl/trade/energy	4	Land, built env	2
Empl/trade/energy	1	Empl/trade/energy	1	Collective consump	2	Law and order	1
Central govt org	0	Central govt org	0	Agriculture	2	Agriculture	0
		Law and order	0	Land, built env	0		
		Agriculture	0	Central govt org	0		
		Collective con	0				
Total	**5**	**Total**	**16**	**Total**	**64**	**Total**	**14**

Notes: A figure of 0 in (b) indicates a percentage of all central state core budgets which is below 0.5%.

Source: Dunleavy, 1989b, pp. 412–3.

agencies is highly unfavourable for new right budget-maximizing models because across virtually all welfare state areas national policy is controlled by bureaus whose core budgets absorb only a tiny proportion of overall program budgets – and whose interest in maximizing PB levels is correspondingly reduced.

A crude measure of how these different types of agencies fared in practice is provided by public expenditure figures under the Thatcher government's new right policies (Table 8.3). While overall spending (unadjusted for inflation) more than doubled over the 1980s, four policy areas did much better than the average. One of these, social security spending, reflected almost entirely the unplanned growth of payments due to the expansion of mass unemployment; government policy consistently cut entitlements over the decade without offsetting the spending expansion triggered as a by-product of monetarist economic policies. But spending growth was much better than average in law and order and defence, seen by the new right as a priority spending areas, and agriculture, where the farming industry is a key Conservative support group receiving large subsidies. The collective consumption total covering all other welfare state spending (on education, health care, social housing, transport and environmental services) grew by less than the average, and in many areas real spending fell. Only the tiny overseas aid budget and subsidies to nationalized industries fared worse. The prima facie conclusion seems clear. Intended (as opposed to reactive) spending growth in this period was concentrated on the few remaining large line agencies in UK central government in the defence and law-and-order areas, plus a transfer agency (agriculture) dealing in a closed relationship with an industry well able to organize a flowback of benefits for officials and politicians.

Table 8.3   *Average annual percentage increase in UK public expenditure planning totals across functional categories, 1978–9 to 1987–8*

Law and order	21.7
Social security	18.1
Agriculture	17.0
Defence	15.1
All public spending	*12.8*
Collective consumption	10.4
Overseas aid	6.1
Industry, trade, energy	4.1*

Notes: * this figure is artificially low because of major privatization and nationalized industry receipts at the end of the period.

Source: Treasury (1987b), p. 36, Table 2.27.

217

Bureaucrats' role in the expansion of government

The part played by officials in public sector growth remains disputed despite numerous studies documenting substantial institutional changes in virtually all liberal democracies, especially in the post-war period (Nutter, 1978; Peacock and Wiseman, 1968; Bennett and Johnson, 1980). Evidence of this kind does no more than establish a generally favourable background for budget-maximizing models. The causal origins of expenditure or personnel expansion remain unclear. The existing explanatory literature is too vast to reference in detail, but suggests that government growth can be plausibly correlated with:

- situational factors (such as an open economy, size of polity, unitary government structures, changing demographics increasing the size of state-dependent and public service consumer groups, average per capita incomes, level of income inequality);
- historical factors (such as a country's position in terms of military and strategic alliances, a prolonged and unbroken history as a democratic polity, involvement in large-scale wars allowing military spending to be subsequently displaced into civilian governmental expenditures);
- political demand side pressures (such as the level of voter turnout, the strength of left voting, level of union membership, the number of interest groups, fragmentation and weakness of right parties, the role of Catholic parties);
- supply-side pressures (proportion of voters who are public employees, extent of government centralization, mix of tax types); and
- policy orientations (the extent of redistribution, reliance on direct provision vs transfers, level of corporatism in policy-making).

The relative contribution of all these variables and of budget-maximizing behaviour by bureaucrats still remains largely conjectural with different empirical studies producing sharply varying estimates.

> Bureaucrats and interest groups stand equally high on all lists of the causes of the growth of government, and much case study evidence is consistent with the [budget-maximizing] hypothesis. . . . But more systematic support for the bureaucracy-size [of government] relationship is sparse and contradictory. (Mueller, 1989, p. 339)

Even if substantial government expansion is consistent with budget-maximizing models, only independent measures of demand-side and situational pressures for growth and of the levels of social welfare deriving from policy outputs could establish whether or not oversupply behaviour has occurred, or how great the bureaucratic impetus to growth has been. The careful empirical research by Meyer (1985) is exceptional in directly linking the timing of local spending growth to evidence of increased sectionalization. He showed that the expansion in the numbers of financial divisions and departments in the city governments of Chicago, Philadelphia and Detroit from 1890 to 1975 could not be explained solely in terms of increasing tasks or environmental pressures. Equally, more sectionalization preceded expansion in bureaus' sizes, rather than being a consequence of it. In addition, the bureaus which became more sectionalized survived much better than those bureaus which did not. However, these results are open to counter-interpretation. For example, if municipal bureaus are operating in a hostile political climate close to the implementation limits of the existing organization, then the process of sectionalization may lag behind the accumulation of demand pressures for more spending. Here organizational change may cure bottlenecks and allow budgets to expand, but without thereby proving that the organizational changes themselves *caused* the expansion.

Growth across tiers of government

Surprisingly, the relative expansion of central and sub-central agencies has not featured much in existing empirical tests. Yet the budget-maximizing approach explicitly explains state growth in terms of an increasing national government role (Niskanen, 1975).

[It] implies that high and increasing centralization of government produces large and growing governments. . . . Niskanen's model contemplates a bureaucracy that values larger budgets and always has some power to extract budget dollars from a legislature that values bureaucratic ouput. An important constraint on the bureaucracy's ability to gain unproductive budget dollars is competition among bureaus and among jurisdictions. Thus, institutional developments that weaken competition imply growing budgets. Among these developments, Niskanen cites centralization of government functions [and] the consolidation of government functions into fewer bureaus. . . .

However there are clear factual problems with the general concentration hypothesis taken on its own terms. . . . What seems most impressive about (measured) centralization is its temporal stability in the face of considerable worldwide expansion of public sectors in the past two decades. (Peltzman, 1980, pp. 214–15)

For the 1950–73 period Peltzman's measure of centralization – the proportion of government revenues collected nationally – shows only a meagre relationship with government growth across sixteen countries (explaining 5 per cent of the variance with a high standard error) (Peltzman, 1980, p. 216). This index is anyway unduly favourable to a budget-maximizing view, since much of the revenues collected centrally are actually paid out in grants or transfers to sub-national governments rather than spent directly by central or federal agencies on policy implementation (see below, Table 8.5c).

On the budget-maximizing view national-level officials closest to the centres of legislative and financial power in liberal democracies will want to maintain or increase their share of a generally growing cake. Hence a great deal of public sector growth must take the form of already sizeable agencies becoming larger. For example, national bureaus should follow 'vertical integration' strategies akin to those of modern corporations, extending their control over implementation, and reducing the extent to which they must pass on budgets to other bureaus. Alternatively, national bureaus might follow 'conglomerate' strategies, creating subsidiary sections in new policy fields remote from their previous activities. If central agencies' core budgets or staff numbers only remain stable in a period of overall state expansion, then their relative importance declines – while any direct transfers of core budgets or staffs to other agencies imply national bureaus' absolute decline on a budget-maximizing view. Staffing growth is likely to be intimately bound up in budgetary expansion because the public sector has been and remains far more labour intensive than most large modern corporations. Only in a few areas, such as the heavily equipped armed forces and 'big science' ventures like nuclear power, has capital intensification radically redrawn the link between budgets and staffing. And on the demand side, budget-maximizing models stress that boosting the numbers of bureaucrats is important in fuelling electoral demands for government growth (Garand, 1988; Tullock, 1974; McLean, 1982, pp. 98–100).

In practice, long-term patterns of growth in US and British public employment as a share of overall employment suggest a diametrically opposite picture (Table 8.4). The greatest peacetime expansion of bureaucracy has occurred outside the central or federal government, in the United Kingdom in local authorities and the health service, and in the United States at the state and local government levels. Central and federal employment has been stable or fluctuated for most of the post-war period, while military personnel (a key central responsibility) have fairly consistently declined since the wartime boost.

Of course, Britain and the United States have lower proportions of all public employment at the centre than some other liberal democracies, notably France and Italy where central departments run education (teachers counting as civil servants) and also other substantial field services (Table 8.5a). However, the pattern of employment growth in these countries shows almost exactly the same concentration of growth in implementation-level public services (especially education and health care) found in other liberal democracies (Rose et al., 1985, p. 21). The sectionalization of education and other 'field service' ministries in France and Italy is such that a plausible case could be made for treating them akin to the National Health Service in Britain rather than as single line

Table 8.4 *Long-term patterns of employment growth at different tiers of government, UK and US, 1851–1981*

	% of total labour force in										
	1851	1891	1901	1911	1921	1931	1938	1951	1961	1971	1981
UK											
Civil service[†]	0.3	0.8	1.0	0.7	1.5	1.0	1.5	3.2	2.7	2.9	2.6
Armed forces	1.7	1.7	2.5	1.8	2.4	1.7	1.7	3.5	1.9	1.5	1.2
Local government[*]	0.3	1.2	2.3	3.6	5.0	5.9	5.6	8.2	10.1	13.9	15.6
USA											
Federal civil service[†]	0.2	0.25	–	0.5	0.7	1.2	1.7	3.9	2.6	3.1	1.8
Armed forces	0.4	0.16	–	0.4	0.6	0.5	0.6	5.5	3.8	2.6	1.9
State governments	–	–	–	–	–	5.3	5.6	1.6	2.2	3.2	3.3
Local governments	–	–	–	–	–			5.3	7.1	8.9	8.3

Notes: [†] = excludes Post Office.
   [*] = includes National Health Service staff from 1951 on.

Table 8.5 *Measures of the importance of central governments in six advanced industrial states*

	Central government	Local or regional government	Other (quasi-government)
(a) Percentage of all governmental employment in 1981:			
France	54	28	18
Italy	53	19	28
Sweden	25	70	1
USA	24	75	1
W. Germany	20	64	16
UK	19	52	29
(b) Percentage change in employment at each tier 1950–81:			
W. Germany	+10	+3	+1
France	−2	+9	+7
Italy	−9	+1	+8
UK	−17	+15	+12
Sweden	−17	+25	+3
USA	−35	+28	0

(c) Central government's share of taxes raised and of governmental employment in 1981:

% Taxes raised	% Governmental employment	Country	Difference (%)
90	19	Britain	71
68	20	W. Germany	48
99	53	Italy	46
70	24	USA	46

bureaucracies (Cassesse, 1988; Rigaud and Delcros, 1986): 'The numerous bureaux that exist within a French or Italian ministry do have an identity and often a legally defined mission, [although] they still exist within a hierarchical ministerial structure' (Peters, 1989b, p. 8).

The share of total governmental employment absorbed by central agencies in West Germany and Sweden is comparable with the US and UK levels, and in Germany a conventional ministry structure exists. However, within the Swedish central government level itself there is a key and long-standing organizational distinction between the policy-making ministries absorbing less than 10 per cent of all central personnel, and numerous statutory boards and commissions which carry out all policy implementation not allocated to local authorities (Peters, 1985). All the

Swedish ministries fit within a single office block in Stockholm, placing them at the extreme of non-executant central government and creating an important paradox for budget-maximizing models to explain. The liberal democracy with the largest public sector on most indices is also the country where senior central bureaucrats' core budgets and, presumably, welfare levels are most extensively insulated from dependence upon high program budgets.

The post-war patterns of change across these six countries at different tiers of government also show considerable similarities (Table 8.5b). In Sweden, Britain and the United States central government personnel numbers fell sharply between 1950 and 1980, while regional or local governments (and quasi-governmental agencies in Britain) expanded sharply. In France and Italy the growth in the education service compensated for reductions elsewhere in central ministries, but staffing still fell overall, compared with significant net growth in sub-central government. In West Germany the central bureaucracy in 1950 was extremely limited by the Allies' post-war settlement (for example, in not having any national defence role). Modest growth since then still leaves the German federal bureaucracy proportionately amongst the smallest of any liberal democracy. Most public employment growth was concentrated in the regional Lande governments.

A final dimension of institutional patterns in liberal democracies is the gap between central government's control over taxation and its share of public sector employment pointed out by Rose *et al.* (1985, p. 29). Reworking Rose's figures to refer only to governmental employment (i.e. excluding the trading enterprises sector, which in most countries is basically self-financing) shows that Britain has the largest gap between central government control over taxes and its subsidiary role in directly employing staff (Table 8.5c). The final column here provides a rough indication of the scale of the transfers by central government to private firms and citizens or to sub-central agencies. (Of course, some central government tasks may also be more capital intensive than those in other tiers of government.) The remaining five countries are broadly comparable, with extensive inter-governmental transfers implied.

Summing up this evidence, post-war state growth in most liberal democracies has not generally taken the form of large line agencies at the central or federal government level getting larger. Most state expansion has focused on lower-tier implementing organizations, quasi-governmental agencies and decentralized regional or local governments (see also Sharpe, 1985; Dunleavy, 1984). National governments have played a key role in funding public sector expansion, but at this level pressures for 'keeping the centre small' (Hood, 1978) have meant that large line agencies have tended to lose functions to the other parts of the state apparatus. A shift by central agencies towards a non-executant role, concentrating on progressively

223

higher-grade managerial and policy tasks, and achieving desired policy effects by money-moving, regulatory initiatives and other control mechanisms has been widely noted (Hood, 1983; Hood, 1989; Sharpe, 1979).

The countries of Mediterranean Europe (France, Spain, Italy and Greece) held out longest against this pattern, with strong central department field services and tight prefectural control of localities. But even here most public sector growth has taken place outside central departments, or in heavily sectionalized bottom-tier levels within large ministries. And in the late 1970s and 1980s a wave of regional devolution and decentralization reforms began significantly to alter these last bastions of the Napoleonic approach to administration. In almost all countries (except Greece), civil service numbers and directly related funding have been stable or even declining in absolute terms, while their relative significance in the growing public sector has generally declined.

These results run strongly counter to the budget-maximizing model's implication. Two options seem open. Either disciples of Niskanen can continue to claim that central government bureaucrats critically determine the *extent* of overall state expansion, while acknowledging that they have apparently not been able to influence its *institutional form*. This position seems logically inconsistent except under very odd conditions. Why should implementation-level bureaucrats (or professionals or trade unions) be so powerful and able to secure central funding for the expansion of local or regional delivery agencies, while senior central bureaucrats, operating at the heart of political and legislative power centres, cannot? Alternatively, advocates of the budget-maximizing model must conclude that national bureaucracies' lack of influence on the form of state expansion also reflects their supernumerary role in determining its extent. This position effectively negates the thrust of Niskanen's model or any similar approach. It anyway seems implausible to suppose that large bureaucratic agencies have played so uninfluential a role in the growth of the state.

The bureau-shaping model, by contrast, offers a simple and direct way out of this conundrum. For central government agencies in welfare policy areas, bureau-shaping has meant an extensive shift towards a control or transfer agency format, with responsibility for service delivery passing to local governments or to intermediate-tier agencies. For a few central government agencies (especially those in fields like defence), bureau-shaping in the early post-war period primarily involved guiding growth into desired areas (for example, procurement rather than personnel in defence). At the sub-central level in the United States and in many European countries (although less so in the United Kingdom because of its 'statist' approach (Dunleavy, 1989c)), state or regional governments and municipalities have themselves passed on large parts of their program budget increments to bodies below them (Hood and Shuppert, 1988; Lerman, 1982). Private sector non-profit firms (e.g. hospitals), independent charities (especially in the United States), voluntary groups, social housing associations, etc. actually deliver many services. So even at the sub-national level, there is no simple picture of budget-maximizing behaviour. Overall, the bureau-shaping model views the institutional form of state growth as a key reflection of officials' instrumental preferences (for working in smaller, more central, staff bureaus), not as a puzzling anomaly falling outside the scope of effective theoretical explanation.

Major reorganizations in central government

Cases where existing large line agencies directly lose or hand over responsibilities, budgets and staff to other bodies present an even more severe explanatory difficulty for budget-maximizing approaches. Senior officials should fight tooth-and-nail to oppose the dismembering of their existing organizations. Perhaps a few middle-level officials might anticipate a more lucrative remuneration deal or promotional future if their section is hived-off and a 'ring-fence' policy operated on the new senior jobs created. But for the really senior and presumably influential officials left in the 'parent' departments, such a shift represents an unmistakable welfare loss on a budget-maximizing account. These propositions are hard to apply in the United States, where congressional oversight is so detailed that it severely limits the internal restructuring of federal departments' divisions. All such changes can imply reorganization of congressional committee structures – a factor contributing strongly to Kaufman's tongue-in-cheek supposition that federal government organizations are 'immortal' (Kaufman, 1976).

However, in Britain the Thatcher government embarked on a large-scale reorganization of central government, moving away from the conventional integrated ministry structures and towards a Swedish-style distinction between core policy-making ministries and hived-off 'executive agencies'. In language reflecting Niskanen's influence, a key 1988 report recommended:

> The aim should be to establish a quite different way of conducting the business of government. The central Civil Service should consist of a relatively small core engaged in the function of servicing Ministers and managing departments, who will be the 'sponsors' of particular governmental policies and services. Responding to these departments will be a range of agencies employing their own staff, who may or may not have the status of Crown servants, and concentrating on the delivery of their particular services, with clearly defined responsibility between the Secretary of State [i.e. political department head] and the Permanent Secretary [i.e. head of the administrative side in the ministry] on the one hand, and the Chairmen or Chief Executives of the agencies on the other. (Efficiency Unit, 1988, p. 15)

The blocks of work seen by the government as capable of being hived off to executive agencies involved 194,000 out of 575,000 civil servants by mid-1990 (around 34 per cent), and was expected to include half of all personnel by 1991. Some functions are small and involve only a few hundred staff, but others are large – one covering 72,000 staff (Dunleavy and Francis, 1990). Sceptics argue:

> Most of the bodies identified so far as possible agencies and all those already set up are engaged in self-contained activities, often of a routine kind, which do not normally attract much ministerial attention, and they are not entwined with the mainstream work of the parent department in which they are located. (Jones, 1989, p. 252)

None the less a substantial rolling programme of creating separate agencies is already under way, and official estimates are that between 75 and 90 per cent of staff may be hived-off within a decade.

Opposition to this rolling programme has come mainly from the public expenditure sections of the Treasury, the powerful central ministry controlling all departmental spending and most personnel policies. Its existing powers and standardized control procedures have been built up in coral-reef fashion for over 120 years. They are directly threatened by proposals to allow deconcentrated agencies the freedom to transfer monies between budget heads, operate their own salaries and conditions policies, recruit and promote as they see fit, and adopt new technology without clearing their decisions through the Treasury.

Yet most senior officials in other Whitehall ministries have endorsed the government's strategy, many enthusiastically (Hencke, 1988). The full implementation of the reforms would drastically reduce their departments' personnel and core budgets. Yet policy-level officials have generally agreed on the need to separate out their existing under-managed and under-prioritized executive roles, so as to allow them to concentrate on their key tasks of providing policy advice to ministers, managing relations with Parliament, organizing legislation and regulations, and moving money around to individuals, private sector firms, and subordinate public sector bodies. In addition, under the new regime the policy departments would take over from the Treasury most of the detailed supervision of executive agencies. Thus the new core ministries would preserve their capacity to shape the broad development of policy, while losing direct responsibility for detailed implementation issues.

On the bureau-shaping model the hiving-off proposals provide senior bureaucrats with a unique opportunity to engage in wholesale reshaping of their bureaus to attain their ideal form of small, élite, staff agencies. The government report which triggered the reorganization process candidly admitted that political and policy proposals preoccupied policy-level officials and inherently were always likely to do so (Efficiency Unit, 1988).

The Thatcher government's earlier strong efforts to assign a higher priority to 'managing' central departments' executive responsibilities made virtually no impression on the entrenched attitudes of the civil service hierarchy during the 1980s (Ponting, 1985). By contrast, hiving-off creates a streamlined core administration perfectly congruent with the preferences of senior bureaucrats who maximize work-related utilities.

The British reorganization looks like a large-scale example of the general change charted in Figure 7.11 (page 207). The Conservative government obviously believes the reforms are consistent with rolling back the frontiers of the state, perhaps because some executive agencies may proceed in stages to privatization (see next section). More generally, however, as senior officials' discounted marginal utility curves shift from DMU_1 to DMU_2 their optimum program budget falls from Q_1 to Q_2. Yet senior bureaucrats' positive reactions to the proposals can be explained by noting that in Figure 7.11 their area of net welfare gain (lying below the discounted marginal utility curve but above the marginal advocacy costs curve) is larger with DMU_2 than with DMU_1. Hence new right ministers and their senior bureaucratic advisers can both support the reform package – because it simultaneously maximizes officials' welfare while reducing the equilibrium level of program budgets in any given policy area.

EXPLAINING PRIVATIZATION AND DEINSTITUTIONALIZATION

Just as the appeal of budget-maximizing models has not been grounded on detailed empirical support, so it is unlikely to be diminished solely because the evidence reviewed in the previous section is overwhelmingly unfavourable. My concern here is to show that even as a looser framework of explanation, budget-maximizing models cannot satisfactorily account for two major administrative trends, privatization and deinstitutionalization. By contrast, the bureau-shaping model offers clear-cut interpretations which fit our existing knowledge of these shifts well. I first review the general features of privatization and deinstitutionalization, and then analyze budget-maximizing and bureau-shaping explanations in turn.

Two administrative meta-trends

Privatization

American new right authors see privatization as 'the key to better government' (Savas, 1982; Savas, 1987), or (more extravagantly) to 'better government at half the price' (Bennett and Johnson, 1981). For British enthusiasts, changing the organization of public services is a central element in a new 'micro-politics' which can produce a qualitative shift towards rolling back the boundaries of the state (Pirie, 1988a, 1988b). Four mechanisms can be identified. In *competitive tendering* the tasks involved in providing services are specified as government contracts, for which private firms tender, at first against in-house public agency staffs. Alternatively, in *contracting out* blocks of work are transferred directly to a private firm, but still funded by the agency. In *franchising* a public agency authorizes what is to be done but gives a licence to a private firm to operate the service and recoup its expenses via charging. Finally government can fund and allocate *vouchers* to citizens, who exchange them for services with diverse private suppliers.

In the post-war period competitive tendering and contracting out have both been widely used where public administration systems remained undeveloped; to cope with labour shortages (because of uncompetitive public sector wages); for construction and major capital projects; and to accommodate rapid workload increases during 'policy boom' periods (Ascher, 1987; Dunleavy, 1981a). What is new about recent developments has been the self-conscious effort to use these methods not as a supplement to integrated public service provision by mainstream agencies, but instead as an integral part of a shift to multi-sourced production of public services – where the function of authorizing/funding services is decisively separated out from the task of delivering them (New Zealand Treasury, 1987). By challenging the idea of unified public service delivery systems privatization methods imply 'the end of the public bureaucracy state' (Hood, 1989; Pirie, 1988b).

A privatization policy boom has been sustained in some key US states (such as California), Britain, New Zealand and parts of Australia since the 1980s by central or state government encouragement – including, for example, mandatory competitive tendering imposed on British health authorities and local governments (Ascher, 1987); or Reagan's 1987 executive order establishing the Office of Privatization within OMB (Office of Management and Budget) and inaugurating reviews of federal provision of commercial services (Massey, 1990). Political pressure has come from hard-sell efforts by interested corporations (and some professionals) to corner a share of a growing market, with attendant problems of penetration pricing (firms setting prices at zero-profit levels) and loss-leader contracting (firms setting prices below break-even levels). Privatization has been opposed by public service trade unions representing grass roots implementation staff (Ascher, 1987, Chapter 4). But public service managers have generally accepted and implemented competitive tendering and other initiatives with very little evidence of organized resistance.

Deinstitutionalization

There has been a widespread trend in the modern welfare state, and some law-and-order areas, for large facilities run by public agencies (often those

228

which Goffman (1961) labels 'total institutions') to be replaced by new, smaller-scale services run by different kinds of bureaus, or by voluntary organizations and private firms. In Britain the same shift is more commonly called 'care in the community'. In social policy areas deinstitutionalization can involve closing mental hospitals, facilities for the mentally and physically handicapped, large homes for the elderly, facilities for the elderly and mentally infirm, children's homes and facilities for troubled or criminal adolescents; in law-and-order policy, deinstitutionalization chiefly involves getting people out of prison. One key source of this change has been the recognition in social policy areas that clients/patients/inmates 'are entitled to live in the least restrictive environment necessary and [to] live their lives as normally and independently as they can' (Lerman, 1982, p. 2, quoting the US General Accounting Office). But a precise definition of deinstitutionalization in terms of its impacts on clients has proved elusive (Lerman, 1982, pp. 19–68). Accordingly I define this trend organizationally as:

- a trend away from modes of service delivery which are formalized, institutionalized, centralized, continuous-care, permanently staffed and relatively costly; and instead
- a shift towards more community-based, de-concentrated, and less formalized services, often based around episodic care, not continuously staffed, or utilizing relatively cheaper forms of service administration.

Deinstitutionalization (hereafter shortened to the DE process) can involve a *single tier of government*. Here an established bureau runs down its activities in favour of a new bureau, which may be another section of the same overall organization or a completely separate agency. The DE process may also transfer some activities or resources directly to the clients receiving services or use people in the community instead of employees to deliver services (as with the fostering of children in care). At a limit, an established agency may run down its activities by transferring all of them in one way or another to clients or sections of the 'community' caring for them. Alternatively, the DE process can involve *two tiers of government*. Here a top-tier department (at the national or state level) instructs one or more local-level established agencies to run down their activities, and directs resources into building up alternative local agencies or activities.

Whichever pattern applies, deinstitutionalization always implies that budgetary increments are diverted away from established delivery agencies with large staffs and budgets to new or different agencies, or to private organizations, or to community-based provision. Established bureaus or delivery systems therefore decline relative to alternative agencies and systems. In some cases deinstitutionalization involves the run-down of existing agencies or delivery systems in absolute terms, even extending to organizational or programme termination.

In Britain the DE process has focused on large mental hospitals, which have been run down slowly since 1961, with bed numbers falling by 40 per cent since the mid-1970s (Brindle, 1988). Mentally handicapped hospital places also fell by 17 per cent during the 1970s. These changes have been slow-moving because local governments and health authorities have received insufficient central funding to provide full alternative facilities (Wistow, 1985, pp. 74–5). In addition, children's homes have given way to fostering, and old people's homes to greater provision of services for the elderly in their own homes. British evidence about the cost implications of deinstitutionalization suggests that although institutional closures (especially of big hospitals) release valuable assets, running cost savings in many areas from 'care in the community' are fairly modest, since much domiciliary and smaller-scale care is relatively expensive (Audit Commission, 1986).

In the United States deinstitutionalization has been operating on a longer time-scale, principally since the 1935 Social Security Act. Federal social services policy has focused growth in non-traditional, smaller-scale or more privatized institutions, but has not cut the overall number of people living in institutions:

> A probing study of deinstitutionalization reveals a number of
> surprising paradoxes. Whereas traditional institutions have been
> depopulated or reduced in size, new institutional forms have also
> emerged during the last quarter century. Although the welfare state
> has helped deinstitutionalization by subsidizing ex-patients outside of
> institutions, it has also been a major patron of the nursing home
> industry and provided traditional mental retardation institutions with
> a renewed chance of survival for many years. Public welfare has
> increased the number of institutional-type social functions
> supported by federal and state dollars, but it has also introduced more
> opportunities to profit from this welfare expansion. The mentally
> disabled have been granted greater freedom of treatment, care and
> supervision outside of traditional institutions, but they have also
> been subject to new forms of physical, personal and social control.
> And more persons are experiencing a stay – albeit short – in an
> institutional facility in 1980, than occurred twenty, thirty, or fifty
> years ago. (Lerman, 1982, p. 220)

Again, US studies of the comparative costing of traditional and alternative institutional care also suggest that any cost advantage for community-based services is fairly narrow. In the law-and-order area the DE process has centred on finding alternatives to prison sentences, with large cross-national variations in the use of non-custodial alternatives (Rutherford, 1986). In the United States and Britain mainstream prison populations have soared since the 1930s, despite the growing use of fines, suspended sentences, community service, parole and probation. But in the

Netherlands and Japan far more offenders are cautioned without resort to full trials; far fewer people are sentenced, and of these a lower proportion are imprisoned. The DE effort has more recently involved experiments in probation, community service, 'intermediate treatment' facilities for juveniles, and tagging offenders as alternatives to imprisonment.

Budget-maximizing explanations

The budget-maximizing literature hardly discusses contemporary empirical trends, but it is possible to construct from the basic Niskanen model a number of interpretations of privatization and of deinstitutionalization, whether it involves a single level or two tiers of government.

Privatization

This change clearly threatens public bureaucracies by greatly increasing uncertainty and risk for budget-maximizing officials, and creating a much more hostile and turbulent environment for them to operate in. Competition with private firms forces agencies to specify detailed trade-offs between budgets and outputs and explicitly to justify previously customary service standards. It greatly enhances sponsors' power and erodes agencies' capacity to oversupply outputs. Even if in-house teams can win contracts, they must usually cut costs radically to do so.

Public service privatization transfers funding from an agency's core budget to its bureau budget, entailing substantial welfare losses for middle- and low-ranked officials (typically, requiring them to work more intensively for the new contractor or throwing them onto the job market). Senior officials may remain in the public service but see their program budgets shrink because of firms' greater efficiency. Top bureaucrats control fewer staff in an employment relation, find their patronage and perks opportunities curtailed and see their status ranking, promotion prospects and often salaries decline. And privatization attacks the integrity of government organizations, particularly eroding the strong protective ideologies which bureaus (such as social welfare agencies) build up to insulate their oversupply behaviour from external scrutiny or criticism. Hence all ranks of officials should oppose privatization root and branch. The key problem for budget-maximizing models then becomes to explain why privatization has become so widespread and significant despite this predicted bureaucratic resistance.

At this juncture, new right exponents seem to split into two schools of thought. A *heroic variant* explains the rapid implementation of privatization and apparent absence of significant bureaucratic opposition by ascribing special importance to the advent of new right leaders in the United States and Britain during the 1980s. The Thatcher and Reagan administrations demonstrate that there is nothing inherent about the success of supply-side pressures for budgetary growth. Sponsor bodies clearly have (and by implication always have had) the ability to assert their priorities over the state apparatus. However, it was not until the advent of new right governments in London and Washington that political leaders really *wanted* to curtail budget growth or improve efficiency.

The heroic view can be made roughly consistent with observed patterns, but at considerable cost. Niskanen's supposedly deductive derivation of oversupply behaviour from rational officials' motives and powers is downgraded to a special case based only on a contingent state of affairs. Bureaucracy cannot inherently produce oversupply if a simple change of political control is enough to make the state apparatus operate in a basically different way. The realist emphasis of public choice models also takes a knock, since the Thatcher or Reagan trend-breaking governments are ascribed a 'special virtue', allowing them to resist pressures acting on all previous politicians. The empirical fit here is also dubious: privatization efforts in the United States began under Carter (Massey, 1990).

A second *fatalist variant* argues by contrast that privatization has had little impact. It most resembles previous management innovations such as Planning, Programming Budgeting Systems (PPBS), Zero-Based Budgeting (ZBB), and Management by Objectives (MBO) in the USA, or Management Information Systems for Ministers (MINIS) and the Financial Management Initiative (FMI) in Britain (Downs and Larkey, 1986; Gray and Jenkins, 1985; Hennessy, 1989, Chapter 14). All these innovations had a once-for-all impact in the early years of their introduction, but with sharply reduced continuing impacts over time on public policy formulation. Exponents of the fatalist view argue that politicians like Thatcher still suffer from 'weakness of will', shying away from genuinely radical cutback policies in favour of 'façade privatizations' which are easily accepted by incumbent bureaucrats. The empirical emphasis on inherent oversupply in public provision survives via such fatalist disclaimers, but at the cost of impugning a key piece of new right policy analysis and moving instead towards prescriptive utopianism.

Single-tier deinstitutionalization

The DE process must be strongly opposed by officials in established agencies according to budget-maximizing accounts. Such a shift always inaugurates overt competition between established agencies and new bureaus or less formalized alternatives. Even where established agencies maintain a constant share of the cake, they lose monopoly responsibility for given services or client groups, and are forced to disclose much more information about their marginal costs and benefits to sponsors. Sponsors' power is enhanced by the existence of alternative implementation channels; agency clients can more easily exit if dissatisfied; and both politicians and citizens can make direct comparisons between alternative forms of care.

Organizational stasis or stagnation in large established agencies caused by DE threatens senior officials' opportunities for further promotion, and precludes managerial expansion or scaling-up responsibility payments. The DE process encourages debate about and experiments with lower-cost policy technologies, making it more difficult for established agencies to maximize outputs, protect existing budgets, or preserve the patronage powers which go along with control of staffs and budgets. In addition, DE reforms attack the integrity of established agencies, again eroding protective ideologies which bureaus use to insulate themselves from external scrutiny. Hence DE may easily inaugurate established agencies' absolute decline, break-up, or termination. It unequivocally increases uncertainty and longer-term risks for senior budget-maximizing bureaucrats.

So how can this budget-maximizing approach explain the apparently widespread DE trends in the United States, Britain and other liberal democracies. Most new right commentators shrug off this question by claiming (correctly) that there is no evidence that deinstitutionalization has yet reduced overall state spending on social policy or law and order – indeed, the trend has been perfectly compatible with major budgetary growth. The diversification of agencies and delivery systems has served only to maximize job opportunities and promotion prospects for the new class of state-employed professionals. But this gut reaction only highlights a possible collective interest in the DE process, without showing how it is *individually* rational for bureaucrats in established agencies to accept (still less promote) it. As with privatization, the budget-maximizing view bifurcates at this point into heroic and fatalist variants.

The *heroic variant* accepts that the DE process marks a significant change in agency behaviour and that this contradicts budget-maximizing predictions. Again, reforms are ascribed to the strong political backlash against bureaucratic over-provision orchestrated by new right parties and political leaders, especially the Thatcher and Reagan governments which have forced the pace of reforms and changed the parameters of previous bureaucratic behaviour. The heroic view counts the DE process as an effective weapon in new right policy analysis because it breaks up monopoly providers, weakens public services, fragments public service client groups, and is strongly associated with privatization – especially in the United States. Inherent in this perspective is the strong expectation that because the DE process marks the limiting of bureaucratic power over clients and *vis-à-vis* sponsors, it is always implemented against the determined resistance of established agencies.

The *fatalist variant* denies that single-tier deinstitutionalization marks a significant change in bureaus' behaviour, and seeks its causes in agencies' internal environment. Some authors claim that whenever legislative demand for their services shifts down, bureaucrats reduce their diversion of resources for private purposes, and instead invest in raising sponsors' demand again until it has stabilized (Hoenak, 1983, p. 252). Thus DE reforms might be represented as a strategy allowing slow-growing bureaus to trigger re-expansion of their funding. But for an established agency the displacement of budgetary growth to other agencies inherent in the DE process could easily cause cumulative losses of political muscle and status, rendering budget cycle arguments more than usually implausible (see page 166). A more plausible fatalist view sees DE changes as lagging years or even decades behind the realization that institutionalized 'care' does not work or is being rejected by clients. Large public facilities are often anachronistic and unresponsive to consumer demands, with state professionals vetoing alternative provision and using subtle forms of coercion in order to artificially fill otherwise empty places. The key question about DE reforms is not, therefore, why did they happen at all, but why did they take so long?

Two-tier deinstitutionalization

Here the DE process involves national-level control or transfer agencies enforcing a switch of policy on sub-central implementing agencies. Although budget-maximizing explanations generally say little about complex administrative systems and interactions, it is possible to construct more plausible heroic and fatalist explanations of the DE process when the initiative for change is top-down rather than bottom-up, since the central government agency promoting change need no longer suffer direct budget losses.

The *heroic variant* no longer relies solely on political factors to override opposition to the DE process from large established agencies. Instead, central departments can become an important additional source of pressure to run down established institutional provision and to transfer growth budgets to alternative delivery organizations, especially in unitary states. Before the 1980s, top-tier agencies followed conventional public administration doctrines of avoiding duplication and relying on functionally organized delivery systems. A key impact of new right political leaders such as Thatcher or Reagan and 'new public management' thinking amongst administrators has been to shift away from implementation systems monopolized by one particular type of agency, profession, or trade union, and to move instead towards multiple, competing implementation systems (Pirie, 1988b).

Central or federal-level departments are not as threatened by the DE process as established implementing agencies. But reforms can still disrupt their patronage networks, reduce their program budgets, and reveal unwelcome information about the marginal costs and benefits of welfare state outputs. Hence national-level bureaucracies may produce only DE plans which boost overall program budgets in their policy sector and avoid any major policy termination. Changes tend to be offered only where existing policy is obviously failing and public discontent is already high.

Reforms often hinge on 'bribing' vested interests to accept cumulatively significant 'micro-politics' changes (Pirie, 1988a) and on a sophisticated 'public use of private interests' (Schultze, 1977). As before, bottom-tier agencies fiercely resist a top-down DE process. However, in unitary states where national departments dispose of stronger legislative and regulatory powers over sub-central governments, the heroic account can now better explain how relatively timely DE changes can be forced through against established agencies' opposition.

The *fatalist variant* explains a two-tier DE process in terms of cycles of budgetary growth and cutbacks, building on some remarks by Niskanen (1971) and Blais and Dion (1988). Suppose a central bureau C relies on bottom-tier agency B to get its policies implemented. If B becomes politically unpopular or discredited with the party in power nationally, then C's ability to attract program budget increments is impaired by its dependency on B. Here creating alternative more acceptable delivery mechanisms allow the central department to restart program budget growth. For example, the US 1935 Social Security Act switched funding growth from established state and city government hospitals and long-stay homes towards philanthropic and private sector service suppliers, triggering a major expansion in funding and greater popular acceptance of welfare state interventions (Lerman, 1982, p. 11). Similarly, in Britain the central education ministry originally relied solely on local councils as implementation agencies. In the 1980s, however, the Thatcher government was so hostile to local government that rival central departments with more market-oriented implementation systems began to nibble away control over education policy-making. By encouraging schools and colleges to 'opt out' of municipal control, the education ministry was able to escape from its dependence on local government, defend its policy territory from rivals and secure its program budget against attack (see Dunleavy and Rhodes, 1988).

Pruning to promote growth may be especially attractive to national agencies responsible for 'cinderella services' constrained by long-standing budgetary limits. But 'switching horses' organizationally and promoting new approaches to care help to modernize services and compete more effectively for program budget increments with rivals. Similarly, in 'crowded policy space' there are greater pressures to free resources for new initiatives by terminating old policies (Hogwood and Peters, 1982). Budgetary expansion will typically be faster for new or redesigned services, strengthening the attraction of a top-down DE process for budget-maximizing officials in national agencies. Top-tier departments can use legislation or central financial controls to overcome resistance to the DE process, even where this precipitates absolute budget declines or policy termination in bottom-tier organizations. More commonly, however, established implementing agencies suffer only *relative* budgetary decline. And fatalist accounts stress that the aggregate of old and new delivery agencies' budgets (in many cases the program or super-program budget for the top-tier agency) will grow or remain stable.

However, the fatalist explanation still confronts a fundamental problem. Why should rationally self-interested officials in national-level control or transfer agencies care about their program budgets, which go over-whelmingly to other organizations? Why protect the 5 per cent of the program budget absorbed by central agencies' core budgets by maximizing the remaining 95 per cent? Senior bureaucrats in top-tier agencies have much more direct and effective ways of increasing their welfare than by engineering large-scale DE changes. For example, simply recentralizing a fraction of the program budget would boost the top agency's standing far more easily if central officials are budget-maximizers.

Of course, there is some evidence from Washington and Whitehall of strong bureaucratic cultural norms, which assign considerable significance to program budget 'headline totals'. In national budget debates agencies are seen as going up or down in the world on the strength of their global appropriations, almost irrespective of who finally spends the money. Yet the existence of such irrational norms and interpretations cannot save the fatalist view. Why should budget-maximizing bureaucrats (vying with each other for scarce resources) collectively subscribe to norms centring on symbolic 'success' rather than much more directly welfare-boosting objectives? Even supposing that such norms become established at all, how can officials who believe in them survive or secure promotion in competition with bureaucrats with a more objective focus on utility-maximization? The fatalist variant can only explain why national bureaucrats promote top-down deinstitutionalization by assuming that they fetishize program budget levels in ways which no rational choice account can consistently explain.

Bureau-shaping explanations

By contrast, the bureau-shaping model offers a developed account of why senior officials generally accept or promote both deinstitutionalization and privatization, so much so that explaining inappropriate privatization becomes an important task. The general argument is that there are strong internal pressures for facilitating changes which are popularly interpreted as externally imposed, a theme which applies also to some other new right policy changes – such as Reagan's 'revolution' in antitrust policy (Eisner and Meier, 1990). To crudely represent public service bureaucrats as uniformly hostile to institutional change because they are 'a powerful special interest – an interest dedicated to hierarchical control' (Chubb and Moe, 1988, p. 1069) fails to take account of the variable stakes in policy areas held by central, state or local officials; the radically different interests of bureaucrats across types of agency; and the professional pressures in failing administrative systems to devise more adequate alternatives.

Deinstitutionalization

The DE process is not resisted by the professionals and officials running large established agencies, because these traditional social policy or penal organizations are often anachronistic in the modern period. Institutions' staffing structures and treatment methods have little professional content. Most staff are low-paid and semi-skilled carers. Physical arrangements are inappropriate and hard to change. The scale of institutions is often extremely large by modern standards, making them hard to manage in any coherent guided fashion. Therapeutic effects on clients are not very visible. Hence this type of organization is prone to periodic scandals, and is often subject to continuous external criticism.

Many facilities which simply 'warehouse' their inmates (like large mental hospitals, municipal children's homes or prisons) originated in the late nineteenth century as highly bureaucratized attempts to tidy up and centralize previously unsystematic forms of care. In Britain the workhouse tradition and a repressive prison system were founded on strong reactions against 'outdoor relief' and lax and corrupt prison regimes respectively. In the United States similar attitudes still played a key role in governmental and private charity policies in the early twentieth century (Lerman, 1982, Chapter 1). Institutionalization in its day was seen as progressive because it stressed predictable routines, equitable rules and disinterested officials. But from the 1920s onward, and particularly in the post-war period, organizations which pre-date the emergence of coherent professionalized solutions to social welfare or law-and-order problems have become progressively less attractive job locations for senior officials.

In the bureau-shaping model rational senior bureaucrats do not value routine, conflictual work in large organizations staffed mainly by non-élite personnel, exposed to public criticism and risks from mistakes and situated a long way from political power centres. Instead, they value individually innovative work with a developmental rhythm, a broad scope of concerns, low exposure to public criticism, collegial and élite work units, restricted hierarchy, congenial personal relations, high-status organizational and social contacts especially professional ones, and proximity to political power centres. Hence they support a DE process which is consistent with reshaping their bureau into an optimum form for them, that is, a staff unit with a small core budget determining and managing policy by channelling funds to private firms, the voluntary sector or subordinate public agencies.

Forms of deinstitutionalization which simply transfer blocks of funding from an established agency's core budget to its bureau budget or program budget attract the strongest support from senior bureaucrats, whose welfare is only slightly bound up with direct agency control of policy delivery. For example, a shift from running children's homes directly to using foster parents makes little difference to the welfare of top managers in a local social services department. Even where new forms of provision are much more cost-effective, so that their large-scale adoption cuts aggregate program budgets, they are still pursued by senior officials so long as they help reshape their bureau in a favoured direction. For instance, using foster parents is much cheaper than running children's homes, yet it also requires more professional social workers to operate placements and assessments. The clear losers in this example of reorganization are low-paid care workers in the children's homes, and perhaps the children themselves if fostering fails to provide a stable background for them. As with hiving-off (page 225), the DE process moves delivery agencies towards a control or transfer agency configuration, thereby insulating senior officials' welfare from dependence on high program budget levels.

Even if DE reforms mean that established agencies relinquish funding or policy responsibilities to another agency altogether – for example, a British health authority loses a block of work to local government – senior bureaucrats may well support the change. Selective load-shedding which exports troublesome, low-grade, low-status and repetitive tasks to rival agencies (while preserving a viable core of established agency activities), or simply tasks which reduce the coherence of the organization's 'mission', can be fairly easily explained. Large-scale load-shedding which opens the way towards a major redefinition of work tasks or internal structures favourable for policy or professional-level officials is also perfectly consistent with the bureau-shaping model. For example, where a large mental hospital is to be mostly closed but the professionals in post are to create a new smaller, more intensive and more specialist psychiatric unit, the welfare of the senior officials is still protected or expanded. All agencies defend their 'turfs' within an unchanged bureau-definition. But closing down activities in the course of radically reshaping the bureau's role is perfectly feasible, as are policy termination and quite large-scale budget-losses which free resources (such as redundant land and buildings) useful in developing other work tasks. The only case that the bureau-shaping model cannot explain is where an established agency's senior officials support their bureau's termination without any continuity being maintained with replacement organizations. There seem to be few, if any, examples of this kind of change.

Two-tier deinstitutionalization strengthens the bureau-shaping model's expectation that the DE process could effect radical changes with minimal conflict. Senior officials in national control or transfer agencies are not committed to defending their existing program budgets, and may view the prospect of substantial cuts with equanimity, because 95 per cent of this funding only nominally flows through them. Of course, a small amount of patronage power and insurance value (slack creation to cope with crises) may attach to a high level of program budget. Boosting bureau prestige and maintaining good relations with private sector organizations may make senior officials defend high *bureau* budget levels (providing of course that private sector recipients are themselves substantial organizations).

A top-down DE process could threaten these relatively intangible benefits for senior central bureaucrats. But bureau-shaping strategies are better methods of compensating for any losses than defending a status quo where the welfare of senior officials depends on high program budget levels. DE proposals have few positive or negative impacts on central government agencies which are already in a control agency or transfer agency configuration. Senior officials in national agencies must resist DE reforms which would recentralize checking or inspections, or threaten to reinvolve them in line administration, even if their core budget would be re-enlarged.

The DE process involves up to three sets of senior bureaucrats (in top-tier, established agencies and new organizations), all trying to restructure their own activities (and the activities they supervise) in ways which fit with their preferences and ideal image of their bureau. Tensions and contradictions between them are bound to occur, but may not produce the overt organizational conflict predicted by budget-maximizing or even pluralist accounts. Established agencies want their funding to cover run-down costs and hangover-overheads, but none the less they may want to create a coherent reshaped structure for their organizations fairly quickly. New or expanding organizations want funding growth to keep pace with their expanding responsibilities and obligations, but to build up their activities selectively rather than wholesale.

The bureau-shaping model predicts solutions which load costs onto three other participants in the DE process: the low-paid and least powerful workers in established agencies, the clients whose futures are being resolved and redirected, and often also informal carers in the community. This thrust seems to fit well with the closed exclusionary manner in which professional debates about policy change are often handled (Dunleavy, 1981b; Rhodes, 1988, pp. 286–305). The main protection for clients' interests comes from the countervailing forces at work in the triadic relationship between top-tier, established and new agencies, together with a general bureaucratic anxiety to avoid mistakes and scandals. Where the DE process runs down public facilities in favour of community-based provision rather than a new agency, differences between the top-tier and the established agency are particularly likely to be minimized by imposing costs on fragmented and relatively powerless clients and their immediate families. The interests of clients and carers are only fortuitously protected by senior bureaucrats in top-tier, established, and new agencies. A real danger of inappropriate (that is, welfare-reducing) deinstitutionalization consequently exists.

Privatization

Contracting out or competitive tendering does not generally represent a threat to senior bureaucrats in the bureau-shaping model. There are various features of the process which positively favour their interests. In particular, contracting arrangements require legislators to reveal their demand for goods or services in advance of budget setting, curtailing the use of dissimulation strategies in their dealings with the bureaucracy (Miller and Moe, 1983, p. 321). And sponsors must often commit to contracts for services for periods of three to five years, powerfully insulating these programmes in otherwise turbulent political environments. So long as central policy staff are retained in post, these are powerful advantages to gain. Policy-level staffs in almost all types of agency should co-operate in shedding low-level, or routine functions to contractors. What does it matter to senior bureaucrats (any more than to managers in private companies) who changes the towels in the office washrooms, so long as they do get changed? Because senior bureaucrats' utilities attach mainly to the bureau budget, their interests are simply not engaged in these decisions on behalf of preserving the status quo.

Like hiving-off, competitive tendering and contracting out allow policy-level officials in line bureaus to effect radical transformations in their agency's character and status. A delivery agency can metamorphose quite rapidly into a contracts agency dealing with private firms, or perhaps a control agency in social policy areas where service delivery is devolved to smaller-scale bureaus, or to voluntary or non-profit organizations. Either change effectively insulates policy-level staff from reliance on continued high levels of program budget appropriations in order to maintain their welfare levels. Managerial flexibility also increases, as a study of US federal government privatization noted:

> The demand for many government services changes over time and the big advantage for bureau-heads was that contracting-out provided them with the ability to close one thing down and instruct another contractor to do someting else 'more efficiently and rapidly'.
> Unfettered by civil service rules, the public sector union resistance and the requirement to pay superannuation and other benefits, senior managers were able to respond to the challenges of their jobs within a budget that was shrinking in real terms. (Massey, 1990, p. 13)

Policy-level staff are keenest to shift over to contracting where they can deal regularly with a few large corporations which have congruent management structures, are simple to monitor and have higher status and prestige. Large firms can better organize flowbacks of benefits for their official contacts, and they share bureaucrats' well-attested preferences for negotiated or selective tendering procedures rather than open competition (Turpin, 1972). But senior bureaucrats have less to gain from privatizing activities in highly competitive markets. Small businesses are constantly shifting, hard to monitor, prone to failure and their performance is highly sensitive to personnel changes. Bureaucrats' preferences thus distort privatization policy, promoting contracting-out where agencies become dependent upon a few oligopolistic suppliers, but resisting it where highly competitive markets exist.

Contracting-out and competitive tendering often entail considerable transition costs, but these are again borne overwhelmingly by rank-and-file state workers, whose job security, hours of work, working conditions, access to union protection and wage rates all get squeezed when firms take over service delivery. The greater the grade distinctions and social differences between policy-level bureaucrats and implementing staff, the less likely it is that rational managers will oppose privatization. Public service organizations often have a polarized social class profile, with many graduates and professionals, substantial routine white-collar staffs, few skilled workers, and large numbers of low-paid, semi-skilled or unskilled workers. Unionization levels are often high and create some greater solidarity, but policy-level staffs are usually in different unions from manual workers. In addition, senior public officials in Britain and the United States are overwhelmingly males in full-time employment, while grass roots staff are predominantly female and often working part-time, especially in social policy agencies. Sexist management attitudes often regard female part-timers as 'working for pin money': hence redundancies do not involve a loss of 'real jobs'. Finally, the ethnic balance of government agencies may also disincline managers to protect in-house staffs from privatization. In Britain policy-level officials are disproportionately white, while black employees are concentrated in agencies' manual workforces.

Privatization normally entails significant changes in the form of service provision, either reduced quality standards, or decreased public or consumer control over service provision. But again policy-level bureaucrats' welfare is little affected, especially where there is a wide social gap between policy-level officials and their agencies' clients in terms of class, gender, age, or ethnicity – as in most welfare state agencies dealing with the poor, elderly, unemployed, disabled or homeless. Even in policy fields where bureaucrats themselves consume public services, spatial segregation can recreate a wide social gap between senior officials and clients – as when the schooling, health care or environmental services in run-down areas are managed by officials living in more congenial parts of the metropolis.

Inappropriate privatization

Contracting out or competitive tendering may be introduced in conditions where they *reduce* the social welfare. Such inappropriate privatization becomes a general risk in the bureau-shaping account. Senior bureaucrats may go along with organizational changes because they enhance the reshaping of their agencies in ways they find congenial, even if the public interest implications are negative. But why should politicians or legislators want to push ahead with large-scale competitive tendering or contracting out if its net social impacts are deleterious?

The bureau-shaping model points to situations where the 'internal' or financial costs of government agencies' providing public services are different from their full 'social' costs, taking account of externality effects (see Becker, 1983, p. 387). Demands from public opinion and the legislature as a whole (acting in a non-budgetary role) often mean that government agencies are expected to foster desirable social developments which have little if anything to do with their specific objectives. These requirements are monitored and enforced by central control or regulatory agencies, and effectively raise public agencies' internal costs above those of firms carrying out equivalent activities. Examples include:

Employment practices
Paying 'a living wage' or above-minimum wage levels.
Using regular salaried staffs, not casual labour.
Encouraging proper pensions development.
Operating recruitment and promotion policies strictly on a meritocratic basis.
Devising and enforcing good health and safety-at-work measures.
Encouraging racial and sexual equality of opportunity.
Positively helping handicapped clients or employees.
Using above minimal numbers of professional staff in appropriate contexts.

Industrial relations
Recognizing trade unions and practising 'good industrial relations'.
Assessing cases fairly and acting reasonably.

Client orientation
Operating fail-safe and double-check procedures against mistakes.
Thoroughly investigating grievances and complaints.
Thoroughly respecting confidentiality.
Treating people (whether workers or clients) with respect and giving advice on their rights.
Always acting in the letter and spirit of the law.

Consultation
Consulting the public on issues affecting them.
Accepting political interference and guidance.
Generally observing 'good practice' rather than cutting corners.

All of these constraints bear most heavily in cost terms on bureaus with a lot of staff and direct contact with the public, especially delivery agencies. They are such prominent employers that they are a symbolically important leverage point, a sector of the labour market where the government can 'give a lead' to other large organizations. Taxing and trading agencies are also strongly affected, followed after a large gap by service, transfer agencies

242

and perhaps contract agencies. Control and regulatory agencies' small staffs and absence of large-scale implementation responsibilities mean they are little involved.

Majority opinion in Western democracies regards most of these extra requirements on public agencies as improving the social welfare (LeGrand and Robinson, 1984; Heald, 1983). By contrast, the new right argue that these constraints are counter-productive. Yet higher public sector employment and service standards have by and large survived numerous challenges under neo-conservative governments in the United States and Britain (Rose *et al.*, 1985). To establish that the majority view of extra public sector requirements is generally well grounded would involve a lengthy digression away from the mainline of the argument, so I simply note here that my arguments below are underpinned by the premiss that these features normally do enhance the social welfare when applied in public service systems.

In principle the legislature can take into account any 'by-product' benefits of this kind by up-rating the marginal social benefit curve used to appraise an agency's outputs, since costs are defined in most micro-economic analysis simply as forgone utilities (McCormich *et al.*, 1974, pp. 201–18). This seems to be the position implicitly adopted by Niskanen who considers only the legislature's (social) demand curve and the agency's (private) internal cost curve. However, there are four reasons why this strategy of sublimating all externalities in the positioning of the social benefits curve is unsatisfactory, and instead externalities should be accommodated by drawing a separate *marginal social cost curve* for the agency:

1. *Comparability*. Positive (or negative) externalities treated as affecting private firms' costs should be similarly treated for government, or no comparable analysis of the two is feasible.

2. *Generality*. The legislature will perceive positive externalities uniquely produced by one agency's activity, and incorporate them in its marginal social benefit curve. But general benefits produced by *all* government agencies (when compared with having a private organization implementing policy) may not be perceived or incorporated, even though the extra requirements on any given agency 'artificially' boosts its internal costs above those of private firms.

3. *Fragmentation*. As Niskanen argued, the sponsor body (whether a committee of the legislature or a political department head) is normally organized on programme lines. Since the programme committee (rather than the legislature as a whole) effectively defines demand, it may well fail to take into account generalized external benefits (or costs) outside its purview.

4. *Asymmetry between benefits and costs*. If an agency's activities impose costs upon individuals, groups, firms or other organizations they will generate

vocal complaints to the legislature. But generalized benefits from agency operations may not be very visible to the public and certainly will not be concentrated enough to show up in increments of public support for particular programmes. Public appreciation will show through only in diffuse ways, such as overall satisfaction with government or trust in officials (Rose, 1989). Hence legislatures or sponsors differentially perceive external costs more than external benefits, an effect greatly strengthened by the impact of politicians' vote-winning calculus (Wilson, 1973, Chapter 16).

When public agencies externalize benefits, but in a way which is not directly taken account of by the legislature or public opinion in setting their budgets, they have two cost curves: a higher marginal internal cost line and a lower marginal social cost curve. Inappropriate privatization is highly likely in this situation because the agency's internal costs will be above those of private firms. If the committee of the legislature or political department head becomes aware of this differential, perceives a possibility to make financial savings and does not fully appreciate the agency's externalized benefits, then contracting-out may well go ahead despite reducing overall social welfare.

In Figure 8.1 the internal costs optimal level of output is at Q_1. Suppose for argument's sake that the agency (especially a delivery agency) manages to budget-maximize so successfully that it actually pushes output up as far as Q_2, which is the socially optimal level of output – since at B the marginal social benefits and costs of production are equalized. The marginal cost curve for the firm lies in between the two agency cost curves (for simplicity I assume that the firm's internal and social costs are identical at MC_F). Privatization produces a fall in output from Q_2 to Q_3. But this does not indicate – as the new right might claim – that the agency was previously oversupplying outputs. Instead it shows that by not having to meet public sector operating requirements, the privatized firm is able to lower its marginal internal cost curve – from the agency's level at MIC_A to the new level at MC_F. But since this also reduces the generalized benefits accruing to the rest of society, the overall (social cost) consumers' surplus of UBR under the government agency has been reduced to the (internal cost) consumers' surplus UCT after privatization. Variants on this basic picture can allow for contract compliance policies by public agencies maintaining some constraints on corporations taking over bureau functions, so that the firm's social cost curve is lower than its internal costs level. Alternatively, the firm gaining the contract may be particularly freed from constraints on its internal practices, even as a contractor to the government, so that its MSC curve lies above its internal cost curve (Dunleavy, 1986, pp. 26–30).

Suppose that the private firm taking over an agency's functions has an internal cost curve at OT in Figure 8.2, well below that of the public agency

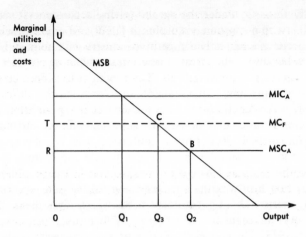

Figure 8.1 **The impact of privatization where an agency externalizes benefits**

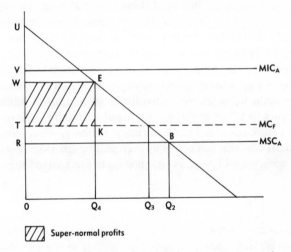

Figure 8.2 **The impact of privatization where contractors can make super-normal profits**

(and again I assume the firm's social and internal costs are identical for simplicity). If the firm can disguise this cost level from the sponsor it has a discretionary ability to charge the legislature a price as high as OV – set by the internal cost levels at which other public agencies are still operating, or by the cost levels involved in restarting an in-house capability. If de-privatization is still feasible, the firm chooses a level such as OW, just below public agency costs, but maximizing the firm's ability to make super-normal profits (equivalent to the area EKTW). Here production has fallen dramatically from Q_2 under the agency (giving a consumers' surplus of UBR) to Q_4 (with a consumers' surplus of UEW). Of course, these losses could not occur in a perfectly competitive industry with no price fixing by contractors, because of the threat of new entrants winning contracts. Some markets, such as those for routine ancillary functions like office-cleaning or catering, may approximate this situation.

However, if the functions to be contracted out are specialized, have no private sector counterpart, or require large amounts of organizational expertise and capital, then private contractors can be oligopolistically organized to jointly maintain super-normal profits and exclude would-be entrants to the market. Changing contractors can also be problematic, because the first firm winning a privatization tender gains special knowledge and expertise about government needs which gives them an unfair advantage over subsequent competitors – Williamson's 'information impactedness' (1975, Chapters 1–2). Taking on a contractor may also create dependency on them, as when agencies build up data on one proprietary computer system and then find that major transition costs attach to shifting to an alternative supplier. In any of these circumstances effective market competition at the recontracting stage is prevented, and firms taking over government functions have every prospect of making super-normal profits with a particularly heavy cost in social welfare terms.

A final aspect of inappropriate privatization concerns bureaus which *externalize costs*, such as a regulatory agency which creates workload or other compliance costs for firms or individuals, or a transfer agency which requires clients to fill in multiple forms and surmount high information thresholds before gaining social security benefits. Here the agency's marginal social cost curve is above its marginal internal cost curve (Figure 8.3). If the agency could persuade its sponsor to fund up to the point where

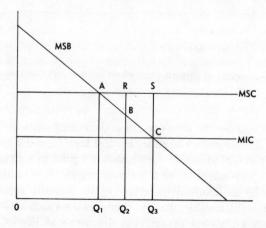

Figure 8.3 **The impact of privatization where an agency externalizes costs**

its internal costs are being covered by social returns on the expenditure, this is still an oversupply situation measured against the social cost curve. But in practice citizens' complaints will normally ensure that the legislature or political department head can determine roughly where the agency's MSC curve lies. Suppose that the sponsor is able to limit output to Q_2, although the consumers surplus is still cut by an area ARB where the social costs of agency activity outweigh social benefits. Privatizing an agency function like this normally entails or coincides with reduced scrutiny by the sponsor. Citizens' complaints go directly to the firm, or at best to the bureau monitoring the contractors, but not to elected representatives, who no longer have a voice in implementation. Assume the sponsor can prevent the firm making super-normal profits. The firm's profitability is tied to output levels, so corporation managers increase activity to Q_3 in order to maximize profits. The area of net socially wasteful production grows to ASC, and again social welfare falls.

Conclusion

This chapter has considered two different ways of assessing the comparative plausibility of budget-maximizing and bureau-shaping models, specific empirical tests and the ability to interpret some broader organizational trends. There is little reason to suppose that Niskanen's demand-side conditions generally exist. The existing empirical support for budget-maximizing models is scanty in the extreme. The various micro-level extrapolations from budget-maximizing accounts which can be directly tested are overwhelmingly unfavourable to these accounts: 'These models seem to have little to recommend them as models of the real world of public bureaucracy' (Peters, 1989a, p. 142). Budget-maximizing models commonly draw casual support from the extent of post-war government growth, but there are multiple other possible explanations and no multi-variate tests which satisfactorily establish any causal link from bureaucratic behaviour to expansion. The more testable implications of budget-maximizing accounts linking growth to increasing centralization of government run contrary to post-war trends. The institutional form of state growth has been as a decentralized network of agencies, not the expansion of large line bureaus which the Niskanen model entails. And the account cannot explain key reorganizations such as large-scale hiving-off in the United Kingdom. Add to this catalogue the public choice literature's astonishing lack of enthusiasm for critically testing or empirically applying budget-maximizing models and it is hard to see their popularity as founded on anything but an intuitive faith in their message or an ideological predisposition to accept them without testing.

The bureau-shaping account also remains to be systematically proved, but despite its recent appearance empirical applications have begun

(Dunleavy, 1989a, 1989b). The model is congruent with a wide range of demand-side conditions and its predictions closely fit with available micro-level evidence about the pattern of budgetary growth in the 1970s and cutbacks in the 1980s. The bureau-shaping approach directly predicts the institutional patterns of post-war growth and easily explains why large-scale hiving-off reorganizations can occur.

Turning to the interpretation of privatization and deinstitutionalization, budget-maximizing models clearly have considerable difficulty in accounting for the emergence and strength of these contemporary meta-trends, or in explaining the low level of bureaucratic resistance to them. Fundamentally, the budget-maximizing account sees these changes as unwelcome and irrational for budget-maximizing officials, and the split between heroic and fatalist variants reflects the new right's difficulty in trying to explain the phenomena away. Heroic accounts posit the parameter-shifting intervention of new right super-figures, endowed with a mysterious insulation from the corrupting influences which affect all other politicians, and able to reverse entrenched (and supposedly deductively necessary) patterns of behaviour. Appealing to such Nietzschean acts of will only begins to look plausible for two-tier deinstitutionalization, but even here the heroic model achieves a descriptive fit at the cost of impugning the causal basis of budget-maximization as a general prediction. Fatalist explanations, by contrast, preserve theoretical consistency at the cost of junking key new right policy prescriptions. Neither privatization nor deinstitutionalization offer any prospect of reducing government spending or bureaucratic power in the policy process. Especially applied to two-tier deinstitutionalization, the argument that budgetary cycles allow 'pruning to promote growth' of top-tier agencies' program budgets fits some empirical trends in the early post-war period. But it still depends on central bureaucrats wanting to maximize global budgets that have only a vestigial connection with their welfare.

By contrast, the bureau-shaping model offers direct, detailed and effective explanations of why privatization and deinstitutionalization should have emerged as major trends in the contemporary period. It predicts that senior managers and officials will accept and promote these changes in order to facilitate reshaping of their bureaus in line with their preferences, and outlines how many of the transition costs involved are likely to be displaced onto rank-and-file public service workers and onto clients and the broader community. The model also highlights the likelihood that inappropriate, welfare-reducing privatization and deinstitutionalization will occur when the financial and welfare costs of public agency provision diverge.

Chapter 9

CONCLUSION – ECONOMIC EXPLANATIONS IN POLITICAL SCIENCE

At root public choice approaches rely heavily on an analogy: 'Politics is seen as a "market" activity, one which serves as an extension of the economic market' (Ware, 1979, p. 5). Every market has demand-side and supply-side actors. Neo-classical economics and public choice theory have traditionally handled these two sets of actors differently, making significantly divergent assumptions about why they behave as they do. The revised accounts of political institutions given here call some of these premisses into question.

DEMAND-SIDE IMPLICATIONS

Properly specified, the rational actor model of consumption involves quite a few requirements: that people have determinant preferences which are easily discovered, ranked, and transitively ordered; that actors do not become satiated with consumption, and hence they continuously maximize; that actors are basically self-regarding and instrumental in their behaviour. Only if all these stages hold, and if decision-makers are unitary actors, will people behave rationally, making choices so as to maximize benefits net of costs. Each of these stages can plausibly be questioned in political contexts. People may not have determinant preferences on most political issues; may not rank political preferences (for example, because there is no common numeraire like money in economic markets); may operate with intransitive preference orderings; may be easily satiated and hence only satisfice in their political 'consumption'; and may behave altruistically in important respects.

These are serious difficulties which cannot be easily dismissed by the bland efforts of public choice enthusiasts to gloss over them. For example Tullock (1976, p. 5) argues:

> Voters and customers are essentially the same people. Mr Smith buys and votes; he is the same man in the supermarket and in the voting

249

booth. There is no strong reason to believe his behaviour is radically different in the two environments. We assume that in both he will choose the product or candidate he thinks is the best bargain for him.

In a restricted sense the analysis given here accepts this public choice approach, the sense of using rationally self-interested behaviour as a working postulate capable of producing developed and potentially useful explanations of political behaviour. But in another sense the import of my accounts of group-joining, voting and even bureaucratic motivations is to insist that the environmental differences between the voting-booth and the supermarket are vitally important to how people make decisions. The two key public choice assumptions queried in my account are that people are fully informed in making their political choices, and that political actors' preferences are exogenously determined and hence unchanging with the political process in which they are involved.

Perfect information assumptions are pervasive in economic analysis. For example, the neo-classical model of perfect competition requires that 'all buyers and sellers have complete information on the prices being asked and offered in all other parts of the market [being analysed]' (Bannock *et al.*, 1979, p. 343). This strong postulate underlies the picture of economic markets as a 'doubly decentralized system', 'both informationally decentralized (decision-makers know only "their own" information) and decisionally decentralized' (Gravelle and Rees, 1981, p. 11). Similarly, the pure theory of consumer decision-making in terms of indifference curves assumes that 'the consumer has full knowledge of the availability of commodities, their technological qualities, and their exact prices' (Miller, 1978, p. 16). In addition, various hidden strategies have been adopted to make stringent information requirements seem plausible, especially the device of redrawing demand and supply curve diagrams whenever the smallest change is made in the goods being marketed. 'It has been the tradition . . . to consider the confrontation between a consumer and possible choices among goods as a direct one. Goods are goods, and a consumer exercises his choice among them' (Lancaster, 1974, p. 217). When the key influences upon product demand are undeniably product innovation and differentiation, it is highly simplifying to assume that goods are undifferentiated or operate in separate 'markets' from each other.

The status of perfect information requirements in economic analysis more generally remains disputed. The orthodox line has followed Robbins (1935, pp. 93–6) in claiming that information conditions are merely simplifying expository devices, adopted temporarily to help build up pure theory, but not fundamental or indispensable elements of developed economic reasoning (and see page 53). Critics argue that unless the assumption of transitive preferences is linked to a perfect information requirement, then rational actor models become contentless and irrefutable (Hutchinson, 1938).

The 'fundamental principle' of economic theory [according to Robbins] is that all agents maximize. . . . But our theory does not tell us how to maximize; rather, it assumes that agents not only strive to reach a maximum position, but are aware of how to reach it. But to [assume] that one knows how to maximize requires that the maximizing agent has full information concerning both current and future prices, incomes and tastes. . . . Thus the maximization principle . . . is based on the wholly unrealistic assumption that expectations are perfect. The major problem encountered by agents in the real world is how to make rational decisions in the face of uncertainty; the neo-classical solution assumes away the crux of [this] problem. (Caldwell, 1984, pp. 109–10)

On this view precisely because they are so contestable, perfect foresight requirements make it feasible to test economic models and see how far they match up with reality. If we find that people in fact act unreflectively, on impulse, or out of habit, then we have grounds for doubting the applicability of the rational actor model – but we can simultaneously be confident that it is after all an empirical model and not an irrefutable set of tautologies.

These criticisms, plus the extraordinary persistence of strong assumptions about information in neo-classical and public choice models, suggest that at the least these premises play a much more important role in economic analysis than the orthodox defence admits. Even when efforts are made to incorporate imperfect information into models, as with Downs's account of voting behaviour, public choice authors committed to model-development rather than empirical applicability constantly reintroduce stringent informational premises on very slender arguments. For example, Breton criticizes Downs because his work is:

primarily a theory of how [electoral] competition can work in a world where information is costly and it is not profitable [*sic*], at least for a large number of agents, to acquire any. . . . But it is difficult to believe, when one observes the large amount of political activity that exists in democratic societies, the large flow of political news put out by media seeking to maximize the level of their rating and/or the value of their advertising revenue and hence the attention of a large number of people, and the large number of individuals who vote, that political information exists in very small amounts. [For example], it was suggested to me that it is probable that not a single day goes by in any given year without an election of some kind taking place in the United States. (Breton, 1974, p. 6)

This simplistic effort to suggest that Downs modelled an information-poor environment does not stand up to analysis for a minute. *An Economic Theory of Democracy* is explicitly about an information-rich world

251

where assembling, screening and evaluating the mass of data transmitted is a costly undertaking:

> Thousands of specialized agencies gather, interpret and transmit [political] information, making it available to the citizenry in a tremendous variety of forms, from television broadcasts to encyclopaedias. But since the resources any citizen can devote to paying for and assimilating data are limited, he finds himself in a situation of economic choice: from among these many sources of information, he must select only a few to tap. (Downs, 1957, pp. 212–13)

Even in more sophisticated accounts, however, the conceptualization of information is extremely limited. For example, I noted above (page 53) that Downs assumed that all 'information' is factually correct and does not need checking for accuracy, although its interpretation or significance might be contentious.

Exogenously fixed preferences were discussed extensively above (pages 98–110), and the assumption's central role in conventional economic analysis and most public choice reasoning is now scarcely disputed. 'Unspecified changes in tastes over time and unspecified differences in tastes between people are, as we know, capable of accounting for just about any behaviour we might observe' (Blaug, 1980, p. 241). Hence economic approaches have tried to exorcise this possibility for evading empirical refutation by fiat. But given the reluctance to test assumptions for 'realism', and the ability to pluralize deductive models quickly by variations taking account of objections and disconfirming evidence, the gains in empirical applicability from subscribing to the exogenous preference assumption remain conjectural (Caldwell, 1984). In political contexts it obviously interacts with stringent information assumptions, and with the premiss that people's preferences are determinant and easily discovered, to preclude examination of a critical area of interest – the extent to which political preferences are formed *within* and conditioned by the choice processes being analyzed.

The analyses of interest groups, voting and bureaucratic motivations given here all qualify one or both of the perfect information and exogenous preferences assumptions in significant ways:

The interest group process as described in Chapter 3 is dominated by the informational problems confronting potential group members. Group-joining depends upon a multi-stage perceptual process in which people's subjective estimations of the relevance of identity sets and group activity, and of the size and viability of interest groups, are likely to exert a much more important influence on their decisions than a rational calculus of the benefits of free-riding. Even if all the perceptual stages are resolved, the group-joining decision is complex, with multiple measures of the size of groups (that is, actual and potential memberships and rates of mobilization) affecting different non-joining considerations. The important category of endogenous groups present inherent difficulties for rational actors because the size of their identity sets (their potential memberships) cannot be established independently.

The critical role played by group identities in joining and mobilization decisions contradicts the exogenously fixed preferences assumption because the visibility of group identities fluctuates. Pure exogenous groups' identity sets are structurally determined, so that a given level of group recruitment and interest-defending activity will produce a relatively strong response. By contrast, pure endogenous groups have no significant structurally-given identity set, and are entirely dependent on their own activity to create identification with their cause. Perceptions of group identities are additionally heavily influenced by the level of environmental hostility, which is of course partly endogenously determined within the interest group process itself. For example, a group leadership which misjudges its course of action can trigger an adverse political and media reaction with consequent implications for subsequent group-joining and mobilization decisions by their potential members. In addition, the analysis of interest group democracy (in the final section of Chapter 3) demonstrated that how leaders guide interest groups – and especially the organizational structures established to integrate members into participation – influences members' and potential members' perceptions and behaviour.

The account of voting behaviour set out in Chapter 4 also infringes the key public choice demand-side assumptions. The decision to turn out and vote depends on a similar (if somewhat simpler) calculus to group-joining, in which inclusion in a party's identity set is a critical influence upon estimations of the party's size and viability. These informational influences are important because they considerably increase voters' dependence upon political leaders and parties in forming preferences (Page, 1978). They create scope for opinion leadership by candidates and for sudden shifts in the salience of issues with voters in response to parties' propaganda or alterations of policy stances. Information deficiency also underlies many forms of preference-shaping, notably in the way that governments use the political-business cycle to maximize short-term gains from myopic voters.

Several previous commentators have argued in passing for a review of the public choice assumption that voters' preferences are exogenously fixed. But the argument in Chapters 4 and 5 is not merely that it is desirable to make this change but that it is logically necessary to do so. The object of party competition is to win control of state power. And more than any other social agency, the government has the capacity to alter voters' preferences. Within a rational choice approach, self-interested incumbents will make use of state power for partisan advantage, hence inherently endogenizing voters' preferences within the process of party competition itself. Empirically, I reviewed a number of arguments for the importance and efficacy of both state power and party power as influences upon the shape of the aggregate distribution of preferences in the electorate.

Bureaucrats' motivations are not demand-side factor, but it is worth briefly considering here how their information and preferences were analyzed in comparison with those of voters and interest group members. Chapter 7 assumed that officials, especially senior bureaucrats, are relatively well informed by comparison with ordinary citizens. In particular, officials' possible maximands were identified as the global budget and the overall shape of a bureau, rather than assuming that their preferences centre around their particular section's budget or organization. These premises effectively mean that all (policy-level) bureaucrats have a strong identity with their agency. There is no counterpart among senior officials to the competing identities problem so important in group-joining and significant too for voters. Bureaucrats' strong pecuniary involvement with their agency, and the importance of rank structures in influencing their remuneration, influence and work tasks, provide strong enough reasons for adopting this different approach.

But in addition there is an important difference to note for policy-level bureaucrats compared with either those in lower ranks or the electorate. I noted in Chapter 7 that budget-maximizing and bureau-shaping are collective activities, which top officials are likely to pursue only if individual strategies for improving their welfare are exhausted or unavailable. Yet the gap between individual and collective avenues is still much less for bureaucrats than it is for citizens in general. Someone who joins an interest group or political party, or even votes in an election, has to undertake a radically different kind of activity from their normal daily round. This is the kernel of truth behind the early pluralist characterization of politics for many people as 'a remote, alien and unrewarding activity' (Dahl, 1961, p. 279); and their insistence that if 'a man's life work is banking, . . . he will spend his time at the bank and not manipulating community decisions' (Polsby, 1963, p. 117). But for senior officials in the modern extended state no such *stark* distinction between private and public spheres can be drawn, as the collapse of the old administration/politics dichotomy eloquently testifies (Aberbach *et al.*, 1981).

Hence the different treatment of bureaucrats' information and identities from those of voters or group members seems well founded. On the other hand, Chapter 7 also argued in line with those in Part I that bureaucrats' preferences are not exogenously fixed, but endogenously determined within the budget-setting and bureau-shaping processes which underlie agencies' activity (see below).

Conclusion

SUPPLY-SIDE IMPLICATIONS

The methodological rules which govern how neo-classical economics makes assumptions about the utilities of economic actors are rarely set out explicitly, but seem to be threefold. First, collective bodies (such as multi-person firms and households) are conventionally regarded as unitary actors, as if they were individuals, which they patently are not. A few authors complain that this involves treating economic molecules as if they are atoms (Liebenstein, 1976, p. 7). In public choice accounts of parties, interest groups and bureaucracies the unitary actor assumption constantly recurs: in the guise of an integrated leadership team fully controlling the group's strategy, or a dominant candidate directing the behaviour of political parties, or Niskanen's hegemonic top bureaucrat.

The second requirement is that different kinds of utilities can be attributed to economic actors only if these variations are strictly *role-related*. We cannot assume that some entrepreneurs derive utility from maximizing profits, while others increase their utilities by producing commodities, and still others maximize their utilities by increasing their leisure time. As I noted in relation to Downs's typology of bureaucratic personalities (page 168), it is inadmissible to make varying substantive assumptions about actors within a given role. But we can properly make different assumptions about all consumers (one role) and all entrepreneurs or firms (another role) to drive a deductive model.

The third requirement is that substantive assumptions about preferences are confined to 'intermediary', that is, supply-side, non-consumer roles. This view is the obverse side of the exogenous preferences assumption:

> As consumers, and therefore [*sic*] as human beings, people are
> themselves. This is the only role in the basic economist's model of
> society in which they indulge their personal eccentricities. We assume
> that the manager of a firm will not insist on producing pink
> automobiles just because he likes pink, but only if it is profitable to do
> so. When he receives his income, as salary or profits, his decisions on
> what to do with it are in his role as consumer, and he may then choose
> to live in a pink house and drive a pink car. . . . (Lancaster, 1974,
> p. 216)

In economics the principal supply-side, intermediary actors are firms and entrepreneurs:

> The firm is, in a sense, an intermediary, [because it is] using inputs
> whose ultimate ownership is in the hands of consumers or
> government, and producing outputs which are ultimately bought by
> consumers or government. . . . Firms and other decision-makers in the
> economy are treated as faceless and nonhuman. (Lancaster, 1974,
> pp. 165, 216)

255

The theory-of-the-firm debate has generated a large number of alternative maximands which managers or owners might pursue (profits, or total sales, growth, market share, etc., all within high or low forms of profit constraint).

Most public choice work accepts all three features of economic work: unitary actors, role-specific assumptions and confining substantive assumptions only to supply-side actors. The unitary actor assumption is rarely questioned. Some authors have criticized making substantive assumptions about supply-side actors, but for reasons which seem confused. For example, Breton and Wintrobe (1982) argue that it is possible to construct a model of how bureaucracies behave by assuming that officials maximize whatever it is that gives them most utility (such as bigger budgets, a quiet life, or more managerial discretion), or whatever gives them most expected utility in conditions of uncertainty.

> We will discard all specific goals and assume [only] that bureaucrats maximize utility functions. . . . This generalization has served economists so well in other areas of analysis that it should also be a sure guide in the analysis of bureaucracy. . . . To understand the meaning of making specific assumptions about objectives for bureaucrats, the reader should imagine the state of demand theory if specific targets had been assumed for consumers. (Breton and Wintrobe, 1982, pp. 29 and 170)

The obvious problem here, however, is that bureaucrats are supply-side actors analogous to firms, not demand-side actors analogous to consumers. As Niskanen noted, and as the vagueness and non-empirical quality of Breton and Wintrobe's own principal/agent analysis demonstrates, some substantive assumptions about supply-side actors are invaluable in driving a model of how markets operate. And so long as variations in these assumptions are role specific (and only role-specific) they can be perfectly legitimate.

In this analysis, I reject the unitary actor view of supply-side actors' behaviour. Instead the constraints on institutional leaders which arise from incomplete organizational control, and from fragmentation inside the leadership group itself, are seen as critically important. Second, role-specific assumptions about preferences are retained, but because demand-side preferences are endogenized in my account, institutional leaderships no longer confront a single, determinant welfare-maximizing course of action. Instead, the concepts of size manipulation, preference-shaping, and bureau-shaping emphasize that the leaders of interest groups, political parties and government agencies all confront significant *choices* between alternative strategies. They must decide whether to accommodate people's preferences (treating them as exogenously fixed), or instead to try to change what people want (treating their preferences as partially endogenized). For all three types of leadership, the circumstances conditioning their choices are themselves determined within the political process being analyzed. Thus political behaviour is doubly endogenized in my account. Leaders of supply-side organizations can restructure the political preferences and reactions of 'consumers'. And their own supply-side choices are heavily influenced by structural, institutional and environmental factors.

Interest group leaders are constrained by the basic logic of mobilizing members to maintain more democratic and devolved patterns of organization than exist in most other social institutions. At the same time, however, group leaders develop selective incentives following Olson's logic of organization, with by-product effects which help to insulate them from control by members. Size manipulation helps resolve the potential tensions between these strategies, by allowing group leaders to send contradictory messages to members and potential members: on the one hand that the group's size makes it highly viable, but on the other that its organizational design means that their individual participation is not irrelevant to the supply of benefits or direction of group policies.

Party leaders are also greatly limited in their strategy choices by the structure of power inside their organization, the views of party activists, consistency with longer-term voter images, the party's history and record in government, etc.

> The issue is not whether leaders of electoral parties seek to maximize the vote or follow ideologies. Leaders of electoral parties prefer to win more votes rather than fewer: this we do not doubt. The question is under what constraints they maximize votes, and the issue may be at most whether there is any room for choice left after all the constraints are considered. To ignore such constraints, to assume that party leaders can pick any strategy, address themselves to any group with any program, reduces the study of parties and elections to empty formalisms. To conclude that party leaders who do not maximize votes must be victims of the irrationalism of ideology is to forget how many obstacles stand in the way of those who would very much like to win elections. (Przeworski and Sprague, 1986, p. 120)

However, my analysis goes much further by stressing that preference-shaping strategies in many circumstances offer party leaders a valuable means of squaring the circle, of operating within their existing constraints while also restructuring the aggregate distribution of preferences amongst voters so as to increase their support. The mix between preference-shaping and preference-accommodating strategies is always an important one for party leaders or political candidates to consider. Other trade-offs include those between 'choice' or 'echo' approaches, and between internal and external popularity. And parties like interest groups also have to regulate

257

their internal organization and operations to help convince activists and voters both that the party is viable electorally and yet that their individual support is not negligible in shaping elements of the party's policy or effectiveness.

Policy-level bureaucrats in government agencies do not behave like a unitary actor. They can choose to invest in either individual or collective modes of improving their welfare, and are likely to encounter collective action problems in pursuing budget-maximizing strategies. The rank-structured quality of bureaucracies does not ameliorate but accentuates this problem, since program budget increments bring few benefits to senior officials. By contrast, collective action problems are less likely with bureau-shaping strategies, from which policy-level bureaucrats benefit more, while their control over the reorganization process is greater.

Senior officials always confront a choice between budget-maximizing and bureau-shaping strategies. The mix of actions adopted depends on: the rank of officials, and associated individual options for welfare maximization; officials' net benefits from a program budget increment or a reorganization increment; the type of agency in which bureaucrats work, its current organizational configuration, administrative technology, task structure and 'client' linkages; the potential for reshaping the bureau into an alternative agency type; and lastly the level of environmental hostility to budget increases or bureau reorganizations, which powerfully conditions the relative probabilities of influence and advocacy costs of the two strategies for policy-level officials. Substantial costs and opportunities turn on the balance of welfare-maximizing strategies which policy-level officials adopt, and the effectiveness with which collective action around their objectives can be sustained. However, Chapters 7 and 8 argued that these factors have pointed decisively towards the superiority of bureau-shaping strategies in the contemporary period in terms of protecting and enhancing most senior officials' welfare. The exceptions remain some large, unreconstructed line bureaus (such as the armed forces or the police), which still seem locked into budget-maximizing strategies.

Conclusions

Much of the recent discussion of economic explanations in political science has not been helpful. Too many contributions still seem to have been written simply to convey an evangelistic fervour that somehow – in the future – public choice is about to transform our understanding. Yet as a research programme, the field is getting long in the tooth while its empirical applications remain at best weakly defined. But equally *generalized* critiques of rational choice explanations as a genre no longer do a great deal to advance knowledge or debate. When a significant body of work has accumulated in any field of science, after a time external queries about the usefulness of that entire approach must get shrugged off. Within any sphere of knowledge development, what becomes used on a large scale is by definition being found useful.

The gains made by public choice theory in extending the scope and methods of debate and research in political science towards new forms of logically and mathematically informed reasoning are in my view now undeniable. But the losses involved in first principles methods also seem regrettable: the retreat into a formalized political 'world'; the fragmenting of 'messy' political experience into tightly circumscribed and non-interacting technical problems; the general non-testing (indeed bolt-on proofing) of theorems against empirical evidence; the non-communication of technical results to the broader political science profession; and the progressively greater barriers erected against informed criticism by outsiders.

The development and refinement of institutional public choice into behaviourally realistic and theoretically diverse explanations of broad classes of political phenomena should provide a much-needed antidote. If public choice methods can also be divorced from their characteristically conservative ideological baggage, and the possibility of different starting assumptions thoroughly explored, then their potential to shed new light on some central questions of political science looks beyond doubt. We still know so little about the mechanisms and operations of democratic control, government power and state institutions – in a world where the number of liberal democracies is growing rapidly, and the striving for democracy is demonstrably near-universal.

BIBLIOGRAPHY

Aberbach, J. D., Putnam, R. D. and Rockman, B.A. (1981), *Bureaucrats and Politicians in Western Democracies* (Cambridge, Mass.: Harvard University Press).

Abrams, R. (1980), *Foundations of Political Analysis: An introduction to the theory of collective choice* (New York: Columbia University Press).

Alford, R. and Friedland, R. (1985), *The Powers of Theory: Capitalism, the state and democracy* (Cambridge: Cambridge University Press).

Allison, G. (1971), *Essence of Decision: Explaining the Cuban missile crisis* (Boston: Little Brown).

Almond, G. and Verba, S. (1963), *The Civic Culture* (Princeton, NJ: Princeton University Press).

Alt, J. and Chrystal, K. (1983), *Political Economics* (Brighton: Wheatsheaf).

Arrow, K. J. (1951), *Social Choice and Individual Values* (New York: Wiley).

Ascher, K. (1987), *The Politics of Privatization: Contracting out in the public services* (London: Macmillan).

Audit Commission (1986), *Making a Reality Out of Community Care* (London: HMSO).

Auster, R. D. and Silver, M. (1979), *The State as a Firm: Economic forces in political development* (Boston: Kluwer and The Hague: Martinus Nijhoff).

Axelrod, R. (1984), *The Evolution of Co-operation* (New York: Basic Books).

Bannock, G., Baxter, R. E. and Rees, R. (1979), *The Penguin Dictionary of Economics* (Harmondsworth: Penguin), Second edition.

Barnes, S., Kaase, M. *et al.* (1979), *Political Action: Mass participation in five Western democracies* (Beverly Hills and London: Sage).

Barry, B. (1974), 'Review article: exit, voice and loyalty', *British Journal of Political Science*, vol. 14, no. 1, pp. 79–107.

Barry, B. (1978), *Sociologists, Economists and Democracy* (Chicago: Chicago University Press). Originally published New York: Collier-Macmillan, 1970.

Barry, N. (1987a) *The New Right* (Beckenham, Kent: Croom Helm).

Barry, N. (1987b) 'Classical liberalism and public policy' (paper to the Annual Conference of the UK Political Studies Association, University of Aberdeen, April).

Bartlett, R. (1973), *Economic Foundations of Political Power* (New York: Free Press).

Bibliography

Bates, R. H. (1981), *Markets and States in Tropical Africa* (Berkeley: University of California Press).

Baumol, W. (ed.) (1980), *Public and Private Enterprise in a Mixed Economy* (London: Macmillan).

Becker, G. S. (1966), *The Economic Approach to Human Behavior* (Chicago: Chicago University Press).

Becker, G. S. (1983), 'A theory of competition among pressure groups for political influence', *Quarterly Journal of Economics*, vol. XCVIII, no. 3, pp. 371–400.

Becker, G. S. (1985), 'Public policies, pressure groups and dead-weight costs', *Journal of Public Economics*, vol. 28, no. 2, pp. 329–47. Reprinted in Stigler (ed.) (1988), Chapter 2.

Becquart-Leclerc, J. (1976), *Paradoxes du Pouvoir Local* (Paris: Presse de la Fondation Nationale des Science Politiques).

Bendor, J. (1988) 'Formal models of bureaucracy', *British Journal of Political Science*, vol. 18, no. 2, pp. 353–95.

Bendor, J. and Moe, T. (1985), 'An adaptive model of bureaucratic politics', *American Political Science Review*, vol. 79, no. 3, pp. 755–74.

Bendor, J. and Mookherjee, D. (1987), 'Institutional structure and the logic of ongoing collective action', *American Political Science Review*, vol. 87, no. 1, pp. 129–54.

Bendor, J., Taylor, S. and Van Gaalen, R. (1985), 'Bureaucratic expertise versus legislative authority: a model of deception and monitoring in budgeting', *American Political Science Review*, vol. 79, no. 4, pp. 1041–60.

Bendor, J., Taylor, S. and Van Gaalen, R. (1987), 'Stacking the deck: bureaucratic missions and policy design', *American Political Science Review*, vol. 81, no. 3, pp. 873–96.

Bennett, D. (1979), 'Deinstitutionalization in two cultures', *Health and Society*, vol. 57, no. 4, pp. 516–32.

Bennett, J. T. and Johnson, M. H. (1980), *The Political Economy of Federal Government Growth, 1959–1978* (College Station, Tex.: A&M University Press).

Bennett, J. T. and Johnson, M. H. (1981), *Better Government at Half the Price: Private production of public services* (Ottowa, Ill.: Caroline House).

Bentley, A. (1967), *The Process of Government* (Chicago: University of Chicago Press), first published 1908.

Birch, A. H. (1975), 'Economic models in political science: the case of "Exit, Voice and Loyalty"', *British Journal of Political Science*, vol. 15, no. 1, pp. 69–82.

Blais, A. and Dion, S. (1988), 'Are bureaucrats budget-maximizers? The Niskanen model and its critics' (unpublished paper, Department of Political Science, University of Montreal).

Blau, P. and Merton, R. (eds) (1981), *Continuities in Structuralist Enquiry* (Beverly Hills and London: Sage).

Blaug, M. (1980), *The Methodology of Economics or How Economists Explain* (Cambridge: Cambridge University Press).

Block, W. and Olsen, E. (1981), *Rent Control: Myths and realities* (Vancouver: Fraser Institute).

Borcherding, T. E. (ed.) (1977), *Budgets and Bureaucrats: The sources of government growth* (Durham, NC: Duke University Press).

Boudon, R. (1977), *Effets pervers et ordre sociale* (Paris: Presses Universitaires de France).

Bibliography

Boudon, R. (1981), 'Undesired consequences and types of systems of inter-dependence', in Blau and Merton (eds) (1981), pp. 255–84.

Brams, S. J. (1975), *Game Theory and Politics* (New York: Free Press).

Brennan, G. and Buchanan, J. M. (1984), 'Voter choice: evaluating political alternatives', *American Behavioral Scientist*, vol. 28, no. 4, pp. 185–201.

Breton, A. (1974), *The Economic Theory of Representative Government* (Chicago: Aldine-Atherton).

Breton, A. (1988), 'The organization of government in congressional and parliamentary governments' (paper to the Law and Economics Workshop, University of Toronto, 14 September).

Breton, A. and Wintrobe, R. (1982), *The Logic of Bureaucratic Control: An economic analysis of competition, exchange and efficiency in private and public organizations* (Cambridge: Cambridge University Press).

Brindle, D. (1988), 'Ministerial foot in the mental hospital door', *The Guardian*, 19 August, p. 19.

Brittan, S. (1975), 'The economic contradictions of democracy', *British Journal of Political Science*, vol. 5, no. 1, pp. 129–59.

Bromley, D. (1989), *Economic Interests and Institutions: The conceptual foundations of public policy* (Oxford: Blackwell).

Buchanan, A. (1979), 'Revolutionary motivation and rationality', *Philosophy and Public Affairs*, vol. 9, no. 1, pp. 59–82.

Buchanan, J. M. (1954), 'Individual choice in voting and the market', *Journal of Political Economy*, vol. 62, no. 3, pp. 334–43.

Buchanan, J. M. (1977), 'Why does government grow?', in Borcherding (ed.) (1977), pp. 3–18.

Buchanan, J. M. (ed.) (1978) *The Economics of Politics* (London: Institute of Economic Affairs).

Buchanan, J. M. and Tullock, G. (1962), *The Calculus of Consent* (Ann Arbor: University of Michigan Press).

Budge, I. and Farlie, D. (1976), 'Placing party identification within a typology of representations of voting and party competition and proposing a synthesis', in Budge, I., Crewe, I. and Farlie, D. (eds) (1976), *Party Competition and Beyond* (London: Wiley).

Budge, I. and Farlie, D. (1977), *Voting and Party Competition* (London: Wiley).

Burton, J. (1985), *Why No Cuts? An Inquiry into the Fiscal Anarchy of Uncontrolled Government Expenditure* (London: Institute of Economic Affairs).

Byrne, P. (1988), *The Campaign for Nuclear Disarmament* (London: Croom Helm).

Cain, B., Ferejohn, J. and Fiorina, M. (1986), *The Personal Vote: Constituency service and electoral independence* (Cambridge, Mass.: Harvard University Press).

Caldwell, B. (1984), *Beyond Positivism: Economic methodology in the twentieth century* (London: Allen and Unwin).

Cameron, D. R. (1978), 'The expansion of the public economy: a comparative analysis', *American Political Science Review*, vol. 72, no. 4, pp. 1243–61.

Cassesse, S. (1988), 'Italy', in Rowat, D. C. (ed.), *Public Administration in Developed Democracies* (New York: Dekker), pp. 293–315.

Castles, F. G. (ed.) (1982), *The Impact of Parties* (Beverly Hills and London: Sage).

Catt, H. (1989), *How Voters Decide: Tactical voting in British politics* (unpublished Ph.D thesis, London School of Economics and Political Science).

Bibliography

Cawson, A. (1982), *Corporatism and Social Policy* (London: Heinemann).

Cawson, A. (ed.) (1985), *Organized Interests and the State: Studies in meso-corporatism* (London: Sage).

Chappell, H. W. and Keech, W. R. (1986), 'Party motivation and party difference in a dynamic spatial model of party competition', *American Political Science Review*, vol. 80, no. 3, pp. 881–99.

Chubb, J. E. and Moe, T. M. (1988), 'Politics, markets and the organization of schools', *American Political Science Review*, vol. 82, no. 4, pp. 1065–87.

Coase, R. H. (1937), 'The nature of the firm', *Economica*, vol. 4, no. 16, pp. 386–405.

Coates, K. and Topham, T. (1988), *Trade Unions in Britain* (London: Fontana), third edition.

Community Development Project (1976), *Whatever Happened to Council Housing?* (London: CDP).

Conybeare, J. (1984), 'Bureaucracy, monopoly and competition: a critical analysis of the budget-maximizing model of bureaucracy', *American Journal of Political Science*, vol. 28, no. 3, pp. 479–502.

Cox, A. (1984), *The Adversary Politics of Land: The conflict over land and property policy in post-war Britain* (Cambridge: Cambridge University Press).

Crewe, I. and Sarlvik, B. (1980), 'Popular attitudes and electoral strategy', in Layton-Henry, Z. (ed.), *Conservative Party Politics* (London: Macmillan) pp. 244–75.

Crouch, C. (1982), *Trade Unions: The logic of collective action* (London: Fontana).

Crouch, C. (1990), 'Industrial relations', in Dunleavy, P. *et al.* (eds) (1990), pp. 318–32.

Crowther-Hunt, N. and Kellner, P. (1980), *The Civil Servants: An inquiry into Britain's ruling class* (London: Macdonald).

Dahl, R. A. (1956), *A Preface to Democratic Theory* (Chicago: University of Chicago Press).

Dahl, R. A. (1961), *Who Governs? Democracy and Power in an American City* (New Haven: Yale University Press).

Dahl, R. A. (1971), *Polyarchy: Participation and opposition* (New Haven: Yale University Press).

Dahl, R. A. and Lindblom, C. (1953), *Politics, Economics and Welfare* (New York: Harper and Brothers).

Dahl, R. and Tufte, E. (1974), *Size and Democracy* (London: Oxford University Press).

Day, G. and Robbins, D. (1987), 'Activists for peace: the social base of a local peace movement', in Creighton, S. and Shaw, M. (eds), *The Sociology of War and Peace* (London: Macmillan), pp. 199–217.

Dean, J. W. (1984), 'Interest groups and political X inefficiency', *European Journal of Political Research*, vol. 12, no. 2, pp. 191–212.

Downs, A. (1957), *An Economic Theory of Democracy* (New York: Harper and Row).

Downs, A. (1967), *Inside Bureaucracy* (Boston: Little, Brown).

Downs, A. (1972), 'Up and down with ecology: the issue attention cycle', *Public Interest*, vol. 28, no. 1, pp. 38–50.

Downs, G. W. and Larkey, P. D. (1986), *The Search for Government Efficiency: From hubris to helplessness* (Philadelphia: Temple University Press).

Bibliography

Dowse, R. and Hughes, J. (1977), 'Sporadic interventionists', *Political Studies*, vol. 25, no. 1, pp. 84–92.

Dunleavy, P. (1980a), 'The political implications of sectoral cleavages and the growth of state employment, Parts I and II', *Political Studies*, vol. 28, no. 3, pp. 364–83 and no. 4, pp. 527–49.

Dunleavy, P. (1980b), *Urban Political Analysis* (London: Macmillan).

Dunleavy, P. (1981a), *The Politics of Mass Housing in Britain, 1945–75: Corporate power and professional influence in the welfare state* (Oxford: Clarendon Press).

Dunleavy, P. (1981b), 'Professions and policy change: notes towards a model of ideological corporatism', *Public Administration Bulletin*, vol. 36, no. 2, pp. 3–16.

Dunleavy, P. (1984), 'The limits to local government', in Boddy, M. and Fudge, C. (eds), *Local Socialism? Labour Councils and New Left Alternatives* (London: Macmillan), pp. 49–81.

Dunleavy, P. (1985), 'Bureaucrats, budgets and the growth of the state: reconstructing an instrumental model', *British Journal of Political Science*, vol. 15, no. 3, pp. 299–328. Also published in Italian in *Problemi di Amministrazione Pubblica* (1986), vol. 9, no. 1, pp. 9–65.

Dunleavy, P. (1986), 'Explaining the privatization boom: public choice versus radical approaches', *Public Administration*, vol. 64, no. 2, pp. 13–34.

Dunleavy, P. (1988), 'Group identities and individual influence: reconstructing the theory of interest groups', *British Journal of Political Science*, vol. 18, no. 1, pp. 21–49.

Dunleavy, P. (1989a), 'The architecture of the British central state: Part I, Framework for analysis', *Public Administration*, vol. 67, no. 3, pp. 249–75.

Dunleavy, P. (1989b), 'The architecture of the British central state: Part II, Empirical findings', *Public Administration*, vol. 67, no. 4, pp. 391–417.

Dunleavy, P. (1989c), 'The United Kingdom: Paradoxes of an ungrounded statism', in Castles, F. (ed.), *The Comparative History of Public Policy* (Cambridge: Polity), pp. 242–91.

Dunleavy, P. and Francis, A. (1990), 'The development of the Next Steps programme, 1988–90', Appendix 5 in House of Commons, Treasury and Civil Service Committee, *Progress in the Next Steps Initiative* (London: HMSO). HC 481, pp. 69–77.

Dunleavy, P. and Ward, H. (1981), 'Exogenous voter preferences and parties with state power: some internal problems of economic models of party competition', *British Journal of Political Science*, vol. 11, no. 3, pp. 351–80.

Dunleavy, P. and Husbands, C. T. (1985), *British Democracy at the Crossroads: Voting and party competition in the 1980s* (London: Allen and Unwin).

Dunleavy, P. and O'Leary, B. (1987), *Theories of the State: The politics of liberal democracy* (London: Macmillan).

Dunleavy, P. and Rhodes, R. A. W. (1988), 'Government beyond Whitehall', in Drucker, H., Dunleavy, P., Gamble, A. and Peele, G. (eds), *Developments in British Politics 2* (London: Macmillan), revised edition, pp. 107–43.

Dunleavy, P., Gamble, A. and Peele, G. (eds) (1990), *Developments in British Politics 3* (London: Macmillan).

Dunsire, A. (1987), 'Testing theories: the contribution of bureaumetrics', in Lane, J. E. (ed.) (1987), pp. 95–145.

Dunsire, A. and Hood, C. with Huby, M. (1989), *Cutback Management in Public*

Bibliography

Bureaucracies: Popular theories and observed outcomes in Whitehall (Cambridge: Cambridge University Press).

Eavey, C. L. (1987), 'Bureaucratic competition and agenda control', *Journal of Conflict Resolution*, vol. 31, no. 3, pp. 503–24.

Edelman, M. (1964), *The Symbolic Uses of Politics* (Urbana: University of Illinois Press).

Efficiency Unit (1988), *Improving Management in Government: The next steps* (London: HMSO).

Eisner, M. A. and Meier, K. J. (1990), 'Presidential control versus bureaucratic power: explaining the Reagan revolution in antitrust', *American Journal of Political Science*, vol. 34, no. 1, pp. 269–87.

Ellis, A. and Heath, A. (1983), 'Positional competition: an offer you can't refuse?', in Ellis, A. and Kumar, K. (eds), *Dilemmas of Liberal Democracies: Studies in Fred Hirsch's 'Social limits to growth'* (London: Tavistock), pp. 1–22.

Elster, J. (1985), *Making Sense of Marx* (Cambridge: Cambridge University Press).

Elster, J. and Hylland, A. (eds) (1986), *Foundations of Social Choice Theory* (Cambridge: Cambridge University Press).

Enelow, J. M. and Hinich, M. J. (1982), 'Ideology, issues and the spatial theory of elections', *American Political Science Review*, vol. 76, no. 3, pp. 493–501.

Enelow, J. M. and Hinich, M. J. (1984), *The Spatial Theory of Voting* (Cambridge: Cambridge University Press).

Erickson, R. S., Wright, G. C. and McIver, J. P. (1989), 'Political parties, public opinion, and state policy', *American Political Science Review*, vol. 83, no. 3, pp. 729–50.

Etzioni, A. (1988), *The Moral Dimension: Towards a new economics* (New York: Free Press).

Etzioni-Halevy, E. (1983), *Bureaucracy and Democracy: A political dilemma* (London: Routledge).

Feld, S. L. and Gofman, B. (1988), 'Ideological consistency as a collective phenomenon', *American Political Science Review*, vol. 82, no. 3, pp. 773–88.

Fenno, R. (1966), *The Power of the Purse: Appropriations Politics in Congress* (Boston: Little, Brown).

Finer, S. E. (1980), *The Changing British Party System, 1945–79* (Washington, DC: American Enterprise Institute).

Finkel, S. E., Muller, E. N. and Opp, K.-D. (1989), 'Personal influence, collective rationality, and mass political action', *American Political Science Review*, vol. 83, no. 3, pp. 885–903.

Forte, F. and Peacock, A. (eds) (1985), *Public Expenditure and Government Growth* (Oxford: Blackwell).

Foster, C. B. (1984), 'The performance of rational voter models in recent Presidential elections', *American Political Science Review*, vol. 78, no. 3, pp. 678–90.

Frey, B. (1978), *Modern Political Economy* (London: Macmillan).

Frey, B. (1984), *International Political Economics* (Oxford: Blackwell).

Frey, B. (1985a), *Democratic Economic Policy: A theoretical introduction* (Oxford: Blackwell).

Frey, B. (1985b), 'The state and prospect of public choice: a European view', *Public Choice*, vol. 46, no. 2, pp. 141–61.

265

Bibliography

Friedman, M. (1953), 'The methodology of positive economics', in his *Essays in Positive Economics* (Chicago: University of Chicago Press).

Friedman, M. (1962), *Price Theory* (Chicago: Aldine).

Frohlich, N. and Oppenheimer, J. (1978), *Modern Political Economy* (Englewood Cliffs, NJ: Prentice Hall).

Frohlich, N., Oppenheimer, J. A. and Young, O. R. (1971) *Political Leadership and Collective Goods* (Princeton: Princeton University Press).

Frohlich, N., Oppenheimer, J. A., Smith, J. and Young, O. R. (1978), 'A test of Downsian voter rationality: 1964 presidential voting', *American Political Science Review*, vol. 72, no. 1, pp. 178–97.

Fry, G. (1986), 'Inside Whitehall', in Drucker, H., Dunleavy, P., Gamble, A. and Peele, G., *Developments in British Politics 2* (London: Macmillan), pp. 88–106.

Galbraith, J. K. (1953), *American Capitalism and the Concept of Countervailing Power* (Boston: Houghton Mifflin).

Galbraith, J. K. (1969), *The New Industrial State* (Harmondsworth: Penguin and Boston: Houghton Mifflin).

Galbraith, J. K. (1974), *Economics and the Public Purpose* (Harmondsworth: Penguin).

Garand, J. C. (1988), 'Explaining government growth in the US states', *American Political Science Review*, vol. 82, no. 3, pp. 837–49.

Gibson, J. L., Frendreis, J. P. and Vertz, L. L. (1989), 'Party dynamics in the 1980s: change in county party organizational strength, 1980–84', *American Journal of Political Science*, vol. 33, no. 1, pp. 67–90.

Goffman, E. (1961), *Asylums* (New York: Doubleday).

Goldwin, R. A. (ed.) (1980), *Political Parties in the Eighties* (Washington, DC: American Enterprise Institute).

Goodin, R. E. (1982a), 'Rational politicians in Washington and Whitehall', *Public Administration*, vol. 62, no. 1, pp. 23–41.

Goodin, R. E. (1982b), *Political Theory and Public Policy* (Chicago: University of Chicago Press).

Goodin, R. E. (1988), *Reasons for Welfare* (Princeton: Princeton University Press).

Gravelle, H. and Rees, R. (1981), *Microeconomics* (London: Longman).

Gray, A. and Jenkins, W. (1985), *Administrative Politics in British Government* (Brighton: Wheatsheaf).

Green, D. (1987), *The New Right* (Brighton: Harvester).

Halperin, M. (1974), *Bureaucratic Politics and Foreign Policy* (Washington, DC: Brookings Institution).

Hanf, K. and Scharpf, F. (eds) (1978) *International Policy-making* (London and Beverly Hills: Sage).

Hansen, J. M. (1985), 'The political economy of group membership', *American Political Science Review*, vol. 79, no. 1, pp. 79–96.

Hanusch, H. (ed.) (1983), *Anatomy of Government Deficiencies* (Berlin: Springer).

Hardin, R. (1982), *Collective Action* (Baltimore: Johns Hopkins University Press).

Hare, R. M. (1952), *The Language of Morals* (Oxford: Clarendon University Press).

Harrop, M. (1986), 'Press coverage of post-war British elections', in Crewe, I. and Harrop, M. (eds), *Political Communications: The general election of 1983* (Cambridge: Cambridge University Press), pp. 137–49.

266

Bibliography

Harrop, M. and Miller, W. L. (1987), *Elections and Voters: A comparative introduction* (London: Macmillan).

Hayek, F. (1948), *Individualism and Economic Order* (Chicago: University of Chicago Press).

Hayek, F. (1960), *The Constitution of Liberty* (London: Routledge).

Heald, D. (1983), *Public Expenditure* (Oxford: Martin Robertson).

Heath, A. (1976), *Rational Choice and Social Exchange* (Cambridge: Cambridge University Press).

Heath, A. (1987), 'Social stratification and political attitudes', in Social and Community Planning Research, *Survey Methods Newsletter*, summer 1988, pp. 9–10.

Heath, A., Jowell, R. and Curtice, J. (1985), *How Britain Votes* (Oxford: Pergamon).

Hemingway, J. (1978), *Conflict and Democracy: Studies in trade union government* (Oxford: Oxford University Press).

Hencke, D. (1988), 'Whitehall eyes Swedish model', *The Guardian*, 29 November.

Hennessy, P. (1989), *Whitehall* (London: Secker and Warburg).

Hibbing, J. (1985), 'On the issues surrounding economic voting: looking to the British case for answers' (paper to the Annual Conference of the UK Political Studies Association, University of Manchester, April).

Hibbs, D. A. (1987), *The Political Economy of Industrial Democracies* (Cambridge, Mass.: Harvard University Press).

Hindess, B. (1988), *Choice, Rationality and Social Theory* (London: Unwin Hyman).

Hindess, B. (1989), *Political Choice and Social Structure* (Farnborough: Edward Elgar).

Hirschman, A. O. (1970), *Exit, Voice and Loyalty: Responses to decline in firms, organizations and states* (Cambridge, Mass.: Harvard University Press).

Hirschman, A. O. (1985), *Shifting Involvements: Private interests and public affairs* (Oxford: Blackwell). Originally published Princeton: Princeton University Press, 1982.

Hirshleifer, J. (1985), 'The expanding domain of economics', *American Economic Review*, vol. 76, no. 1, pp. 53–66.

Hoenak, S. A. (1983), *Economic Behaviour Within Organizations* (Cambridge: Cambridge University Press).

Hogwood, B. and Peters, B. G. (1982), *Policy Dynamics* (Brighton: Wheatsheaf).

Hollis, M. and Nell, E. J. (1975), *Rational Economic Man* (Cambridge: Cambridge University Press).

Home Office (1985), 'The cautioning of offenders' (London: Home Office), circular 14/1985.

Hood, C. (1978), 'Keeping the centre small: explanations of agency type', *Political Studies*, vol. 26, no. 1, pp. 30–46.

Hood, C. (1983), *The Tools of Government* (London: Macmillan).

Hood, C. (1985), *Administrative Analysis: An introduction to rules, enforcement and organization* (Hemel Hempstead: Harvester Wheatsheaf).

Hood, C. (1987), 'British administrative trends and the public choice revolution', in Lane (ed.) (1987), pp. 146–70.

Hood, C. (1989), 'The end of the public bureaucracy state?', (London: London School of Economics), mimeo – inaugural lecture.

267

Bibliography

Hood, C. and Dunsire, A. (1981), *Bureaumetrics* (Farnborough: Gower).

Hood, C. with Dunsire, A. and Thompson, L. (1988), 'Rolling back the state: Thatcherism, Fraserism and bureaucracy', *Governance*, vol. 1, no. 3, pp. 243–70.

Hood, C., Huby, M. and Dunsire, A. (1984), 'Bureaucrats and budgeting benefits: how do British central departments measure up?', *Journal of Public Policy*, vol. 4, no. 3, pp. 163–79.

Hood, C. and Shuppert, G. F. (1988), *Delivering Public Services in Western Europe: Sharing Western European experience of para-governmental organizations* (London and Beverly Hills: Sage).

Hoover, K. and Plant, R. (1988), *Conservative Capitalism* (London: Routledge).

Hotelling, H. (1929), 'Stability in competition', *The Economic Journal*, vol. 39, no. 1, pp. 41–57.

Hutchinson, T. W. (1938), *The Significance and Basic Postulates of Economic Theory* (New York: Augustus M. Kelly) reprinted 1965.

Inglehart, R. (1977), *The Silent Revolution: Changing values and political styles among Western publics* (Princeton: Princeton University Press).

Jackson, P. (1985), 'Economy, democracy and bureaucracy', in Matthews, R. C. (ed.), *Economy and Democracy* (London: Macmillan), pp. 168–204.

Jackson, P. M. (1982), *The Political Economy of Bureaucracy* (Deddington, Oxford: Phillip Allan).

Johnson, T. J. (1972), *Professions and Power* (London: Macmillan).

Jones, B. D. (1981), 'Party and bureaucracy: the influence of intermediary groups on urban public service delivery', *American Political Science Review*, vol. 75, no. 3, pp. 681–700.

Jones, G. W. (1989), 'A revolution in Whitehall? Changes in British central government since 1979', *West European Politics*, vol. 12, no. 3, pp. 238–61.

Katzenstein, P. (1985), *Small States in World Markets* (Ithaca: Cornell University Press).

Kaufman, F., Majone, G. and Ostrom, V. (eds) (1986), *Guidance, Control and Evaluation in the Public Sector* (Berlin: de Gruyter).

Kaufman, H. (1976), *Are Government Organizations Immortal?* (Washington, DC: Brookings Institution).

Kaufman, H. (1981), 'Fear of bureaucracy: a raging pandemic', *Public Administration Review*, vol. 41, no. 1, pp. 1–9.

Kellner, P. and Crowther-Hunt, Lord (1980), *The Civil Servants: An inquiry into Britain's ruling class* (London: Macmillan).

King, D. (1987), *The New Right: Politics, markets and citizenship* (London: Macmillan).

Kingdon, J. (1984), *Agendas, Alternatives and Public Policies* (Boston: Little, Brown).

Kovesi, J. (1971), *Moral Notions* (London: Routledge, Keegan & Paul, 1967).

Lancaster, K. (1974), *Introduction to Modern Microeconomics* (Chicago: Rand McNally).

Lane, J. E. (ed), (1987), *Bureaucracy and Public Choice* (London and Beverly Hills: Sage).

Lane, R. E. (1978), 'Markets and the satisfaction of wants', *Journal of Economic Issues*, vol. 12 , no. 4, pp. 799–828.

Bibliography

Lane, R. E. (1986), 'Market justice, political justice', *American Political Science Review*, vol. 80, no. 2, pp. 383–402.

Latsis, S. J. (1976), 'A research programme in economics', in his (ed.) *Method and Appraisal in Economics* (Cambridge: Cambridge University Press), pp. 1–42.

Laver, M. (1981), *The Politics of Private Desires* (Harmondsworth: Penguin).

LeGrand, J. and Robinson, R. (1984), *Privatizing the Welfare State* (London: Allen and Unwin).

Lehmbruch, G. and Schmitter, P. C. (eds) (1982), *Patterns of Corporatist Policy-making* (Beverly Hills and London: Sage).

Lerman, P. (1982), *Deinstitutionalization and the Welfare State* (New Brunswick, NJ.: Rutgers University Press).

Levi, M. (1988), *Of Rule and Revenue* (Berkeley: University of California Press).

Liebenstein, J. (1976), *Beyond Economic Man: A new foundation for microeconomics* (Cambridge, Mass.: Harvard University Press).

Lijphart, A. (1984), *Democracies* (New Haven: Yale University Press).

Lindblom, C. (1965), *The Intelligence of Democracy* (New York: Free Press).

Lindblom, C. (1977), *Politics and Markets* (New York: Basic Books).

Lindblom, C. and Braybrooke, D. (1963), *A Strategy of Decision* (New York: Free Press).

Lindblom, C. and Cohen, D. (1979), *Useable Knowledge: Social science and social problem solving* (New Haven: Yale University Press).

Lineberry, R. (1989), *Government in America: People, politics and policy* (Glenview, Ill.: Scott, Foresman).

Lipset, S. M. (1959), *Political Man* (Garden City, NY: Doubleday).

Loasby, B. J. (1968), 'The decision-maker in the organization', *Journal of Management Studies*, vol. 5, no. 3, pp. 352–64.

Macdonald, S. E. and Rabinowitz, G. (1987), 'The dynamics of structural realignment', *American Political Science Review*, vol. 81, no. 3, pp. 775–96.

McCormich, B., Kitchin, P., Marshall, G., Sampson, A. and Sedgwick, B. (1974), *Introducing Economics* (London: Penguin).

McCubbins, M. D., Noll, R. G. and Weingast, B. R. (1987), 'Administrative procedures as instruments of political control' (Stanford: Hoover Institution, Stanford University). Working Papers in Economics E-87–36.

McGuire, T. (1981), 'Budget-maximizing governmental agencies: an empirical test', *Public Choice*, vol. 36, no. 3, pp. 313–22.

McLean, I. (1982), *Dealing in Votes* (Oxford: Martin Robertson).

McLean, I. (1987), *Public Choice: An Introduction* (Oxford: Blackwell).

Mahler, V. (1990), 'Exploring the growth of social benefits in advanced capitalist countries', *Environment and Planning C: Government and policy*, vol. 8, no. 1, pp. 13–28.

March, J. G. and Olsen, J. P. (1984), 'The new institutionalism: organizational factors in political life', *American Political Science Review*, vol. 78, no. 3, pp. 734–49.

Margolis, H. (1982), *Selfishness, Altruism and Rationality: A theory of social choice* (Cambridge: Cambridge University Press).

Marris, R. (1964), *The Economic Theory of Managerial Capitalism* (New York: Free Press).

Bibliography

Massey, A. (1990), 'The new public management grows old: privatization in the United States' (paper to the Annual Conference of the UK Political Studies Association).

Mattausch, J. (1989), *A Commitment to Campaign: A sociological study of CND* (Manchester: Manchester University Press).

Mayhew, D. R. (1974), *Congress: The electoral connection* (New Haven: Yale University Press).

Meltzer, A. H. and Richard, S. F. (1978), 'Why government grows (and grows) in a democracy', *Public Interest*, vol. 52, no. 2, pp. 111–18.

Meyer, M. with Stevenson, W. and Webster, S. (1985), *Limits to Bureaucratic Growth* (New York and Berlin: de Gruyter).

Migue, J.-L. and Belanger, G. (1974), 'Towards a general theory of managerial discretion', *Public Choice*, vol. 17, no. 1, pp. 27–43.

Miller, A., Gurin, P., Gurin, G. and Malanchuk, O. (1981), 'Group consciousness and political participation', *American Journal of Political Science*, vol. 25, no. 2, pp. 495–511.

Miller, G. J. and Moe, T. M. (1983), 'Bureaucrats, legislators and the size of government', *American Political Science Review*, vol. 77, no. 2, pp. 297–322.

Miller, R. L. (1978), *Intermediate Microeconomics: Theory, issues and applications* (New York: McGraw Hill).

Miller, W. L. (1980), 'What was the profit in following the crowd?', *British Journal of Political Science*, vol. 10, no. 1, pp. 15–39.

Miller, W. L., Clarke, H., Harrop, M., Leduc, L. and Whiteley, P. (1990), *How Voters Change: The 1987 British election campaign in perspective* (Oxford: Oxford University Press).

Mitchell, W. C. (1983), 'Fiscal behaviour of the modern fiscal state: public choice perspectives and contributions', in Wade, L. (ed.) (1983), pp. 69–122.

Moe, T. M. (1980), *The Organization of Interests: Incentives and the internal dynamics of political interest groups* (Chicago: University of Chicago Press).

Moe, T. M. (1984), 'The new economics of organization', *American Journal of Political Science*, vol. 78, no. 3, pp. 739–77.

Moseley, P. (1984), *The Making of Economic Policy: Theory and evidence from Britain and the US since 1945* (Hemel Hempstead: Harvester Wheatsheaf).

Mueller, D. C. (1979), *Public Choice* (Cambridge: Cambridge University Press).

Mueller, D. C. (ed.) (1982), *The Political Economy of Growth* (New Haven: Yale University Press).

Mueller, D. C. (1987), 'The voting paradox', in Rowley (ed.) (1987), pp. 77–99.

Mueller, D. C. (1989), *Public Choice II: A revised edition* (Cambridge: Cambridge University Press).

Mueller, D. and Murrell, P. (1985), 'Interest groups and the political economy of government size', in Forte, F. and Peacock, A. (eds) (1985), pp. 13–36.

Muller, E. N. and Opp, K.-D. (1986), 'Rational choice and rebellious collective action', *American Political Science Review*, vol. 80, no. 3, pp. 471–87.

Mulvey, C. (1978), *The Economic Analysis of Trade Unions* (Oxford: Martin Robertson).

Murray, C. (1984), *Losing Ground: American social policy, 1950–80* (New York: Basic Books).

Bibliography

Murrell, P. (1984), 'An examination of the factors affecting the formation of interest groups in OECD countries', *Public Choice*, vol. 43, no. 2, pp. 151–71.

Newman, B. I. and Sheth, J. N. (1987), *A Theory of Political Choice Behaviour* (New York: Praeger).

Newton, K. (1976), *Second City Politics* (London: Oxford University Press).

New Zealand Treasury (1987), *Government Management: Brief to the incoming government* (Wellington: Treasury).

Niskanen, W. A. (1971), *Bureaucracy and Representative Government* (Chicago: Aldine-Atherton).

Niskanen, W. A. (1973), *Bureaucracy: Servant or master* (London: Institute of Economic Affairs).

Niskanen, W. A. (1975), 'Bureaucrats and politicians', *Journal of Law and Economics*, vol. 18, no. 4, pp. 617–43.

Niskanen, W. A. (1978), 'Competition among government bureaus', in Buchanan, J. M. (ed.) (1978), pp. 161–70.

Niskanen, W. A. (1987), 'Bureaucracy', in Rowley, C. K. (ed.) (1987), pp. 135–40.

Noelle-Newman, E. (1984), *The Spiral of Silence* (Chicago: Chicago University Press).

Noll, R. G. and Fiorina, M. P. (1979), 'Voters, bureaucrats and legislators: a rational perspective on the growth of bureaucracy', *Journal of Public Economics*, vol. 9, no. 3, pp. 239–54.

North, D. C. (1981), *Structure and Change in Economic History* (New York: Norton).

North, D. C. (1985), 'The growth of government in the United States: an economic historian's perspective', *Journal of Public Economics*, vol. 28, no. 4, pp. 383–99.

Nutter, G. W. (1978), *Growth of Government in the West* (Washington, DC: Brookings Institution).

Offe, C. (1985), 'New social movements: challenging the boundaries of institutional politics', *Social Research*, vol. 52, no. 4, pp. 817–68.

Offe, C. and Wiesenthal, H. (1985), 'Two logics of collective action – theoretical notes on social class and organizational form', in Offe, C., *Disorganized Capitalism: In temporary transformations of work and politics* (Cambridge: Polity Press), pp. 170–220.

O'Leary, B. (1987a), 'The odyssey of Jon Elster', *Government and Opposition*, vol. 22, no. 4, pp. 480–98.

O'Leary, B. (1987b), 'Why was the GLC abolished?', *International Journal of Urban and Regional Research*, vol. 11, no. 2, pp. 197–214.

O'Leary, B. (1990), 'Party support in Northern Ireland, 1969–89', in McGarry, J. and O'Leary, B. (eds), *The Future of Northern Ireland* (Oxford: Oxford University Press), pp. 342–57.

Olson, M. (1978), *The Logic of Collective Action: Public goods and the theory of groups* (Cambridge, Mass.: Harvard University Press), first published 1965.

Olson, M. (1982), *The Rise and Decline of Nations: Economic growth, stagflation and social rigidities* (New Haven: Yale University Press).

Ordeshook, P. C. (1986), *Game Theory and Political Theory: An introduction* (Cambridge: Cambridge University Press).

Orzechowski, W. (1977), 'Economic models of bureaucracy: survey, extensions and evidence', in Borcherding, T. E. (ed.) (1977), pp. 229–59.

Bibliography

Ostrom, V. (1971), 'Public choice: a different approach to the study of public administration', *Public Administration Review*, vol. 31, no. 2, pp. 203–16.

Ostrom, V. (1974), *The Intellectual Crisis in American Public Administration* (Tuscaloosa, Ala.: University of Alabama Press).

Ostrom, V. (1986), 'Multi-organizational arrangements and co-ordination: an application of institutional analysis', in Kaufman, F. *et al.* (eds) (1986), pp. 495–510.

Ostrom, V. (1989), 'Some developments in the study of market choice, public choice and institutional choice', in Rabin, J., Hildreth, W. B. and Miller, G. J. (eds), *Handbook of Public Administration* (New York: Marcel Dekker), pp. 861–82.

Ouchi, V. (1980), 'Markets, bureaucracies and clans', *Administrative Science Quarterly*, vol. 25, no. 1, pp. 129–41.

Page, B. (1978), *Choices and Echoes in American Elections: Rational man and electoral democracy* (Chicago: University of Chicago Press).

Page, B. I. and Jones, C. C. (1979), 'Reciprocal effects of policy preferences, party loyalties and the vote', *American Political Science Review*, vol. 73, no. 4, pp. 1071–89.

Page, B. I. and Schapiro, R. Y. (1982), 'Changes in Americans' public policy preferences, 1935–79', *Public Opinion Quarterly*, vol. 46, no. 1, pp. 24–42.

Page, B. I. and Schapiro, R. Y. (1983), 'Effects of public opinion on policy', *American Political Science Review*, vol. 77, no. 1, pp. 175–90.

Page, B. I., Schapiro, R. Y. and Dempsey, G. R. (1987), 'What moves public opinion?', *American Political Science Review*, vol. 81, no. 1, pp. 23–43.

Parry, G. and Moyser, G. (1990), 'A map of political participation in Britain', *Government and Opposition*, vol. 25, no. 2, pp. 147–69.

Peacock, A. T. (1979), *The Economic Analysis of Government, and Related Themes* (Oxford: Martin Robertson).

Peacock, A. T. (1983), 'X-inefficiency: informational and institutional constraints', in Hanusch, H. (ed.) (1983), pp. 125–48.

Peacock, A. T. and Wiseman, J. (1968), *The Growth of Public Expenditure in the United Kingdom* (Princeton: Princeton University Press).

Pelling, H. (1987), *A History of British Trade Unionism* (London: Macmillan), fourth edition.

Peltzman, S. (1980), 'The growth of government', *Journal of Law and Economics*, vol. 27, no. 3, pp. 209–88.

Perlman, M. (1976), 'Party politics and bureaucracy in economic policy', in Tullock, G. (1976), pp. 61–80.

Peters, B. G. (1985), 'Sweden: the explosion of public employment', in Rose, R. *et al.* (1985), pp. 201–26.

Peters, B. G. (1989a), *Comparing Public Bureaucracies: Problems of theories and method* (Tuscaloosa, Ala.: University of Alabama press).

Peters, B. G. (1989b), 'The European bureaucrat: the applicability of "Bureaucracy and Representative Government" to non-American settings' (paper to a conference on 'The Budget-Maximizing Bureaucrat', University of Montreal, Montreal, Quebec, 13–15 April).

Piaget, J. (1971), *Structuralism* (London: Routledge).

Bibliography

Pirie, M. (1988a), *Privatization: Theory, Practice and Choice* (London: Wildwood House).

Pirie, M. (1988b), *Micropolitics* (London: Wildwood House).

Plamenatz, J. (1973), *Democracy and Illusion* (London: Longman).

Plott, C. (1987), 'The robustness of the voting paradox', in Rowley, C. K. (ed.) (1987), pp. 100–2.

Pollitt, C. (1983), *Manipulating the Machine* (London: Allen and Unwin).

Polsby, N. (1963), *Community Power and Political Theory* (New Haven: Yale University Press).

Polsby, N. (1980), 'The newsmedia as an alternative to party in the Presidential selection process', in Goldwin, R. A. (ed) (1980), pp. 50–66.

Ponting, C. (1985), *Whitehall: Tragedy and farce* (London: Hamilton).

Poole, K. T. and Daniels, R. S. (1985), 'Ideology, party and voting in the US Congress, 1959–80', *American Political Science Review*, vol. 79, no. 2, pp. 373–99.

Poole, K. T. and Rosenthal, H. (1984), 'The polarization of American politics', *Journal of Politics*, vol. 46, no. 4, pp. 1061–79.

Powell, G. B. (1981), 'Party systems and political system performance: voting participation, government stability, and mass violence in contemporary democracies', *American Political Science Review*, vol. 75, no. 4, pp. 861–79.

Powell, G. B. (1982), *Contemporary Democracies: Participation, stability and violence* (Cambridge, Mass.: Harvard University Press).

Przeworski, A. (1985), *Capitalism and Social Democracy* (Cambridge: Cambridge University Press).

Przeworski, A. and Sprague, J. (1986), *Paper Stones: A history of electoral socialism* (Chicago: University of Chicago Press).

Quattrone, G. and Tversky, A. (1988), 'Contrasting rational and psychological analyses of political choice', *American Political Science Review*, vol. 82, no. 3, pp. 719–36.

Rabinowitz, G. and Macdonald, S. E. (1986), 'The power of the states in US presidential elections', *American Political Science Review*, vol. 80, no. 1, pp. 66–87.

Rabinowitz, G. and Macdonald, S. E. (1989), 'A directional theory of issue voting', *American Political Science Review*, vol. 83, no. 1, pp. 93–121.

Rees, R. (1985), 'The theory of principal and agent: Parts 1 and 2', *Bulletin of Economic Research*, vol. 37, no. 1, pp. 46–69; and vol. 37, no. 2, pp. 70–90.

Rhodes, R. A. W. (1988), *Beyond Westminster and Whitehall: The sub-central governments of Britain* (London: Allen and Unwin).

Richardson, J. and Jordan, G. (1979), *Governing Under Pressure: The policy process in a post-parliamentary democracy* (Oxford: Blackwell).

Rigaud, J. and Delcros, X. (1986), *Les Institutions Administratives Françaises, La Fonctionnement* (Paris: Dalloz).

Riker, W. H. (1962), *The Theory of Political Coalitions* (New Haven and London: Yale University Press).

Riker, W. H. (1982), *Liberalism Against Populism* (San Francisco: Freeman).

Robbins, L. (1935), *An Essay on the Nature and Significance of Economic Science* (London: Macmillan), second edition.

Robertson, D. (1976), *A Theory of Party Competition* (London: Wiley).

273

Bibliography

Robinson, J. (1964), *Economic Philosophy* (Harmondsworth: Penguin).

Roemer, J. (ed.) (1986), *Analytical Marxism* (Cambridge: Cambridge University Press).

Rogowski, R. (1974), *Rational Legitimacy: A theory of political support* (Princeton: Princeton University Press).

Romer, T. and Rosenthal, H. (1978), 'Political resource allocation, controlled agendas and the status quo', *Public Choice*, vol. 33, no. 1, pp. 27–43.

Romer, T. and Rosenthal, H. (1984), 'Voting models and empirical evidence', *American Scientist*, vol. 72, no. 2, pp. 465–73.

Rose, R. (1981), *Understanding Big Government: The programme approach* (London and Beverly Hills: Sage).

Rose, R. (1989), *Ordinary People and Public Policy* (London: Sage).

Rose, R. and Karran, T. (1988), *Taxation by Political Inertia: Financing the growth of government* (London: Allen and Unwin).

Rose, R., Page, E., Parry, R., Peters, B. G., Pignatelli, A. and Schmidt, K. D. (1985), *Public Employment in Western Nations* (Cambridge: Cambridge University Press).

Rosenberg, A. (1979), 'Can economic theory explain everything?', *Philosophy and the Social Sciences*, vol. 9, no. 4, pp. 509–29.

Rothenberg, L. S. (1988), 'Organizational maintenance and retention decisions in groups', *American Political Science Review*, vol. 82, no. 4, pp. 1129–52.

Rowley, C. K. (ed.) (1987), *Democracy and Public Choice* (Oxford: Blackwell).

Rutherford, A. (1986), *Prisons and the Process of Justice* (Oxford: Oxford University Press).

Samuelson, P. A. (1954), 'The pure theory of public expenditure', *Review of Economics and Statistics*, vol. 36, no. 4, pp. 386–9.

Saunders, P. and Klau, F. (1985), *The Role of the Public Sector: Causes and consequences of the growth of government* (Paris: Organization for Economic Co-operation and Development), OECD Economic Studies, no. 4.

Savas, E. S. (1982), *Privatizing the Public Sector: How to shrink government* (Chatham House, NJ: Chatham House).

Savas, E. S. (1987), *Privatization: The Key to Better Government* (Chatham House, NJ: Chatham House).

Schlesinger, J. A. (1985), 'The new American political party', *American Political Science Review*, vol. 79, no. 4, pp. 1152–89.

Schmitter, P. C. and Lehmbruch, G. (eds) (1979), *Trends Towards Corporatist Intermediation* (London: Sage).

Schultze, C. (1977), *The Public Use of Private Interests* (Washington, DC: Brookings Institution).

Schumpeter, J. A. (1944), *Capitalism, Socialism and Democracy* (New York: Harper and Row and London: Allen and Unwin).

Self, P. (1985), *The Political Theory of Modern Government* (Sydney: Allen and Unwin).

Sen, A. K. (1970), *Collective Choice and Social Welfare* (San Francisco: Holden-Day and Edinburgh: Oliver and Boyd).

Sen, A. K. (1977), 'Rational fools: a critique of the behavioural foundations of economic theory', *Philosophy and Public Affairs*, vol. 6, no. 4, pp. 317–44.

Bibliography

Shackle, G. (1969), *Decision, Order and Time in Human Affairs* (Cambridge: Cambridge University Press), second edition.

Sharpe, L. J. (ed.) (1979), *Decentralist Trends in Western Democracies* (London: Sage).

Sharpe, L. J. (1985), 'Central coordination and the policy network', *Political Studies*, vol. 33, no. 3, pp. 361–81.

Sigelman, L. (1986), 'The bureaucrat as budget-maximizer: an assumption re-examined', *Public Budgeting and Finance*, vol. 6, no. 1, pp. 50–9.

Simms, M. (1990), 'Political feminism and women candidates: some implications for pluralism and democracy' (paper to the International Colloquium on Organized Interests and Democracy, Cortone, Italy, 29–31 May).

Smithies, A. (1941), 'Optimal location in spatial competition', *Journal of Political Economy*, vol. 49, pp. 429–39.

Sorenson, R. (1987), 'Bureaucratic decision-making and the growth of public expenditure', in Lane, R. E. (ed.) (1987), pp. 64–76.

Steinfels, P. (1979), *The Neo-Conservatives* (New York: Simon and Schuster).

Stigler, G. J. (ed.) (1988), *Chicago Studies in Political Economy* (Chicago: University of Chicago Press).

Stigler, G. J. and Becker, G. (1977), '*De gustibus non est disputandum*', *American Economic Review*, vol. 67, no. 1, pp. 76–90.

Stokes, D. E. (1963), 'Spatial models of party competition', *American Political Science Review*, vol. 57, no. 2, pp. 368–77.

Taagepera, R. and Shugart, M. S. (1989), *Seats and Votes: The effects and determinants of electoral systems* (New Haven: Yale University Press).

Tarschys, D. (1975), 'The growth of public expenditures: nine modes of explanation', *Yearbook of Scandinavian Political Studies*, vol. 61, no. 4, pp. 1010–19.

Taylor, M. (1987), *The Possibility of Cooperation* (Cambridge: Cambridge University Press.

Taylor, M. and Laver, M. (1973), 'Government coalitions in Western Europe', *European Journal of Political Research*, vol. 1, no. 3, pp. 205–48.

Thain, C. and Wright, M. (1989), 'Running costs: a new agenda for controlling public spending?' (paper to the UK Political Studies Association Annual Conference, University of Warwick, 4 April).

Treasury (1987a), *Supply Estimates* (London: HMSO).

Treasury (1987b), *The Government's Expenditure Plans, 1987–88* (London: HMSO). Cm 56, vol. II.

Trueman, D. (1951), *The Process of Government* (New York: Knopf Press).

Tufte, E. R. (1978), *Political Control of the Economy* (Princeton: Princeton University Press).

Tullock, G. (1965), *The Politics of Bureaucracy* (Washington, DC: Public Affairs Press).

Tullock, G. (1967), *Towards a Mathematics of Politics* (Ann Arbor: University of Michigan Press).

Tullock, G. (1974), 'Dynamic hypotheses on bureaucracy', *Public Choice*, vol. 17, no. 2, pp. 128–32.

Bibliography

Tullock, G. (1976), *The Vote Motive: An essay in the economics of politics, with applications to the British economy* (London: Institute of Economic Affairs).

Turpin, C. (1972), *Government Contracts* (Harmondsworth: Penguin).

Tzserbelis, G. (1990) *Nested Games: Rational choice in comparative politics* (Berkeley: University of California Press).

Uhlaner, C. (1989), 'Rational turnout: the neglected role of groups', *American Journal of Political Science*, vol. 33, no. 2, pp. 390–422.

Veljanowski, C. J. (1982), *The New Law-and-Economics* (Oxford: Centre for Socio-Legal Studies).

Veljanowski, C. J. (1987), *Selling the State: Privatization in Britain* (London: Weidenfeld and Nicolson).

Verba, S. and Nie, N. H. (1972), *Participation in America* (New York: Harper and Row).

von Mises, L. (1944), *Bureaucracy* (New Haven: Yale University Press).

von Weizsacker, C. C. (1971), 'Notes on endogenous change of tastes', *Economic Theory*, vol. 3, no. 4, pp. 345–72.

Wade, L. (ed.) (1983), *Political Economy: Recent views* (Boston: Kluwer-Nijhoff).

Walker, J. L. (1983), 'The origins and maintenance of interest groups in America', *American Political Science Review*, vol. 77, no. 2, pp. 390–406.

Wallerstein, M. (1989), 'Union organization in advanced industrial democracies', *American Political Science Review*, vol. 83, no. 2, pp. 481–501.

Ware, A. (1979), *The Logic of Party Democracy* (London: Macmillan).

Ware, A. (1989), *Between Profit and the State: Intermediate organizations and the United States* (Cambridge: Polity).

Weatherford, M. S. (1983), 'Economic voting and the "symbolic politics" argument: a reinterpretation and synthesis', *American Political Science Review*, vol. 77, no. 1, pp. 158–74.

Weingast, B. (1984), 'The Congressional-bureaucratic system: a principal-agent perspective (with applications to the SEC)', *Public Choice*, vol. 44, no. 2, pp. 147–91.

Whiteley, P. (1990), 'Economic policy', in Dunleavy *et al.* (eds) (1990), pp. 175–96.

Whynes, D. K. and Bowles, R. A. (1981), *The Economic Theory of the State* (Oxford: Martin Robertson).

Wildavsky, A. (1979), *The Politics of the Budgetary Process* (Boston: Little Brown).

Wilding, P. (1982), *Professional Power and Social Welfare* (London: Routledge).

Williamson, O. E. (1964), *The Economics of Discretionary Behaviour* (Englewood Cliffs, NJ: Prentice Hall).

Williamson, O. E. (1975), *Markets and Hierarchies* (New York: Free Press).

Williamson, O. E. (1985), *Economic Institutions of Capitalism* (New York: Free Press).

Wilson, G. (1981), *Interest Groups in the United States* (Oxford: Oxford University Press).

Wilson, J. Q. (1973), *Political Organization* (New York: Basic Books).

Wistow, G. (1985), 'Community care for the mentally handicapped: disappointing progress', in Harrison, A. and Gretton, J. (eds), *Health Care UK, 1985* (Hermitage, Berkshire: Policy Journals), pp. 69–78.

Bibliography

Wittman, D. A. (1973), 'Parties as utility maximizers', *American Political Science Review*, vol. 68, no. 2, pp. 490–8.

Wootton, G. (1970), *Interest Groups* (Englewood Cliffs, NJ: Prentice Hall).

Zipp, J. (1985), 'Perceived representativeness and voting: an assessment of the impact of "choices" vs "echoes"', *American Political Science Review*, vol. 79, no. 1, pp. 50–61.

AUTHOR INDEX

278

Author index

SUBJECT INDEX

activists
  in groups, 35, 71–7
  in parties, 133–5, 143
  in politics, 89, 105
adjusting social relativities, 121
administrative sociology, 201
ADP *see* aggregate distribution of
  preferences
adversary politics, 133–5
advocacy costs (for bureaucrats), 179–81,
  197–200, 205–8
advocates, 150–1, 168
  defined, 150
AFL-CIO, 74
agency types, 183–91, 193–4, 197–9, 205–8,
  215–17, 234–9, 242–3
agenda-setting, 127–8, 157–8, 211–13
aggregate distribution of preferences (ADP),
  92–110, 113, 116, 118–19, 121, 124,
  127, 128, 133–4, 143–4
agriculture, 216–17
Agriculture (US), Department of, 184
Air Force (US), 163
American Farm Bureau Federation, 52
American Medical Association, 74
analytical Marxism, 5
Anderson, J., 126
armed forces, 152–3, 163, 190–1, 194, 258
Australia
  Liberal party, 123
  politics, 4, 123, 138, 228
Austria
  local government, 137
  pay bargaining, 29–30
Austrian school, 6

BB *see* bureau budget
Birmingham (UK), 54, 196

blacklisting, 89
Britain
  1974 election, 122
  care in the community, 229–31
  central departments, 175, 187–91, 195,
    203, 204, 213–17, 219–27
  central–local relations, 170, 219–25
  civil service, 200, 219–25
  Conservative party, 75, 87, 105–7, 120–1,
    122, 123, 128, 136, 203, 217, 227
  constitution, 138
  economic policy, 30
  Falklands war, 108–10
  history, 106–7
  housing policies, 120–1, 196–7
  interest groups, 23–4, 42, 54
  Labour party, 105–7, 126–7, 133
  land policy, 127
  Liberal party, 132
  local government, 120–1, 123, 136, 196–7,
    204, 220–5, 229–30, 236
  mass media, 87
  miners strike, 23–4
  National Health Service, 120, 220–5
  politics, 4, 142
  press, 25
  prisons, 230–1
  privatization policies, 120, 228
  retail opening hours, 23–4
  secrecy, 157
  social contract, 26
  Social Democratic Party, 131–2
  trade unions, 71–5
  Trades Union Congress, 29
  union laws, 72
  voting, 83, 89, 94, 103, 105–9, 120–1
  Westminster system, 138–9
  'winter of discontent', 27
  workhouses, 237

281

Subject index

Subject index

de Gaulle, Charles, 123–4
DE *see* deinstitutionalization
deinstitutionalization (DE), 228–30, 232–9
  one tier, 229, 232–4, 236–9
  two-tier, 229n, 234–9
delivery agencies, 183–5, 188–91, 193–4,
  198–200, 205–8, 215–17, 242–3, 244
demand-side models, 4, 249–54
Democratic party, 84, 126, 132–3, 138
Denmark, 136–7
Detroit, 218–19
'directional model' of voting, 96–8
discounted marginal utility (DMU) curves,
  197–200, 205–8, 212
  rotating, 207–8, 227
DMU *see* discounted marginal utility

economics
  neo-classical, 4, 6
Education, Department of (US), 194
Education and Science, Department of
  (UK), 194
Eire, 136, 141, 183
Electoral College (US), 126
electoral systems, 140–2
employers, 59
employment/trade/energy, 216–17
'end of ideology', 13
endogenous groups, 55, 57–9, 66–71, 84–5,
  143
Energy, Department of (US), 187
entrepreneurs, 34–5, 39, 143, 148
  bureaucratic, 148
  political, 34–5, 39, 143
equilibrium
  budget levels, 166–7, 197–200, 205–8
  in party competition, 79–80, 94, 114
ethnicity, 241
'exit' options, 16–19, 65
exogenous groups, 54–5, 56–9, 63–5, 68–71,
  84–5, 143
exogenous preferences, 4, 8, 90–111, 144,
  252–4
externalities, 241–7

Falkland Islands war, 108–10, 122
fatalist variant, new right, 232–6, 248
Federal Highways Administration (US), 186
federalism, 137–8, 219–25
Financial Management Initiative (FMI), 232
'first principles' public choice, 1–2, 5, 9, 259
First World War, 122
Food Safety and Inspection Service (US), 184
France
  central government, 220–4
  constitution, 123–4, 138
  corporatism, 30
  economic growth, 42

legislature, 139, 157
local government, 136, 220–4
National Front, 125
pantouflage, 194
politics, 123–4, 129–30
voting, 83, 129–30
franchising, 228 *see* also privatization

game theory, 9
gender biases
  in bureaucracies, 155, 241
General Services Agency (US), 187
Germany, 42, 83, 129–30, 137, 200
gerrymandering, 123
Gladstone, William, 125
government agencies *see* bureaucracies
grants systems, 172
Greece, 89, 224
Greenpeace, 67, 75
Grenada, 125
groups *see* interest groups
group identity, 3, 54–9, 60–2, 84, 253
  defined, 57
group-joining, 32–4, 45–62, 83–5, 252–3
growth of government, 149, 155–8, 218–25

Health and Social Security, Department of
  (UK), 204
Heath, Edward, 122
heroic variant, new right, 232–6, 248
hierarchies, 72–3, 149, 162–5, 171–2, 177–
  81, 191–3
hiving-off, 204–5, 225–7 *see* also
  deinstitutionalization
Home Office, 160
homes for elderly, 229–30, 237–8
Horton, Willie, 125–6
hospitals, 229–30, 237–8
housing policy, 120–1
Hume, David, 100

identity sets, 54–9, 60–7
ideology, 131–2, 257–8
Illinois, 126
inappropriate privatization, 241–8
incumbency
  advantages of, 117–44
  bias against, 114–17
indifference curves, 90–2
individualism, 6–7
information, 4, 9, 53–4, 95, 112–17, 128–9,
  131, 149
information impactedness, 246–7
Institute for Defence Analysis, 163
institutional care, 237
institutional manipulation, 123–4, 128
  joint, 126–7
institutional public choice, 1–7

283

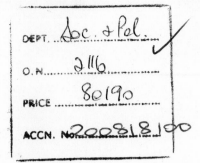